# Triumph and Tragedy

## The Story of the Kennedys

by the writers, photographers, and editors of

**The Associated Press**

*Project Director*
Keith Fuller

*Editor*
Sidney C. Moody Jr.

*Manuscript Authors*
Sidney C. Moody Jr., Jules Loh,
John Barbour, Bernard Gavzer,
Robert Price, Harry F. Rosenthal,
Ben Funk

*Art*
Hal Buell

*Design*
Barbara White

*Special Material Contributors*
Washington—Jean Heller,
   Richard Barnes, Robert Gray,
   Garven Hudgins
Boston—Cornelius Hurley
Ireland and England—
   Thomas A. Reedy,
   Arthur Gavshon
Los Angeles—Bob Thomas
New York—Relman Morin

*Editorial Research*
Cissy Steinfort, Jane Gallagher,
Carol Cartaino, Elizabeth Basset

*Promotion and Distribution*
M. J. Wing, Edward T. Fleming

*Photo Researchers*
New York—Robert White
Washington—Joe Jamieson,
   Bob Daugherty
Boston—Donald Guy
Miami—Toby Massey
Los Angeles—Richard Strobel

Pictures were made by staff photographers of The Associated Press and
its member newspapers. Additional photographs are from *Life* Magazine,
Black Star, Underwood & Underwood, Brown Bros. and James Vance.

# Contents

# Foreword

The Kennedy family story is a mosaic of contrasts. It moves from relative poverty to extreme wealth. From obscurity to an unquestionable place in history. From high positions in government to violent death.

Without the sudden intrusions of death, the Kennedy chronicle would be an American success story to rival the most far-fetched fiction.

But death took three of Joseph P. Kennedy's sons in turn and, ironically, while each was in the service of this nation.

This work records in words and pictures an account of the family from its origins in Ireland to its most recent tragedy, the assassination of Senator Robert F. Kennedy.

We purport to do nothing more than let the ambition and achievement of this American family emerge from their words and actions.

To do more would be an attempt to speak for the Kennedys. The Kennedys always have spoken for themselves.

*The Authors*

New York City
July 10, 1968

Eunice, Jean, Rosemary, Bobby, Teddy, Joe, Jack, Rose, Pat, Kathleen, and Joe Jr.

# An American Family

For one one-hundredth of a second in the year 1940 the Kennedys stood still.

Ready. Smile. Click.

Only a camera shutter, it would seem, could halt for a fragment of a moment the perpetual stir at the home of Joseph Patrick Kennedy. A friend, visiting the Kennedys that summer, watched in fascination:

"Jack was autographing copies of *Why England Slept* while Grandfather Fitzgerald was reading to him a political story from a newspaper. Young Joe was telling about something that happened to him in Russia. Mrs. Kennedy was talking on the phone with Cardinal Spellman. A tall and very attractive girl in a sweatshirt and dungarees, who turned out to be Pat, was describing how a German Messerschmitt plane had crashed near her father's house outside of London. Bobby was trying to get everybody to play charades. The next thing I knew all of us were choosing up sides for touch football, and Kathleen was calling the plays in the huddle for the team I was on. There was something doing every minute."

Thus the Kennedys, eleven of them, at home.

When they spoke of home—and to them the word meant more than shallow sentiment, an emotion they deplored—Joseph Kennedy and the members of his sizable tribe referred to only one of the several places they could claim as residences. The others were perhaps more stately, more grand, but none was quite as comfortable, quite as relaxed, quite as gracious, quite as fit for their lusty, unpretentious style of living as the rambling old house by the sea. That was home.

It was a large house, seventeen rooms and nine baths, spacious enough for nine personalities to grow and develop the sort of initiative and self-reliance Joe Kennedy wished for his children. The house, like Joe himself, was sturdy and competent if not elegant. It was, in fact, rather undistinguished among all the others at The Port, as the inhabitants referred familiarly to the Cape Cod village of Hyannis Port where the house stood. It was finished in white-painted shingles, green shutters, and rested with easy nonchalance overlooking Nantucket Sound. Its gabled roof was visible from far at sea, and the young Kennedys could swing the prows of their sailboats toward it as an unfailing landmark when it was time to race home for meals.

A two-and-a-half-acre lawn sloped down from the house to the harsh dune grass and the soft, warm sand of the beach. For all its size and space it was a simple place, really, and an excellent place to raise a family. That, after all, was to Joe Kennedy's mind what life was all about. "The measure of a man's success in life," Joe once said, "is not the money he's made. It's the kind of family he's raised."

Joe Kennedy had positive notions about success. It was not measured, as he said, solely by personal fortune, but was entwined with a sense of self-esteem, professional excellence and public acceptance. By the late 1930s Joseph P. Kennedy had amassed a fortune in the financial world, given counsel in the top echelons of the diplomatic world, participated in the loftiest decisions of the political world. Still, by some in the city of his birth whose accomplishments were far less he was regarded not as financier, diplomat or politician but as Joe Kennedy, son of a barkeeper and politico.

For Joe Kennedy was an Irishman, an Irish Catholic. And in Boston during the years of his rise to prominence, his every knock on the door of Yankee society was greeted by the same message, albeit muted, as greeted his father and grandfather when they sought jobs: No Irish Need Apply.

Early in his career Joe, after months of delay as a result of anti-Irish bias, finally landed a seat on the board of trustees of a Massachusetts electric company. Some of his friends wondered why he had been so persistent, so determined to join what many considered a moribund firm. Replied Kennedy: "Do you know a better way to meet people like the Saltonstalls?" Later, in the 1920s, Joe rented a place at Cohasset, which was a favorite summering place for Boston Brahmins. When he applied for membership in the Cohasset Country Club, he was blackballed. That hurt. Nor were his daughters invited to join the debutante clubs, and that hurt too, despite Joe's disclaimer to a reporter: "Not that our girls would have joined anyway; they never gave two cents for that society stuff."

At length, in 1926, millionaire Joe Kennedy, the tavern owner's son, bundled his family aboard a private railroad car and moved to Riverdale, New York. Boston, he muttered, "was no place to bring up Irish Catholic children." The following year he bought a handsome Georgian mansion on a five-acre plot in fashionable Bronxville, New York, and during the next six years acquired the Hyannis Port home as well as a $100,000 Moorish-style home in Palm Beach, Florida.

Odd, in a way, that Hyannis Port, which was not an address to match Newport or Bar Harbor, should be the place the Kennedy roots would sink deepest. On the other hand, it did prove to be a fine place to bring up Irish Catholic children.

Brought up in the manner Joseph Kennedy thought right, a manner which reflected in many ways his own upbringing, a manner which taught them, in the words of his daughter Eunice, that "the important thing was to win; don't come in second or third, that doesn't count, but win, win, win"—brought up in that manner and with the help of time's

steady erosion of prejudice, the offspring of Joseph P. Kennedy, a hyphenated Irish-American, might discover, as he had not, that faith and ancestry were only artificial barriers even to his exacting definition of success. If he himself could not complete the journey he could at least, as one of his biographers, Richard Whalen, expressed it, provide the driving will, his children the legs, to go the distance.

What prize lay in the distance he could not know, not specifically, but if excellence and drive and determination and skill could attain it, it would not be beyond the reach of a child of Joseph P. Kennedy. Nor was any goal excluded, any at all, not even, for example, the Presidency of the United States. Such would be Joseph Kennedy's legacy to his children.

The sunlit family in the photograph numbered eleven: Joe, his wife Rose, a model of patience and womanly fortitude whom he took as his bride in 1914, and their bright, adventurous brood.

The first was his father's namesake, Joseph Patrick Kennedy Junior, whose arrival cheered the first home of Joe and Rose, a modest frame house in Brookline, Massachusetts, within a year of their marriage.

Young Joe was the heir apparent, the embodiment of his father's dream: editor of his prep school yearbook; winner of his prep school's trophy for combining athletic and scholastic excellence; delegate to the coming National Democratic Convention; self-confident; poised; capable; witty; impatient with those whose pace did not match his. He had his mother's gentle looks and his father's audacious drive, and there seemed no limit to the things he might accomplish. Young Joe even discussed, in a quite confident way, about someday becoming President. To him it did not seem an unnatural ambition.

The tall, thin youth of the photograph was Jack—John Fitzgerald Kennedy—named for his mother's father, his narrow face surmounted by an uncontrollable mop of brown hair. He was neither as husky nor as handsome as Joe, nor as outgoing and sociable. Illness plagued him repeatedly: he had scarlet fever when he was four; appendicitis in prep school; jaundice in college. But his frequent afflictions never dimmed the Irishness of his sense of humor or dulled his typical Kennedy drive. At Harvard he slipped out of the infirmary, where he was recovering from flu, to practice his backstroke so he could make the swimming team that would face Yale. Weakened, he lost out. As an end on Harvard's junior varsity football team, Jack suffered a back injury that nagged him periodically. Though Joe was the one cut out to carry the family's political ambitions, clearly Jack would be no disappointment to his father either—though there were times when his father was not so sure. For example, when he received a note from Jack's prep school master complaining that Jack's room, which served as a clubhouse for his friends, was forever a mess. Furthermore, wrote the master, Jack "is casual and disorderly in almost all of his organiza-

tion projects. Jack studies at the last minute, keeps appointments late, has little sense of material value, and can seldom locate his possessions." But the schoolmaster was not all despairing:

"I would be willing to bet anything," he wrote, "that within two years you will be as proud of Jack as you are now of Joe. Jack has a clever, individualist mind. It is a harder mind to put in harness than Joe's—harder for Jack himself to put in harness. When he learns the right place for humor and learns to use his individual way of looking at things as an asset instead of a handicap, his natural gift of an individual outlook and witty expression are going to help him. . . . We must allow for a period of adjustment and growing up; and the final product is often more interesting and more effective than the boy with a more conventional mind who has been to us parents and teachers much less trouble."

The schoolmaster's faith was well placed, for Jack in that year of 1940 graduated cum laude from Harvard, and his senior thesis became a best-selling book, *Why England Slept.* Would he continue writing? Or become a teacher? Jack was undecided, but he had the goods, as his father once put it, to succeed.

Joe Kennedy's next son was Bobby—Robert Francis, born in 1925. Joe, with typical carefree inelegance, called Bobby the runt of the litter. Runt he might have been, strong-willed he might have been too, but in other respects he was typically Kennedy—loyal to friends, dependable, faithful.

When Bobby was ten, his governess, Elizabeth Dunn, took him and his baby brother, Teddy, to visit the Miles Standish monument at Duxbury. Having climbed with the two boys to the top, the governess became frozen with fear at the height, unable to descend the steep spiral staircase. Bobby took Teddy to the bottom, then climbed back up. "Don't worry, Miss Dunn," he said. "Take my hand and close your eyes and I will lead you down." Safe on the ground, Bobby smiled at the shaken governess. "I won't tell anyone," he said. And he didn't.

Bobby regarded his brothers, Joe and Jack, with a respect approaching awe. They taught him to sail, to kick a football, to swing a bat. He approached every challenge with perhaps even stronger determination than other Kennedys. One friend said of Bobby, "He feels that when a challenge exists and you have said you will meet it, you destroy

yourself if you run away from it." This attitude typified Bobby in his later years, but during his boyhood he had, on an least one occasion, a more pragmatic outlook. One day he and the chauffeur's son decided to jump off the roof of the house using bedsheets as parachutes. The chauffeur's son jumped first —and broke his leg. Bobby didn't jump.

The youngest son in the picture, a smiling boy still chubby with baby fat, was Edward M. Kennedy, friendly Teddy, just eight. In 1940, of course, it was too soon to discuss Teddy's potentialities as, say, a future President though the possibility would not seem at all remote to his father. Teddy was, after all, a Kennedy.

The five girls were Kennedys, too, with all that that implied: The fierce tribal loyalty, audacity, drive. Rosemary, Kathleen, Eunice and Patricia arrived between Jack and Bobby, and after Bobby came Jean. They brought their father the sort of solace daughters bring to devoted fathers, and their jaunty personalities brightened his hearth.

Rosemary, a loving child, was an exception. Rosie was shy, retiring, unlike the rest, a concern to her parents. For such a child, however, one could hardly imagine better sur-

*Hyannis Port, 1940: Eunice, Mrs. Kennedy, Robert, Patricia, Edward*

roundings. Mutual support was a characteristic of Joe Kennedy's gang. If one Kennedy required an extra share of help and attention, the other Kennedys gave it freely and without question. Rarely did one of them forget to include in a letter from school or from a trip abroad "Give my love to Rosie." As one family friend remarked, "If one Kennedy was threatened, it became the Kennedys against the world."

On one occasion, in 1934, Rose Kennedy wrote a letter to her son Jack's schoolmaster which showed the tender concern of the family for Rosemary.

*Dear Mr. Steele:*

*Would it be possible for Jack to attend a tea-dance in Providence on Friday, January 19th?*

*The reason I am making this seemingly absurd request is because the young lady who is inviting him is his sister, and she has an inferiority complex. I know it would help her if he went with her. She is fifteen years old, and is trying to adjust herself. I am sure you understand my point of view. It is not tremendously important, but we do all we can to help her. . . .*

All we can. That was the Kennedy way. They did all they could for one another and for themselves, for that was the way Joe taught them. "My husband," remarked Rose, "was quite a strict father. He liked the boys to win at sports and everything they tried. If they didn't win he would discuss their failure with them. But he did not have much patience with the loser."

His sons inherited the trait. Once young Joe was in a sailing race and ordered little Teddy, his crew: "Get the jib!" Teddy didn't respond; he didn't know what the jib was. Whereupon Joe knocked Teddy overboard and held him underwater for a long moment. Teddy learned what the jib was.

"Joe wanted his children to be thinkers and doers," commented a friend, Thomas Schriber. "He'd get them to sit down and he'd tell them, 'I don't care what you do in life, but whatever you do be the best person in the world when you do it. Even if you're going to be a ditchdigger, be the best ditchdigger in the world.' " Joe demanded that they give it all they had. In a sailing race, for instance, if a Kennedy boy didn't go all out, didn't try, he ate his dinner in the kitchen.

A boyhood friend recalled visiting the Kennedys at their home in Bronxville, New York, and playing touch football. "You had to remember there were a lot of trees around the lawn. I always ran looking for the trees and the ball at the same time. But Joe and Jack and Bobby never did, and WHANG! that was that. They were always knocking themselves out. I can remember many occasions when one or the other of the boys would be picked up unconscious. They were always bandaged and bruised all over."

Nothing short of total effort, total commitment, would do if they would attain what he considered success. Joe Kennedy removed all obstacles. He set up a million-dollar trust fund for each of the children so each would receive income at twenty-one and one-half the principal at forty-five—a fund that would eventually be worth ten million dollars per child. This was the foundation for a secure social position; the rest was up to them.

How could they miss cracking the barrier of pettiness and bias that had so wounded Joe Sr. personally, that had caused him once to explode in rage: "I was born here. My children were born here. What the hell do I have to do to be an American?"

At the gay, competitive, loving home at Hyannis Port, Joe Kennedy was doing all he could.

# To a New World

To be Americans: that the Kennedys were. And their fathers before them. Born in America, the only land they knew. But they were of Ireland, too. Not of the shamrock veneer of the wearing of the green but of something deeper, as strong as it was invisible. They were of a people that had borne much, a proud, gregarious, able strain tormented and oppressed in the land of their birth, scorned and exploited in the land of their adoption.

This marked them. It had always marked them, the Irish. That they survived marked them, too: with pride, with ambition, with a deep sense of family and clan sharpened in struggle with countless foes as ancient as the oldest ballad. The Vikings. The Normans. Cromwell, "The Protector" who brutalized them. Nameless landlords and storied British kings who for generations took what their peasant hands could produce but left their minds empty of even the alphabet of the language they spoke.

All this the Kennedys and O'Kennedys of Ireland knew. The hills and valleys of County Wexford, too, have known Kennedy blood and accepted Kennedy bodies, fallen in battle, beneath their sod.

There was the rising in 1798. Poverty caused it. British nobles and even some of their Irish supporters levied harsh taxes, ousted tenants and seized land from many farmers, bringing the whole to uncontrollable ferment. The decisive struggle came at Vinegar Hill, near Enniscorthy. Led by a priest, Father Murphy, the remnants of the rebels charged with only simple pikes. It was their doom.

That day has come down in Irish lore in a song, "The Boys of Wexford":

> To free my land I'd gladly give
> The red drops from my heart . . .
> And if for want of leaders
> We lost at Vinegar Hill,
> We're ready for another fight,
> And love our country still.

Among the boys of Wexford were two brothers, John and Patrick Kennedy of Dunganstown. John was wounded. Patrick gathered him up and brought him down the River Barrow to their homestead. But John had died of his injury. Another Kennedy victim of his people's battle. In Cromwell's day thirty-seven other Kennedys had been hanged until dead, the records show. A printed history is a perishable thing, but persecution and valor are not so readily forgotten. They seep into the bloodlines of a people, from generation to generation.

The survivor of Vinegar Hill, Patrick Kennedy, was a farmer as were almost all the Irish of his time. The Industrial Revolution that was about to thrust Britain into her glorious century of empire never crossed the sea to Ireland. Yet the life of a peasant in a land as green as Ireland need not be destitute. But in fact, it was.

Ireland was garotted by choking land laws that made land acquisition by the peasant difficult, if not impossible. Landholdings were minute, scattered. The situation was all the more aggravated by an upward burst of the population in the first half of the nineteenth century. The poor became poorer.

Because there were no Poor Laws—nineteenth century welfare—in Ireland as there were in Britain, no almshouses for the indigent, the Irish sought what security they could in begetting large families in the hope that enough children could survive to support their parents in their old age.

Life, at best, was hard. In 1837 nine thousand people lived in Tullahobagly in County Donegal. There were ten beds counted among them. Half the families in the country lived in single-room, windowless mud huts, sharing the dirt floor with the family pig and any other livestock they were lucky enough to own.

The English had forbidden the teaching of

*The docks of New Ross, the last step to a new world*

13

The New Ross shipping office. America: one way, twenty dollars.

any who clung to their Catholic faith. Priests defiantly conducted what were called "hedge" schools, instructing the young clandestinely among the hedgerows.

There had been some emigration, particularly to America, in the early part of the century, but even the few dollars required for passage were a fortune to most of the Irish. Those who did go were largely the relatively prosperous farmers, not the peasants.

Those who went wrote home much as one emigrant from America: "If a man likes work, he need not want for victuals. There is a great many ill conveniences here, but no empty bellies." America, wrote one John Doyle of New York to his wife in Ireland, was free from "visits from tax gatherers, constables or soldiers . . . every one is at liberty to act and speak as he likes." That was a far cry from Ireland under the Penal Laws imposed by Britain in 1695 and not repealed until 1829, which forbade Catholics even to buy land.

But land, even tenanted land, was becoming scarce for a country whose population rose an extraordinary 172 percent between 1779 and 1841. Because of the competition for acreage, rents became exceedingly high. The 1841 census showed that almost half the holdings in Ireland were smaller than five acres.

Yet that was almost enough, for one and a half acres was usually adequate to support a family of four or five with that nourishing staple of the Irish diet—the potato. It was an admirable food, the potato. It was easy to harvest, easy to cook, and could be used to feed animals as well as humans. It had a weakness, however. It could not be stored for long periods. So in the summer months—when the Irish poor were on the brink of hunger until the crop came in—the peasants sometimes had to buy corn meal at exorbitant rates. Not only was meal beyond the fiscal reach of the poor, there wasn't enough of it, anyway.

So, to the Irish, the potato was life. And without it . . . ?

July 1845 in Ireland was dry and hot, promising a bumper potato harvest. Then there was a sudden change to unseasonably cold and, even for Ireland, wet weather. Yet as late as July 23 the *Freeman's Journal* reported that "the poor man's property, the potato crop, was never before so large and at the same time abundant." But in August came disquieting news: the potato crop in England was failing in scattered areas. It seemed it was afflicted with the same blight that had struck in North America a year earlier, a blight that somehow had made its way across the Atlantic.

After a tour, Sir James Graham, the Home Secretary, said he had found "fearful destruction" and said it would be "a shocking calamity for the poor" if the failure became general. First harvest reports from Ireland indicated a good crop but within a few days the potatoes inexplicably blackened and rotted. Ireland's potato famine had begun. In 1846 the crop failed entirely and did so again in 1848.

It had been said the only thing that could drive the Irish from their home was the choice between flight and death. For over a million people the choice came too late, if at all. They died—along the hedgerows, in their hovels, in the fields.

Nor was flight that simple an alternative. Although passage to the New World was only $20, few peasants had even that kind of money. The trip itself could take up to 160 days in ships little better than slavers. "Ship fever," a kind of typhus, was common. Passengers were crammed between decks with no privacy, sleeping on straw. They usually brought their own food with them, and when it ran out, as it often did, hunger at sea replaced hunger on land.

Among those to leave was Patrick Kennedy of Dunganstown, the son of the veteran of

Vinegar Hill. Patrick Kennedy the younger was not typical. His family owned eighty acres —mostly in barley—and cattle, and were people of substance. And yet he went.

"Patrick Kennedy left, we are convinced, out of a sheer sense of adventure and the courage to start a new life," said a local historian more than a century later. The shipping office where he probably booked his passage is still standing in New Ross along the banks of the Barrow, a wide, deep stream that could handle the 500-tonners which came up from the sea to the walled town of slate houses and thatched cottages.

Customarily a departure was celebrated with a night of merrymaking followed by a cavalcade of relatives and neighbors down to the port after a blessing from the local priest. And there was a song favored of the emigrants. It went:

*The heart that now bleeds for thy sorrows*
*And will waste on a far distant shore.*

Little is recorded of Patrick's leave-taking, but it would seem fate rather than design brought him to Boston, as was true of many of his countrymen. Some years earlier the Cunard Line, with the encouragement of a local bank, had decided on Boston as its principal terminal in the United States. And the Cunard Line was one of the main carriers of the Irish fleeing the famine.

Patrick Kennedy survived a trip that many Irish did not and stepped ashore in 1848 on Noddle's Island, now part of East Boston. If he would find it a land without "empty bellies," Patrick Kennedy would also find America a land of "ill conveniences." To be an Irishman among Americans was not much better than to be an Irishman among Irishmen. There was discrimination and poverty for the Irish in the New World just as there had been in the Old. But at least in America a man could work and, perhaps some day, succeed.

The Irish in Boston and elsewhere were crammed into "paddyvilles" where smallpox and cholera and tuberculosis were commonplace. One privy sometimes served a whole neighborhood. Whole families would share a single bed. A study in 1848 in Boston reported a "hive of human beings without comforts and mostly without common necessaries . . . huddled together like brutes without regard to sex or age or sense of decency. . . . "

In 1849 a resident thought it "something of a sensation" to see an Irishman in South Boston, but the sensation would soon be replaced with alarm and scorn at the illiterate masses that were filling up Boston from Ireland.

Employers retained "padrones" who would meet the immigrant ships and hustle their unwitting human cargo off to the most menial jobs at pitiable wages. Colleens off the farm found work as lowly domestics where they were called "biddies" and "kitchen canaries." Many newspaper want ads carried the initials NINA: No Irish Need Apply. Walt Whitman visited Boston and said the Irish were worse off than the Negroes.

The Irish had long been a target of suspicion and hate in America. Their God, for one, was not the austere deity of the Puritans, and as early as 1829 Irish Catholic homes had been stoned in Boston. Rumors of fiendish activities in Catholic convents were frequent, and in 1834 an Ursuline convent in Charlestown was burned by vigilantes who believed Protestant children were being forced to adopt Catholicism, and nuns were kept locked in the basement. Three years later a riot over the Irish broke out in Boston, and the militia had to be called.

The Yankees could laugh at the awkward ways of their domestics, "girls fresh out of the bogs," such as one who came downstairs backwards because stairs had been unknown in her home in Erin. She had always used a ladder.

But they could not laugh off another aspect of the Irish invasion. "Men," said one Yankee, "were led up to the desk like dumb brutes, their hands guided to make a straight mark." The mark was made on a ballot. The Irish had discovered a key to their establishment in America: the vote.

It was a natural reaction. The portrait of Irish conviviality is no caricature. It is fact. In effect prisoners in their own land in Ireland, the Irish togetherness had no political outlet other than sporadic uprisings. In America, crowded into ghettoes that concentrated by necessity their sociability, they gathered in saloons and social clubs. Shared suffering was nothing new to the Irish. An opportunity to do something about it was. Aside from their cohesiveness, the Irish had another asset that other immigrant groups lacked. They spoke English.

Knowing the language, they quickly learned the ways of politics, but just as their speech was blurred by a brogue, so was their politics blurred by a genial disregard of textbook procedures. They were a person-to-person people, and so was their politics. A dollar loaned until payday was an IOU for a favor or vote to be redeemed at some future date. If Paddy got drunk Saturday night, it was the duty of any good ward politician to put up bail just as it was Paddy's, when sobered, to vote for him—and more than once if need be.

Martin Lomasney, a Boston boss who if he didn't write the textbook on precinct politics failed to do so because he was too busy tending his flock, once said:

"I think that there's got to be in every ward somebody that any bloke can come to—no matter what he's done—and get help. Help, you understand. None of your law and your justice, but help."

Lomasney had no better disciple than his brother, Joseph, who was once found influen-

*In the hills of Wexford, Cousin Jim Kennedy still tends the family fields.*

The homes of the Brahmins. Beacon Street, 1855.

Kennedy

cing a deaf and dumb voter at the polls by talking to him in sign language. If such shenanigans were unseemly and ill-mannered in so proper a cradle of liberty as Boston, the Irish could well be excused. Their political life in Ireland had been a struggle for survival, transformed in America into a struggle for success. Why should they play the game any more uprightly than their oppressors? The battle was all the more appealing to the jollity in the Irish in that it pitted them against that most austere, frugal, aloof, Calvinistic fellow, the New England Yankee, the Brahmin of Boston who readily acknowledged the gap between himself and the uncouth Papist overflowing the very heart of "the land of the Pilgrim's pride."

"Our Celtic fellow citizens," said one Brahmin, George Templeton Strong, "are almost as remote from us in temperament and constitution as the Chinese."

"Scratch a convict or pauper and the chances that you tickle the skin of an Irish Catholic," said a newspaper, faithful to the feeling of the times.

It was a time for anti-Irish sentiment, culminating in mid-century with the Know Nothing movement, which was directed against immigrants in general and Catholic immigrants in particular. For a time the movement had national significance although its quasi-secret nature gave it its name: when questioned about the movement its adherents would answer they knew nothing about it.

The defensive reaction of the Irish was a political flowering that found its nutriment in two quarters, the neighborhood grog shop and the Democratic Party. The grog shop was the neighborhood social center as the Democratic Party became nationally for the poor immigrants of the city. The Irish found themselves at home in both places, as did Patrick Kennedy.

On his arrival in Boston, Patrick took a job as a cooper, making the barrels that held the whiskey that brightened the world that his countrymen had come to. It was a time when men worked for a dollar or less for a fourteen-hour day. Said a Negro slave in 1850:

"My master is a great tyrant. He treats me as if I was a common Irishman."

In time Patrick Kennedy took a wife, Bridget Murphy, who was two years older than he. They had three children: two daughters, and a son born January 8, 1858. They named their son Patrick Joseph.

Within a year the father died of cholera. He was only thirty-five. Had Patrick remained in Ireland and survived the famine, his descendants would almost certainly have remained the farmers that the Kennedy relations are in Ireland today, relatively prosperous countrymen still tilling the green hills about Wexford.

But fate had written otherwise for Patrick Kennedy. Although he did not know it, he had begun a dynasty, and the name Kennedy through his seed would know glory and tragedy in the new land to which he had come.

# Days of the Dearos

Along with the cod and the baked bean the Irish ward boss was a staple of life in Boston in the late nineteenth century. Draped in the smoke of a blunt cigar from the top of his derby hat to the bottom of his button shoes, the ward boss set out to see that his countrymen from Erin—not overlooking himself —got their due slice of the American Dream. While their tactics might have discomfited a graduate of the Electoral College, the Irish nonetheless took to politics with a zesty, humorous and realistic appraisal of the frailities of mankind. In exchange for the tender, loving care with which they administered their people, they expected and got their return, a scrawled signature on a ballot come election day. It was not always parliamentary. But it was fun.

"Don't get mad, get even," was one of the first principles of the game. "Do to others or they will do you," decreed James Michael Curley, who served part of a term as mayor of Boston from a prison cell.

Another rule was handed down by one John I. Fitzgerald, who said of course elections in his ward were honest. The polls were too closely watched. "Ballot boxes are never stuffed," he proclaimed, "unless it's absolutely necessary."

It is often overlooked that Jack and Robert Kennedy had not one, but two grandfathers who were noteworthy achievers in the game. One, of course, was John F. "Honey Fitz" Fitzgerald (no relation to John I.), a chipper, flamboyant man who paraded through Boston's political life with a song on his lips— he would sing "Sweet Adeline" at the drop of a derby—and a smile on his jut-jawed face that one observer said "looked like it had been built from the bottom up." He was friend of Presidents and peddlers and also friend and ally of Patrick J. Kennedy, who was a marked contrast to Honey Fitz, pre-

ferring to work behind the scenes while Fitzgerald strutted on center stage, slapping backs and charming his constituents of "the Dear Old North End" who, at length, came to be known as the Dearos.

Patrick, or P. J. as he came to be known, was the son of the same Patrick Kennedy of Dunganstown. Patrick was educated as a good Irishman should be, in church schools taught by nuns. His mother would not have her son contaminated by the public schools which did not feel that religion, particularly the religion of Rome, was one of the three R's. Afternoons and Saturdays Patrick helped his mother at her work and in his teens left school entirely to help support the family by working along the docks in East Boston.

"His deep urge to get ahead was practically his only resource," wrote Richard Whalen. The Irish developed a canny and colorful nomenclature to determine where one stood in the social and economic pecking order. At the bottom were the shanty Irish, followed in ascending order by such as the lace curtain Irish, two-bathroom Irish, wall-to-wall Irish and Irish who "had fruit in the home when no one was sick."

P. J. was a cut above the shanty and capitalized on his countrymen's chronic thirst to move higher. He was a frugal youth, husbanding his savings until he finally had enough to purchase a rundown saloon on Haymarket Square. He later bought into two other saloons and a whiskey-distributing business. Then he acquired a coal business and a share of a bank he helped organize, the Columbia Trust Company, where his son and grandsons would later work.

Patrick's growing affluence matched the substance of his bride, Mary Híckey, whose brothers included a mayor of Brockton, a doctor, and a police captain.

As a saloon keeper Patrick Kennedy found

*The progenitor: Patrick J. Kennedy*

That was the meetingplace of the so-called "Board of Strategy," a group of six men which was described as "practically the dictatorate of the Democratic city machine." The Board was the final and often first say in who got what in city, county and state jobs.

Thus Room 8 was the hub of the Hub. The Quincy House itself was one of the few places that accepted City Hall vouchers for meals, refreshments or rent-a-carriage; the place where the pols celebrated their flocks' weddings and mourned their funerals. It was a natural environment for P. J., a quiet, cigar-smoking man who liked good stories, never raised his voice, spoke kindly of one and all except the few whom he characterized as "no-good loafers." P. J. understood the value of hard work and was even a broad-minded enough barkeeper and politician to have promised his support to one of his customers provided he never touched a drop again.

Another member of the Board with P. J. was the other Kennedy grandfather, Honey Fitz. Fitzgerald was born to Irish immigrant parents in 1863 in a third-floor tenement apartment that could have qualified for lace curtains but had no toilet. Honey Fitz's father had worked on a farm when he arrived in America but later moved to Boston where he opened a grocery-liquor store. (Liquor long has been friend to the family fortune. P. J.'s son was to make a killing in whiskey and gin upon repeal of Prohibition).

It may have been the store that gave the young Fitzgerald his nickname. Legend has it that he used to dip into his father's sugar barrel to appease a sweet tooth. Others say it was the result of a typographical error of Johnny Fitz, the name he raced under in his early political years.

In any event, his parents sent him off to the prestigious Boston Latin school, and he later almost finished a year at Harvard Medi-

himself cast in the role of a Good Samaritan, Father Confessor and friend in need. He soon saw the political possibilities of such a position, saw politics as "the substance of power," says Whalen, and ran in 1886 for the state house of representatives—as a Democrat, naturally. He served four years, was elected to the state senate in 1892 and was a delegate to the national Democratic conventions in 1888, 1896 and 1900.

Patrick Kennedy also held various city posts in Boston, but it was not in the limelight but in Room 8 of the old Quincy House, now torn down, that P. J. wielded his power.

cal School, but had to leave to support his family when his father died. Fitzgerald went into the fire insurance business and carried the protection for P. J. Kennedy's stable, the beginning of a long relationship. Honey Fitz naturally gravitated to politics—and prosperity. At one political ball, he had the water in the hall turned off so the parched guests would buy soft drinks and fatten the party treasury.

In 1892 Honey Fitz was elected to the City Council, and to insure he stayed there, he used to read the obituaries and send out his henchmen as a "wake squad" to show the bereaved that he cared. In 1894 he was elected to Con-

gress and again in '96 and '98. In Washington he was called "Boston Johnny" for his perseverance in getting the Charlestown Naval Yard reopened. He was a familiar figure at the White House and once introduced his young daughter, Rose, to President McKinley while passing through on his way to Palm Beach. Rose would later know much of both places.

Honey Fitz's brother, James, was often referred to as the man who discovered Palm Beach for Bostonians. He first went there in the winter of 1898-9 because someone told James, who liked to swim in the summer,

*The Honorable John F. Fitzgerald, Mayor of Boston*

that it was a good place to swim in the winter.

Honey Fitz, meanwhile, was making another big splash in Boston, getting elected mayor in 1905. He popped up all over town wherever he could find enough people to make up an audience—wakes, parties, meetings—and earned the title as "the Number One Uninvited Guest in America."

Defeated in 1907 for reelection, he tried again in 1910 and rode into office on the wings of song after wowing an audience with his rendition of "Sweet Adeline," which became his lifelong theme song. Once, when run over by a truck, Honey Fitz reassured worried bystanders by singing "Sweet Adeline" to show he was all right and then went home for six weeks to recover.

Honey Fitz could use his tongue for other than lyrics. When Teddy Roosevelt said he felt as vigorous as a bull moose and organized the splinter Republican faction that bore that animal's name, Honey Fitz said it was "one-ninth moose and eight-ninths bull," a piece of Americana that has survived the Bull Moosers. He was a man of action, if nothing else. On his fiftieth birthday he celebrated by running the 100-yard dash in the morning and boxing in the afternoon. He loved to travel with the Red Sox and pose with Babe Ruth for photographers. He was a friend of the famous, such as sportsman and tea tycoon Sir Thomas Lipton. Honey Fitz said he had known every President since Grant, whose hand he had shaken as a schoolboy.

The life of a Boston politician of the time was one of glorious skulduggery and oratory. A favorite trick on election eve was to send henchmen through the tenements banging on doors and rousing the sleeping to tell them to vote for the opposing candidate. "Mattress voters"—men brought into rooming houses the night before registration so they could claim residency in the ward and thus swell the boss's list of available names to vote for him—were commonplace. Fitzgerald used to have his volunteer workers arrive early at the polls and then give up their places in line to later arrivals "compliments of Honey Fitz."

Toughs called "bullpushers" because they worked the cattle boats that plied back and forth to Europe did heavy work when needed. One hefty bullpusher was seen to have decked a man he recognized as on his way to vote for the opposition and then leaned solicitously over him, saying: "Oh dear, I'm afraid the poor man has fainted."

When pressure was too blatant, strategem was resorted to. Once P. J. Kennedy was feuding with Martin Lomasney, dictator of the Eighth Ward, over control of a nominating convention and put up roadblocks to keep Lomasney's supporters at bay. Lomasney sneaked his men through the lines disguised as a funeral procession. There was another pol who placed glue in the lock of a polling place to keep early risers from voting before heading for work for the day. Honey Fitz himself ran into trouble in 1918 when his election to Congress was voided after a hearing on voting fraud in some precincts. There was testimony about how Honey Fitz's opponent had printed stickers with his name on it and distributed them to voters so they wouldn't have to go to the trouble of writing in his name. Some of Fitzgerald's supporters got wind of it and began passing out their own stickers, charitably still bearing the opposing candidate's name but having no glue on the back so the labels fell off in the ballot box, negating the vote.

Irish loyalty to clan was not forgotten when the Dearos moved to power in City Hall. Nepotism was as common as graft. One did not forget friends—or enemies. Honey Fitz when mayor created the post of City Dermatologist, filling the post with a party faithful at $4,000

a year. When Losmasney did a favor for a party worker back in 1895, the man sent the ward boss a thank-you note. Thirty-seven years later he received back the yellowed piece of paper from Lomasney with a notation to get out and vote for a Lomasney candidate.

Boston politics had a long memory, and few events were remembered longer than Honey Fitz's notable political defeat in 1916. (He was not to win another election after 1918 although he ran a number of times for various offices, including governor.) In that year Fitzgerald challenged Henry Cabot Lodge for the latter's Senate seat. If any election showed how far the Irish had come, it was that one. Lodge was a Brahmin's Brahmin, a prototype of the sublimely self-confident Yankee aristocracy, one dowager member of which reportedly said she could not comprehend all the fuss being made about the painting by James Whistler of his mother. "After all, she's only a McNeill from North Carolina."

That an upstart born of Irish immigrants could challenge nobility may have horrified Back Bay Boston, but not other areas of Massachusetts, and Lodge won by only 33,000 votes, a defeat that would not be soon forgotten by the Fitzgeralds—or the Kennedys.

Nor would the family forget Honey Fitz's classic battles with James Michael Curley, the darling of the Dearos, who could have sat for Edwin O'Connor's portrait of the roguish, but lovable, Frank Skeffington in his novel, *The Last Hurrah.* It was during a Curley campaign for mayor when he countered an attack by Honey Fitz, his opponent, by announcing:

"I am preparing three addresses which, if necessary, I shall deliver in the fall and which, if a certain individual had the right to restrict free speech, I would not be permitted to deliver. One of these addresses is entitled: Graft,

Ancient and Modern,' another, 'Great Lovers, from Cleopatra to Toodles,' and last, but not least interesting, 'Libertines, from Henry VIII to the Present Day.' "

Toodles?

Curley was referring to Miss Elizabeth M. "Toodles" Ryan, a self-described "cloak model" in her twenties who had once appeared in a "morality play," titled *Experience,* in New York. She also appeared in a breach of promise suit in Boston in 1915 in which it was testified that she had been kissed by four men one Sunday afternoon in an upper room of the Ferncroft Inn near Boston.

The following colloquy took place during the trial between James F. Mullen, a 71-year-old retired wine salesman; Daniel Coakley, Toodles's lawyer; and Michael L. Sullivan, attorney for Henry K. Mansfield, target of Miss Ryan's suit and proprietor of the Ferncroft Inn.

Coakley: "Who were the four men?"

Mullen: "Frank Hall, John F. Fitzgerald, Gus Seeley and myself."

Coakley: "Is the John F. Fitzgerald you mention the ex-mayor of Boston?"

Mullen: "Yes."

Coakley: "You kissed Bessie Ryan?"

Mullen: "Yes."

Coakley: "You're a gay old dog, aren't you?"

Sullivan: "I object!"

Honey Fitz likewise objected later to reporters. Mullen's story, he said, was "silly and untrue." He later testified he had never heard of Miss Ryan. She, too, denied Mullen's testimony and then wrote her memoirs for the Boston *American* beginning: "Oh, girls, girls! Don't think it's cute to start out for a good time after decent people have gone to bed. . . . If you live in a farm, stay there. That's where I was raised and I wish I never had left it."

Such color may have been the despair of Boston's Watch and Ward Society, but it could only provide ammunition to those who felt the proper place for the Irish was Ireland.

Honey Fitz knew the prejudice against the Irish and their religion. It had been a major factor in his 1910 mayoralty race.

"You have plenty of Irish depositors, why don't you have some Irishmen on your board of directors?" he once asked a bank president.

"Well, a couple of the tellers are Irish Catholics," the executive replied.

"Yes," Fitzgerald shot back, "and I suppose the charwomen are too."

Not too far from the madding crowds, both Honey Fitz and P. J. Kennedy were raising their broods. P. J. had had two sons. One, Joseph Patrick, was born in 1887; the other died in infancy. There were also two daughters, Loretta and Margaret. Honey Fitz's daughter, Rose, was the apple of his eye—and of Boston's. A very bright student, she graduated from high school at the age of fifteen and was voted the prettiest graduate that year. After studying at a convent in Europe for a year, she returned and became her father's official

hostess in place of her shy and retiring mother. Thus Rose at an early age learned the political game.

P. J.'s boy, meanwhile, was making a name for himself as an athlete at Boston Latin and one year won the city batting championship with an average of .667. Honey Fitz was on hand to present the trophy to his old ally's son. Despite occasional fallings-out politically, the two had remained good friends and spent a summer with their families at Old Orchard Beach in Maine where their two children, Rose and Joe, saw quite a bit of each other.

Honey Fitz had another daughter, Eunice, who died at twenty-three of tuberculosis apparently contracted when she was doing Red Cross work during World War I. It was a hard blow for the aging warrior. He suffered another loss in 1929 when his friend, P. J. Kennedy, died of a heart attack. A newspaper said in his obituary:

"He represented a type of political leader that is fast disappearing in this city and was noted as a discreet counsellor and strong adherence to party organization. He very seldom made speeches, but discussed political issues and candidates in a calm, constructive and conservative manner."

They had called him "one of the shrewdest men in Boston politics." And now P. J. and many of the others who had brought the Irish to political power in Boston were gone.

But Honey Fitz survived, and there were the grandchildren coming along. Perhaps they could fill the ranks some day. Honey Fitz no doubt beamed with pride the day when he brought his little grandson, Jack, to a political rally, propped him on a table and heard the child give perhaps his first public speech.

"My grandpa is the finest grandpa in the world," said the little boy.

*The Mayor and Rose sail for South America.*

# The Founding Fortune

"He was an outstanding progenitor. He was always thinking about his family as a unit and promoting it and what he hoped to make of them."

The words from an associate of the New Deal days in Washington bit to the core of Joseph Patrick Kennedy's purpose in life—to build a family that would be big and rich and powerful. It may or may not have been part of the ambition that, in the building, he would become the most remarkable member of a remarkable clan, not only the founding father but the central strength, the cohesive force and the rallying point.

Precisely when his family ambition was born is not recorded, but his financial ambition was established early. Soon after he graduated from Harvard in 1912 with a small nest egg—his half of the profits from a moonlighting venture that began with $600 capital—he decided to be a millionaire by the time he was thirty-five.

Some romantic chroniclers of the Kennedy story endeavored to give it a Horatio Alger tint, a rags-to-riches theme. Possibly the fact that the Kennedys emigrated from an Ireland beset by economic ills inspired the effort, but the subject did not fit the frame.

By the time Joseph P. Kennedy was born— September 6, 1888—his father was firmly established in the strata of lace curtain Irish.

Joe Kennedy's boyhood was like that of a multitude of other Irish Catholic youngsters in the Boston of the late nineteenth and early twentieth centuries: strict religious upbringing, pranks and scrapes, parental punishments and admonishments, the first recognition of girls and the expenditure of a tremendous amount of energy in doing not much of anything. His variety of odd jobs sprung not just from a need for the money but from an urge to compete.

One youthful enterprise involved raising pigeons for the dinner plates of East Boston fanciers of roast squab. Kennedy's contribution to the business was a scheme to replenish the flock without expense. He and his partner took birds from their coop and released them on Boston Common where the pigeon population was both numerous and hungry. By nightfall, if nature prevailed as expected, the boys' birds would be home, accompanied by a few guests.

Kennedy emerged from the anonymity of youth when, after attending two parochial schools, his father transferred him to Boston Latin, an institution of high prestige since 1635. Among its former students were such luminaries of American and New England history as Cotton Mather, John Hancock, four other signers of the Declaration of Independence, Ralph Waldo Emerson, Charles Sumner—and, of course, Honey Fitz, class of 1884.

Kennedy's mark at Boston Latin was as an indifferent but popular student. He was president of his class (1908) in his senior year, led the school's cadet corps to a city championship, and was captain of the baseball team for two years. Teammates remembered him as a tough competitor and a poor loser. "I can still see him glaring at the umpire and pounding his fist in his glove," said one of them.

The class yearbook predicted that Kennedy would make his fortune in "a very roundabout way"—a farsighted observation if the routes of Wall Street, Hollywood and Scotch whiskey could be considered roundabout.

Harvard was a different nut to crack. Virtually the only non-scholastic requirement for admission was enough money to pay the student's way, but getting into the school's social and athletic life was another matter. Cliques divided the campus, and Boston's Irish Catholics believed firmly that the few Irish students were targets of a subtle but nonetheless effective discrimination. Irish

*The door said: Joseph P. Kennedy, banker.*

names of athletes such as Eddie Mahan, Eddie Casey and Charley Brickley were among the hallowed heroes of Cambridge, but they were All-Americans in any company, possessing such talent that even discrimination could not keep them off the team.

Kennedy had at least one experience with discrimination of this sort. He failed to make the baseball team in 1911 but showed up on the bench for the climactic game against Yale and got into action only long enough to win his "H" by making the final putout in Harvard's 4–1 victory. He pocketed the ball, saying: "I made the putout, didn't I?"

Off the ball field, Kennedy did "all right" by his own definition. He was elected to the Hasty Pudding club in his sophomore year and made Delta Upsilon fraternity as a senior. It was not the top but not the bottom, either. He earned passable grades with history and economics getting his best attention. Paradoxically, he withdrew from a course in accounting when he was on the brink of flunking, but graduated with honors in mathematics.

During summer vacations, Kennedy played baseball in a league representing New England hotels and was hired at space rates to report on resort society and sports for the Boston *Globe*. There was a hint of future acumen: he persuaded a friend who had journalistic ambitions to do the reporting, but he kept the money, sometimes $30 per week.

The love of sports, fostered in Kennedy's school days, never left him. Years later, an associate in government would say, "He had tremendous energy that he conserved wisely. I never saw a man take better care of himself physically." He became an accomplished horseman and, even in his seventies, could and did brag that none of his sons was his equal at golf. And, like everything else he touched, sport yielded its lessons for the Kennedy

*Honey Fitz pitched, Rose batted, Joe captained the team.*

*October 7, 1914: Mr. and Mrs. Joseph P. Kennedy.*

career. "Remember," he liked to say, "if you can't be captain, don't play."

Another off-campus Kennedy activity was a venture into the sightseeing business. Kennedy and a friend bought a battered bus for $600 and began escorting tourists around historic Boston. Joe handled the lecturer's spiel, his friend the driving. When Joe went off to New Hampshire to play baseball in the summer, the friend ran the business. At the end of college days they split $10,000.

Kennedy's first post-Harvard job was modest, giving no hint of the explosive career ahead. He used his father's influence to get an appointment as a state bank examiner for $1,500 per year. The true payoff was an insight into the worlds of finance and banking and a chance to meet important people and make important friends.

Then, in 1913, he put over a coup which, more than anything theretofore, bore the Kennedy stamp of bold maneuver and friendly persuasion.

The Columbia Trust Company — P. J.'s bank—was a small neighborhood concern in East Boston with a capital of $200,000 and surplus of $37,000. In a wave of bank mergers, the big First Ward National wanted to absorb it. Patrick Kennedy lacked the means to counterattack, and Joe took charge. He borrowed money to buy stock, scurried around town to get proxies, used his Harvard contacts to raise more money. Two days before the decisive stockholders' meeting, Columbia's independence was assured, and First Ward National withdrew.

Columbia's grateful directors elected Kennedy president. He was twenty-five years old, the youngest bank president in the state and perhaps, as Boston papers suggested, the country. Kennedy was irritated by the idea that he had done something extraordinary. "It's no crime to be young," he said.

The bank affair had another benefit for Kennedy. The presidency gave him the prestige to qualify as a suitor for the hand of Rose Fitzgerald, eldest of Honey Fitz's three daughters.

Rose was a slim, attractive girl who resembled her mother. She was the youngest member of the Boston Public Library committee which selected reading matter for children, was a Sunday School teacher, and a member of the Cecilian League, the Irish counterpart of the Junior League.

In their first dating days, Honey Fitz did not look upon the prospective wooer with favor. He figured on his daughter landing a bigger fish than Joe Kennedy. There was one story that Joe had to give Rose her engagement ring on the sidewalk because Honey Fitz wouldn't allow him to enter the house.

For that matter, Kennedy wasn't overly enchanted with his sweetheart's father, regarding him as a bit on the breezy side. Another story was told that on motor trips (prime sport in those early days of autos), Fitzgerald would talk incessantly, to the irritation and boredom of the captive listener beside him. Joe's defense took advantage of his father-in-law's sweet tooth. When they went for a ride, Joe would deposit a box of the chewiest caramels he could find beside the driver's seat. Honey Fitz would concentrate his jawing on the candy.

Rose Fitzgerald and Joseph P. Kennedy were married in October 1914, to the delight of the Dearos at the joining of the clans. William Cardinal O'Connell celebrated the Nuptial Mass in the private chapel at his residence. The couple honeymooned at White Sulphur Springs, and then began housekeeping in their first home in suburban Brookline. The bridegroom, in debt as a result of the bank exploit, had to borrow for the down payment.

*Miss Rose Fitzgerald, the belle of Boston—and Palm Beach*

With children coming along—Joseph P. Jr. in July 1915, John F. in May 1917—it didn't take Kennedy long to decide that suburban banking and a modest whirl in real estate would not produce the big money he wanted. He was ready to seek new worlds.

The opening came through the good offices of Guy Currier, a wealthy lawyer and one of the powers behind the state legislature. Kennedy had met him while angling to be elected a trustee of the Massachusetts Electric Company and, as he invariably did, made a good impression and was remembered.

The proposition was a position as assistant general manager of the Fore River shipyard at Quincy, Massachusetts, being built by Bethlehem Steel as part of shipbuilding's rapid expansion in anticipation of war needs. The salary was $20,000 per year, plus bonuses, but that wasn't all for Joe Kennedy. Restaurant facilities were scarce, far from enough to feed the foot-loose among a working force of 22,000 men. Kennedy opened a cafeteria—the Victory Lunchroom—and fed thousands of men daily.

Early in his Fore River career, an incident occurred which revealed much about Joe Kennedy's foresighted methods of making potentially valuable friendships. Charles M. Schwab, dynamic chairman of Bethlehem Steel and Kennedy's boss in the last analysis, was coming to Quincy on an inspection tour. A mix-up in plans was to bring him to town without a hotel reservation or luncheon arrangements. Kennedy's secretary told him of Schwab's impending arrival, along with the casual observation that the tycoon liked chicken livers as a luncheon dish.

Whalen told the story in his biography of Kennedy:

"Next day [Kennedy] greeted Schwab at Back Bay station and whisked him to a suite at the Copley-Plaza. Later, Kennedy led the way to the dining room for a lunch of chicken livers, meticulously prepared by a chef who had been alerted 24 hours earlier. Afterward, Kennedy drove Schwab to Fore River and stuck close to his side during a tour of the yard. His invitation to dinner and the theater was accepted. That evening, the men talked for more than two hours. When swung aboard an early train the next morning, he must have made a mental note to keep tabs on the able young man he had discovered."

Joe Kennedy did not enlist when the United States entered World War I, an inaction he was said to have regretted in later years. But it is a question whether Joe Kennedy in a doughboy's uniform would have contributed more to victory than he did as assistant general manager at Fore River. He was a working executive in a blazing effort which delivered thirty-six destroyers in twenty-seven months, as well as many submarines. And that's where he met Franklin Delano Roosevelt.

Roosevelt was an assistant secretary of the Navy. One of his jobs was supervision of the shipyards, prodding them to ever greater effort, an assignment which threw him into contact—and conflict—with Kennedy. They had one tussle over two battleships built for Argentina.

The ships had been completed but not delivered when the United States went to war. Kennedy had orders not to release them until they were paid for. Roosevelt, anxious to avoid international friction, was willing to extend credit. Kennedy wasn't. Roosevelt broke the deadlock by sending Navy tugs to tow the big ships out of the yard. "Roosevelt

was the hardest trader I'd ever run up against," said Kennedy.

When peace came, the shipbuilding business went. Kennedy was ready to move on, as he always was when he figured he had finished the job he wanted to do. "I'll work for nothing, but it's got to be interesting," he said.

Wall Street was the arena which invited him, and Galen Stone was the key he used to get in. Stone was a portly financier, one of the shrewdest in New England, director in a score of companies and partner in the firm of Hayden, Stone and Company. One of his interests was a steamship line; maybe he would like to buy a few liners from Fore River?

Kennedy was able to set up only a fifteen-minute interview, and that was canceled when Stone was called out of town. Kennedy found out which train he was taking, hurried to the station, slid into the seat beside Stone and talked with him all the way to New York. Despite all the persuasiveness he could muster, Stone wasn't interested in buying ships. He was interested in the ship salesman. Two weeks later—after more Kennedy manipulations—the ship salesman was offered the job of managing the stock department in Hayden, Stone's Boston office. He accepted a salary of $10,000 per year, half what he was getting at Fore River. The return he sought wasn't in pay checks.

Kennedy's first adventure in the stock market wasn't encouraging. Acting on a tip that a certain issue was about to be split, he bought it at 160 and watched it slide to 80. The experience was reflected in a later rueful comment: "I always said that with enough 'inside information' and unlimited credit you are sure to go broke."

In his behalf, it might be said that the market just then was unusually tricky. The economy had slowed, a natural reaction after the boom years of war, but the expected recovery had not materialized. Even veteran speculators were baffled and groping.

From 1919 to 1922, Kennedy sat literally at Stone's right hand, listening and absorbing information for future reference, learning the ins and outs of the freewheeling market. In particular, he learned about stock pools, the maneuver by which a group of traders would take heavy options on a stock at a low quotation, stimulate interest by exchanges among themselves, and then, when the gullible public rushed to buy, sell out at an inflated price.

When Stone retired in 1922, Kennedy branched out on his own, in an office which said JOSEPH P. KENNEDY, BANKER on the door. He operated as a lone wolf, alert for tips and information, but secretive about his own dealings. Said an industrialist who knew him: "He was the kind that either told you nothing, but if he did it was 100 per cent the facts and truth. If he liked you, there wasn't anything he wouldn't do for you, and if he didn't like you, there wasn't anything he would do with you."

Joe Kennedy was not a gambler like Jesse Livermore, the "Boy Plunger," or Frank Bliss, the "Silver Fox," or others of their strain. He was a speculator, more modest in the scale of his operations and interested in the long haul rather than the quick profit. He had the temperament for the required restraint; in the words of a close associate: "a passion for facts, a complete lack of sentiment, a marvelous sense of timing." That last attribute would appear in many an appraisal of the Kennedy talent.

Kennedy, himself, once analyzed the difference between gambling and speculating: "I think the prime motive back of most gambling is the excitement of it. While gamblers naturally want to win, the majority of them derive pleasure even if they lose. The desire to win, rather than the excitement involved,

seems to me to be the compelling force behind speculation."

Legends aplenty surrounded Kennedy's exploits in the Street. One that seemed to have more fact than fancy concerned the fluctuations of stock of the Yellow Cab Company. One night in April 1924, Kennedy had a visitor at his home in Brookline (not the one in which he and his bride had lived first, but a twelve-room affair in a more fashionable section. The move was impelled by the growing family. Rosemary had arrived in 1918, Kathleen in 1920, Eunice in 1921.)

Kennedy's visitor was Walter Howey, a Chicago newspaper editor to whom Kennedy owed a favor. Yellow Cab, in which Howey had invested, was skidding, from 85 to 50; the belief was that Wall Street bears were on the prowl. Kennedy was ill. Nevertheless he went to New York, moved into a hotel room, installed a battery of telephones and a market ticker and went to work to frustrate the raiders.

He holed up in that room for seven weeks. Working much of the time from bed, he went through a bewildering series of maneuvers, now buying, now selling, all around the country, sending the stock on an erratic course that only he could understand. His manipulations confused the raiders. They were beaten off, and the stock stabilized around 50. Then Kennedy went home to see for the first time his new daughter Patricia, aged one month.

Months later, Yellow Cab slumped again. A poor earnings report was the obvious explanation, but there were suspicions—totally unproved—that Kennedy was selling short and profiting handsomely thereby.

Only Joseph P. Kennedy could tell how much he made in the market. But it probably would not be overstatement to say that, on his thirty-fifth birthday in 1923, he had attained the millionaire status that was his early goal. That was only the beginning.

*Wall Street 1929: When the bootblacks got in, Joe Kennedy got out.*

*Wall Street: The canyon where Joe Kennedy struck it rich.*

Perhaps there was no better evidence of Kennedy's sagacity than the fact that he was a spectator when the market crashed in 1929. He liked to tell an anecdote about a shoeshine boy who had accurately predicted market fluctuations. "When the time comes that a shoeshine boy knows as much as I do, there's something wrong with either me or the market, and it's time for me to get out." He had made up his mind months earlier when he had time for a leisurely study of the market and didn't like what he saw. Anyway, Hollywood had beckoned. "There are only two pursuits that get into your blood," he believed, "politics and the motion picture business."

To go back a bit. In 1919 Kennedy had seen a small-town banker build a $120,000 investment into more than $3 million with just one movie, *The Miracle Man.* It was enough to put Hollywood in Kennedy's book as a source of important money. For the time, he was content to share in the purchase of a chain of thirty-one moviehouses in New England.

Hollywood and the movies were growing fast, as fast as the lore of glamor around them. Again quoting Whalen:

"There was no business remotely like the picture business; within the movie world and outside, many doubted that it was a business at all. Each film involved fresh problems and different risks. Individual and organizational fortunes swung dizzily from year to year. Kennedy caught on quickly.

"Sixty million Americans went to the movies each week in 21,000 theaters across the country. Statistics of this sort supported the claim that the movies were Big Business. But the men at the corporate heights who guessed the whims of millions of movie-goers were an odd assortment of risen petty entrepreneurs. They included the former furriers, Adolph Zukor and Marcus Loew, the ex-ragman Louis B. Mayer, the one-time glove salesman Samuel

Goldwyn . . . Only a few, like vaudeville producer Jesse L. Lasky, had been established showmen . . . Haphazard, intuitive, uninhibited, the founders of the movie business were a new breed of self-made mogul. . . .

"As happened often in his career, Kennedy came on the scene at the right time, arriving on a flood tide of prosperity . . . With his quick grin, open manner, and direct speech laced with slang and profanity, he was refreshingly unlike the aloof, cold-eyed gentlemen who usually appeared from Wall Street. He looked and behaved like a picture man."

Kennedy went to Hollywood by way of London. He learned that British owners of the Robertson-Cole studios were caught in a credit pinch and wanted to sell their production company and booking office. Reportedly a letter of introduction from the Prince of Wales—there is a variety of stories about how Kennedy got it—was influential in opening the proper doors. In February 1926, Joseph P. Kennedy, the Wall Street tycoon, became president and chairman of the board of Film Booking Office of America, Inc.

FBO, as it was known familiarly, was not a creaking concern. It had a reputation for successful, low-budget, action films. The trouble was financing. The Britons could not afford the high interest rates they were paying at long range. Kennedy's knowledge of banking and finance erased the problem. He also overhauled personnel and injected some members of his own team into management.

He also solved a personal problem. Boston was an inconvenient headquarters for his enterprises. Besides, whatever he did, Boston regarded him as the son-in-law of Honey Fitz. A headline of his acquisition of FBO, announced to the Boston papers by the former mayor, read: FITZGERALD A FILM MAGNATE. Kennedy moved his family to Riverdale, a wealthy suburb north of Manhattan. Then he went to Hollywood for a personal look at his new property.

He found a studio that lacked the prestige of the giants but was doing good business in grinding out a picture per week at a bargain basement cost of $30,000 each. The biggest asset on the lot was Fred Thomson, the first movie cowboy to give star billing to his horse, a mount known as Silver King, who traveled to work in a Packard van. Kennedy tied up Thomson, a Princeton Ph.D., with a new contract for $15,000 per week, almost twice his former salary.

There was one weak spot in FBO's business: its output was popular in small towns but had not cracked the metropolitan markets and their big box-office receipts. Kennedy went to a New York theater owner; try a Fred Thomson picture, he urged. No, said the exhibitor, his audiences wanted flesh and the devil and plenty of both. "It won't cost you anything," Kennedy coaxed and won his point. Sometime later he was able to report, "He simply did not know his own audience. Now he plays westerns every week."

Another test of Kennedy's showmanship was an episode involving Red Grange, the "Galloping Ghost" of University of Illinois football and later a star attraction for the professionals. Grange was available for a movie, but studio after studio turned him down. Kennedy went to the potential audience to find the answer. "Would you like to see Red Grange on the screen?" he asked his sons. "Yes!" chorused Joe, eleven, and Jack, nine. *One Minute to Play* was a moneymaker.

All was not wine and roses for the industry in the 1920s. A series of unsavory scandals made Hollywood appear to be a modern Sodom. The magnates undertook to clean house and installed Will Hays, former postmaster general, in the Harding cabinet, as a czar of film morals.

Joe Kennedy had another idea to make Hollywood respectable: a series of lectures to Harvard University's graduate school of business administration by cinema leaders. Harvard was willing, and Kennedy corralled a stellar stable of guest lecturers, most of whom had never graduated from high school. In the opening lecture, Joseph P. Kennedy offered his own views on the industry:

"In our business, quick sales are necessary. You can never put your product on the shelf. It will not keep. Its value is perishable in the sense that it is worth more when first released than it will be six months later. Hence, the struggle is to get playing time—dates. You are always running a race with the calendar. The minute a picture plays in a given territory, it loses value there, and your opportunity is gone." (Obviously, he did not foresee television and the delayed profits from Late Shows and Late, Late Shows.)

With FBO in profitable order, Kennedy sought a broader field. He thought his company should own theaters. He went after the empire of aging Edward F. Albee, offering $4.2 million for Albee's stock in the Keith-Albee-Orpheum circuit. At the time, KAO was selling for about $16 per share; Kennedy's offer rounded out to $21.

Albee had fought the intrusion of movies into houses which he regarded as sacred for vaudeville. At first, he rejected the proposal, then changed his mind and accepted. Two weeks later, KAO was selling for $50 per share. The golden Kennedy touch again.

The time was 1928. Kennedy was drawing $2,000 a week from each of three sources —FBO, KAO and Pathé, where he was an adviser on production. It also was time for the family to move again. With the birth of Jean in February, the brood now numbered eight (Edward would complete the lineup in 1932) and resided in a home in Bronxville, New York. Another move was decisive and historic —to the rambling white house in Hyannis Port. There the Kennedys put down roots that endured.

One of the biggest strikes of Kennedy's career came in October 1928, when Kennedy swung FBO and KAO into a merger with David Sarnoff's Radio Corporation of America. The new giant was Radio-Keith-Orpheum with RCA in control. Kennedy sold his stock for $5 million, picked up $150,000 for arranging the merger and profited additionally by options on RKO stock.

Meanwhile, Gloria Swanson, the most glamorous of the glamorous queens, had appeared on the Kennedy scene. Kennedy met her while she was the Marquise de la Falaise de la Coudrave and had just returned from France with an imperious command to her studio: "Please arrange ovation." Kennedy was charmed, and so was she. "Joe, you're the best actor in Hollywood," she told him.

Kennedy undertook to finance her in independent films under the banner of Gloria Productions, Inc. Their first venture was *Queen Kelly,* and their first mistake was to take on as director Erich von Stroheim, an undisputed genius, but an erratic one. His idea of making movies was to expose miles of film, improvising on the script as he went along, with uninhibited attention to sexual didoes. In *Queen Kelly,* his improvisations included the device of a convent-bred girl inheriting a string of bordellos in Africa. The climactic scene would show the onetime innocent, now a prosperous madam, on her deathbed, receiving the last rites of the Church from an admiring young priest.

Gloria was appalled. "There's a madman in charge here," she told Kennedy. Kennedy's Catholic mind was appalled, too, and he knew the scenes never would get by the Hays office. Von Stroheim was fired; efforts were

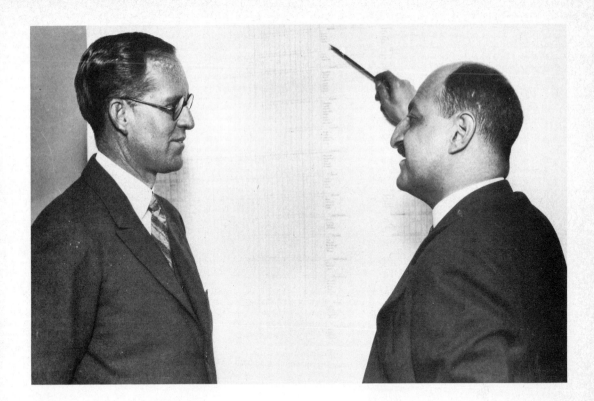

made to salvage the picture, but it was too far along. The film never was shown in the United States, and an investment measured at $800,000 went down the drain. Kennedy could lose money as impressively as he made it.

Kennedy backed the lady in two more films, both financial winners, but the bloom was off the peach, and they parted company. "I questioned his judgment," Gloria said. "He did not like to be questioned."

Kennedy turned his attention to economic affairs. As the Depression deepened, so did his gloom. In later years, he would write, "I am not ashamed to record that in those days I felt and said I would be willing to part with half of what I had if I could be sure of keeping, under law and order, the other half. Then it seemed that I should be able to hold nothing for the protection of my family." In such a state of mind, he looked to Franklin D. Roosevelt for salvation.

The association of World War days was renewed at a luncheon at the governor's mansion in Albany. Kennedy came away convinced that FDR "was a man of action. He had the capacity to get things done . . . I think that I was the first man with more than $12 in the bank who openly supported him. I did this because I had seen him in action.

I knew what he could do, and how he did it, and I felt that after a long period of inactivity we needed a leader who would lead." For a man who later would be criticized as too conservative, that was quite a move.

Once convinced, Kennedy threw himself into the cause with his usual unstinting enthusiasm. At the Democratic convention in 1932, he helped to clinch Roosevelt's nomination with a crucial phone call that induced William Randolph Hearst to switch his support from Jack Garner to FDR. Kennedy was a contributor and a solicitor of campaign funds. He took a campaign tour with Roosevelt and suggested speeches (including one which called for reforms in the nation's financial systems, among them federal regulation of securities and commodities exchanges.)

After the election victory, Kennedy accompanied Roosevelt on a relaxing cruise, then retired to Palm Beach to await his reward. He thought Secretary of the Treasury would be an appropriate New Deal offer. The expected summons from the White House did not come. Some of those close to the new President had little liking for the wheeler and dealer from Boston.

While he waited, Kennedy was active in Wall Street and other fields. He also broke

*The SEC. He knew the tricks of the traders.*

into new ground, in a deal that became one of his most controversial.

In midsummer of 1933, enough states had ratified the repeal amendment to assure the death of Prohibition. A hot scramble was on for liquor franchises, and Kennedy, the son of a saloon keeper, saw an opportunity too good to miss. British distillers had agents active in the United States—and their brands were the tried and true ones—but, typically, Kennedy went to the source. In September, he and Mrs. Kennedy sailed for England. Their traveling companions were James Roosevelt, with whom Kennedy had become close friends during the campaign, and his wife Betsey.

The role of the new President's son in Kennedy's activities in England was a matter of who told the story. One version had him aspiring to a cut in the proceeds. Another

had it that Roosevelt's company wrote the insurance on Kennedy's whiskey. A third saw Jimmy as no more than "a good connection." Whatever the circumstances, Kennedy came home with appointments as United States agent for Haig & Haig Ltd., John Dewar and Sons Ltd., and Gordon Dry Gin Company Ltd.

His next move was to import a vast quantity of liquors under "medicinal" licenses. When Prohibition died, Joseph P. Kennedy had warehouses full of beverages ready to slake America's pent-up thirst.

The next chapter of the Kennedy story was written in Washington. Beginning in 1932 and continuing for the better part of two years, the Senate Banking and Currency Committee had exposed in public hearings the unvarnished skeletons of Wall Street. One by one, the princes of the market marched to the witness stand to tell of their parts in boom, bust and aftermath. Joseph P. Kennedy was not among them, but he was moved to comment, in a book he wrote in 1936:

"For month after month, the country was treated to a series of amazing revelations which involved practically all the important names of the financial community in practices which, to say the least, were highly unethical. The belief that those in control of the corporate life in America was motivated by honesty and ideals of honorable conduct was completely shattered."

Was Kennedy involved in those "highly unethical" practices? Listen to Ferdinand Pecora, a former justice of the New York Supreme Court and counsel to the Senate committee in 1933: "Among those practices were the operation of manipulated stock pools by little groups of brokers. There was no rule among the regulations of the New York Stock Exchange which made these pools illegal, but they certainly were highhanded operations in which the public had no chance except to lose . . . Joseph Kennedy was a participant in seven or eight of these pools, and their operations were outrageous. They were just a case of manipulation of stocks on the floor of the exchange . . . I put in evidence coverage of many pool operations, including the ones in which Kennedy participated."

An early result of the investigation was the Truth-in-Securities Act of 1933—a fruit of the feverish Hundred Days—which required disclosure of pertinent data about new securities. Administration was put into the hands of the Federal Trade Commission, and President Roosevelt said the legislation "at last translates some elementary standards of right and wrong into law."

That was only the first step. In 1934, Congress passed the Securities Exchange Act which brought stock markets under federal regulation. Under the weight of Wall Street resistance, the provisions were less harsh than originally proposed: a new Securities and Exchange Commission would be the overseer, but much of its authority, mandatory under early drafts, would be exerted at the commission's discretion. That meant that in large part the effectiveness of the new act would depend upon the new commissioners.

Competition for the chairmanship was intense. James M. Landis, a former professor at Harvard law school who had helped to draft the acts of both 1933 and 1934, was a strong candidate. Pecora was mentioned prominently. So were a half-dozen others. One of them was Joseph P. Kennedy. Raymond Moley, one of the New Deal's inner circle, wrote beside Kennedy's name on a list of possibilities submitted to the President: "The best bet for chairman because of executive ability, knowledge of habits and customs of business to be regulated and ability to moderate different points of view on the Commission."

Some sharp infighting preceded the final choice but eventually Roosevelt decided that Kennedy was his man. The appointment was announced on July 1, 1934.

Wall Street and New Dealers were stunned. The idea of a celebrated speculator policing the speculators was startling. Harold L. Ickes, the old curmudgeon of the Interior Department, inscribed in his diary, "I am afraid I do not agree" with the President's choice of Kennedy, "a former stock market plunger. The President has great confidence in him because he has made his pile, has invested all his money in government securities, and knows all the tricks of the trade." John T. Flynn, a columnist and an outspoken critic of Wall Street, refused to believe the news: "I say it isn't true. It is impossible. It could not happen."

Kennedy's first gesture was at once conciliatory and a head-on counterattack. One day after he took office, the new chairman of the SEC sat down to lunch with Landis, Ben Cohen and Thomas J. (Tommy) Corcoran who had worked on the regulatory statute. Kennedy greeted them with these words: "Why the hell do you fellows hate me?"

Theirs weren't the only animosities Kennedy had to overcome. If Wall Street did not actually hate, it at least had small liking for the job he was to do. At the same time, Wall Streeters would take from Kennedy what they wouldn't take from other people. He had been one of them.

The SEC chairmanship turned out to be one of the high spots of Kennedy's accomplishment, at least in public esteem. Francis P. Brassor, who was the first secretary of the SEC and held the post until 1942, recalled, "I thought at the time the commission was organized he was exactly the right kind of man to head it . . . Wall Street was scared of [the SEC act]. He had the tenacity to stick with it, to talk with them, to get them to agree to regulations which, when they were first written, were highly opposed. Many of the regulations fostered and promoted [by Kennedy] were self-policing. He told the brokers and the dealers, you have to police yourselves. He convinced them that it was to their interest to do this. At the beginning, it took a man with his courage, guts and ability."

A picture of Kennedy's methods came from Orval DuBois, who was James Landis's personal secretary and later became recording secretary of the commission: "We didn't have very good office accommodations, and the Commission meetings were held in his office . . . It was very crowded. He finally arranged to get some window air conditioners because it was pretty sweaty and smoky a good bit of the time.

"Most everybody called him Joe. He put

in a lot of hours. I never thought of him as being a hard driver . . . You'd walk into his office, and if you didn't know he was a multimillionaire, you wouldn't know it by looking at him because he'd be sitting there with his shirtsleeves rolled up and his tie loose."

One view of Kennedy's work came from Robert Sobel in his book, *The Big Board:*

"Kennedy did a good job in setting the Commission on its feet and, when he resigned after a year, the SEC had become a firm fixture on the Street and was even being spoken of kindly in some financial circles. Kennedy gained the bankers' trust through his moderate interpretation of his powers, and won over some New Dealers by supporting Landis' attempts to develop the SEC's administrative law. Under his leadership, the Commission took a moderate course, prodding but not pushing the district into compliance."

With SEC affairs rolling so smoothly, Kennedy inevitably became restless. He wanted more time with his family. He was losing money because he could not play the stock market. He complained that his government salary wouldn't pay his telephone bill.

Twice he postponed resignation. Finally, on his forty-seventh birthday in 1935, he wrote a letter to President Roosevelt:

*To discontinue my official relations with you is not an easy task. Rather it is one involving genuine regret assuaged only by the privilege of your friendship. . . .*

FDR replied in a "Dear Joe" letter, full of praise for Kennedy's "skill, resourcefulness, good sense and devotion to the public interest."

On September 25, Kennedy, his wife and daughter Kathleen boarded ship, intent on touring Europe, then settling down to "a quiet, peaceful life."

"I'm all through with public life," he had told reporters. He was—for two years.

*Mrs. Kennedy, Eunice, Kathleen, Rosemary, John, Joe Jr.*

# Bringing up Kennedys

Among the summer residents of Hyannis Port, a relaxed and ruminative populace whose taste in recreational activities inclined toward hammock reading and croquet, the tanned, athletic, on-the-go Kennedy children acquired a nickname. They were the Barefoots.

The Kennedys, not surprisingly, had their own ball team, and each Fourth of July the Barefoots took on a team composed of the other summer colonists—for whom a nickname also evolved: the Pansies. The annual Fourth of July softball game between the Barefoots and the Pansies became a Hyannis Port tradition. To the dismay of the Barefoots, they usually got licked. Yet they steadfastly refused to seek beyond their own backyard for players to replace a young Kennedy in the lineup. Losing surely was a most wretched eventuality for a Kennedy but if one thing meant more to them than winning it was loyalty. Family loyalty. "Why go outside the family when we can take care of something ourselves?" was the philosophy Joe Kennedy preached to his children. If the precept was not unfailing against the superior forces of the Pansies in Fourth of July softball, it was one the Kennedys would follow with amazing success in other areas throughout their lives. Whatever the odds, the family first was the Kennedy way of going.

Joe Kennedy always said he would never interfere in a family squabble so long as his siblings stuck together against outsiders. A reporter once noticed that very trait in the family:

"Each Kennedy takes pride in the achievements of the others," he wrote. "Each, instinctively, would rather win the approval of the family than of outsiders. And when an outsider threatens to thwart the ambitions of any of them, the whole family forms a close-packed ring, horns lowered, like a herd of bison beset by wolves."

Family approval began at the top. As a family friend remarked: "Every single kid was raised to think; first, what shall I do about this problem; second, what will Dad say about my solution of it?" Joe and Rose Kennedy were deeply interested in every aspect of their children's lives. If a son was playing in a critical football game, his parents were in the stands. If a daughter was in a school play, her parents were in the audience. Joe was a demanding father, but his insistence on excellence could be done gently. Once he wrote to his son in prep school:

*Now, Jack, I don't want to give the impression that I am a nagger, for goodness knows that is the worst thing a parent can be. After long experience in sizing-up people, I definitely know you have the goods, and you can go a long way. Now aren't you foolish not to get all there is out of what God has given you?*

*After all, I would be lacking even as a friend if I did not urge you to take advantage of the qualities you have. It is very difficult to make up the fundamentals that you have neglected when you were very young, and that is why I am urging you to do the best you can. I am not expecting too much, and I will not be disappointed if you don't turn out to be a real genius, but I think you can be a really worthwhile citizen with good judgment and understanding.*

His son, chastened, replied:

*Dear Dad: I really feel, now that I think it over, that I have been bluffing myself about how much real work I have been doing.*

Joe once remarked about another wealthy family, "Yes, they do have money, but no direction." No growing Kennedy child ever lacked for direction, and the place where Joe dispensed it in concentrated doses was around the big family dinner table. Joe would choose the topic: a current political situation, say, or a sports event or a Broadway play. Then he would sit back and listen to the dialogue. No

Kennedy, however young, was interrupted while presenting his views or in even the mildest way ridiculed for them. But let one of them preface a remark with "They say..." and Joe would leap right in: "*Who* says?" Or should anyone cite a questionable source, Joe would demand to know his qualifications. "Now, are you *sure* he said that? Just that way?" Source examined and documented, the conversation continued.

Only one subject was taboo: money.

Practically from the time they could read, the children would study the "News of the Week in Review" section of the Sunday *New York Times* and then quiz one another at the table. Jack even subscribed to the *Times* while at prep school and read it every day.

The children became accustomed to dining with prominent persons, friends of their father. Many national figures, merely names in the newspaper to most American children, were familiar friends to the Kennedys, and they could discuss a political situation, for example, with no trace of awe for the people involved. Their table talk was always alive, stimulating, witty, prodded out of conversational ruts by the questions of the paterfamilias. A lifelong chum of Jack's, K. LeMoyne Billings, found the experience fascinating.

"I don't ever remember, when Mr. Kennedy was at the table, talking small-talk," said Billings. "He was so interesting that you wanted to read and study so that you could take part. I remember the way the children slowly did. First it was just Jack and Joe, and then, later on, the girls would come into it. But if you weren't qualified to talk, you didn't. He never lectured. He would encourage them completely to disagree with him, and of course they did disagree with him." (Indeed they did. Years later Kay Halle, the Washington hostess, told how old Joe asked her at a cocktail party to try to persuade Jack to change his

mind regarding a piece of legislation. Jack turned to his father and said: "There's one thing we've always agreed on: you keep out of my politics." Joe could only smile. "Well, Kay," he said, "that's why I gave them each a million dollars—so they could spit in my eye if they wished.")

Nurses and governesses were always a part of the Kennedy household, but they in no way increased the distance between children and parents. When Joe bought their fashionable home in Bronxville, New York, and Rose discovered the fine silk upholstery on her bedroom furniture, she had it recovered immediately in a tougher fabric. The room, she reasoned, was no good to her unless her children could romp in it. "Most youngsters, as they grow up, seek their main stimulation and interests outside the home," observed Supreme Court Justice William O. Douglas, "but the Kennedys found these things in their own family circle. After all, it was an exciting home, a good place to be, full of fun and games and plenty of fascinating talk about world affairs and world leaders. It was hard for them to find anything as attractive outside. This is why they are so attached to each other, and so secure."

It was true that at the Kennedy home there seemed to be something doing every minute. Joe had a farm at Osterville, near Hyannis Port, where they stabled riding horses, a pastime in which he and Rose and their daughters—and later their daughters-in-law and granddaughters—excelled. On weekends there were dances at nearby Yarmouth. (Eunice recalled how her brothers would see to it no Kennedy girl remained a wallflower: "Jack would always, you know, dance with you when you didn't have enough partners.") During the Hollywood years, Joe had a miniature theater, complete with projection booth and regulation theater seats for an audience of

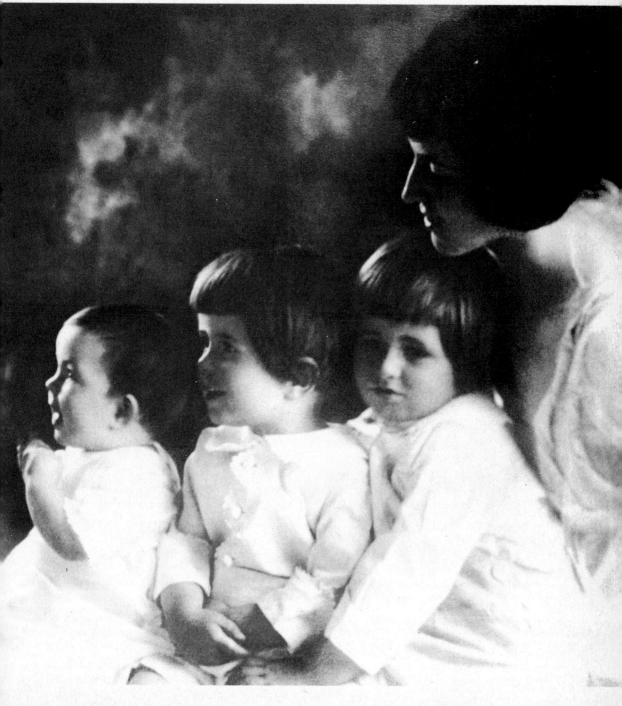

*Young mother of three: Rosemary, John, Joseph Jr.*

when they were so small their parents could barely see their heads above the gunwales. Later, Jack acquired an eighteen-foot boat and named it *Victura,* which he took to be a Latin word "meaning something about winning," although some Latinists don't think it meant anything. He often sailed it across Nantucket Sound from Hyannis Port to Martha's Vineyard. On such a trip in the summer of 1941, he came upon a new type of speedy vessel the Navy was trying out, a patrol torpedo boat, and it so fascinated him he inspected it at close range—a fleet, plywood vessel that could hit forty-plus knots.

Speed and dash seemed to fascinate all the Kennedys. As when they played touch football on the lawn at Bronxville, whacking heads and limbs against the trees, so did a sense of abandon characterize all their pursuits. Once young Joe and Jack decided to have a bicycle race around the block. Just a common, ordinary race? Certainly not: the two pedaled furiously in opposite directions and collided head-on at the finish line. It required twenty-eight stitches to repair Jack. One summer vacation, Jack toured Europe with a friend, Torbert Macdonald. Driving from Paris hellbent for a party on the Riviera, their rented jalopy flipped over and skidded thirty feet on its roof. When it came to a stop, with both occupants literally standing on their heads in the overturned car, Jack grinned at Torbert and said, "Well, pal, we didn't make it, did we?"

The Kennedys were such furious competitors and put such a high premium on winning that, as Eunice recalled, "Daddy always entered us in public swimming races in the different age categories so we didn't have to swim against each other." That would have meant that at least one Kennedy would have to lose. Jack and Joe did compete against each other in sailing races (one year Jack won the Nan-

forty, built at one end of the basement at the Hyannis Port home. Even so, his children often went with their friends to the neighborhood theater and tried to convince the ticket-seller they were all under twelve so they could get in for ten cents apiece.

Down at the water behind the house was a harbor full of sailboats, the Kennedy boys' first love. Just before the last child, Edward, was born, Joe bought a new family sailboat and christened it *Tenovus.* When Edward arrived another boat was added to the fleet and called *Onemore.* Still later, a runabout was acquired for Joe's grandchildren and named *Restovus.* The *Tenovus* and the *Onemore* were both sixteen-foot gaff-rigged sloops, and Jack and Joe Kennedy Jr. learned to sail in them

A Plea for a raise
by Jack Kennedy
Dedicated to my
Mr. J. P. Kennedy

Chapter I

My recent allowance is 40¢. This I used for areoplanes and other playthings of childhood but now I am a scout and I put away my childish things. Before I would spend 20¢ of my 40¢ allowance and in five minutes I would have an empty pocket and nothing to gain and 20¢ to lose. When I a a scout I have to buy canteens, haversacks, blankets searchlights poncho things that will last for years and I can always use it while I can use a chocolate marshmellow sunday with vanilla ice cream and so I put in my plea for a raise of thirty cents for me to buy scout things and pay my own way more around.

Finis

John Fitzgerald Kennedy
Finis

tucket Sound Championship in his Star Class boat, *Flash II*), but more frequently they entered races together as captain and crew. Both were members of Harvard's 1938 Intercollegiate Championship sailing crew.

Reflecting their father's demand for excellence, the Kennedy children apparently had a penchant for throwing recalcitrant crew members over the sides of sailboats. Joe threw Teddy over. Jack dumped Eunice. She said her brother used to "yell a lot and lose his temper like all captains do." And Lem Billings tells of a time when, crewing for Jack in a regatta, he fell overboard, and Jack didn't even stop to fish him back aboard.

To the Kennedys games weren't mere childhood frolics but enterprises involving an outcome. When the children came in for supper after a touch football game their father would always ask who won. "I learnt how to play baggamon today," Jack the atrocious speller wrote from prep school, "and in learning I got licked both games."

Joe Kennedy knew little about sailing, but that didn't prevent him from seeing to it that his boys did well. His wife recalled that when the boys came in, their father would say: "Why was your sail not as large as the other one? Why was it flapping when the other one was straight, and the other one won the race and you didn't?" The boys would reply, she said: "Well, we bought our sails three years ago." And their father would say: 'Well, why don't you tend to those things and find out

what's going on? If you're in a race, do it right."

Their competitiveness was fierce, their pride in achievement strong, their feeling of family instinctive. Once a college friend made a joking slur about grandfather Honey Fitz, and Joe Kennedy Jr. cocked his fist and ordered the fellow out of his room.

These were the attributes Joe Kennedy implanted in his children as he shaped each to the purpose he had conceived for the family as a whole. These, and more. He taught them, for instance, that they were blessed by their American citizenship. "Our father used to say," recalled Robert, "that he couldn't have done any of the things he did, and we couldn't have lived the way we did, in any other country. He said we owed a debt to the government and that is why we ought to work for it." He taught them, too, that those who were well off had an obligation to those who were not. He taught them that because a person held a different opinion, it did not mean he was wrong. "I never knew any of them to be overpowering or give the impression that they were superior," said Mrs. Elizabeth Dunn Anderson, a former Kennedy governess.

But Joe Kennedy's mind and will were not the only ones that worked to shape his offspring. There was, of course, Rose, and her motherly influence was powerful. Indeed, with her husband away much of the time pursuing his ambitions, hers was the more constant hand.

Joe was devoted to Rose, and admired her deeply. "In all the years we've been married," Joe remarked when those years totaled forty-six, "I never heard her complain. That's a quality children are quick to see." Other qualities were equally obvious. Said one close friend of Rose Kennedy: "If I tried to tell you how kind and gentle Rose is, you wouldn't believe it. In all the years I've known her I've never heard her say an unkind word about anybody." Once Rose silenced the ladies at her bridge table when the talk turned toward divorced Mrs. Simpson's romance with King Edward VIII. She said she wouldn't have such slander in her house.

Rose was a deeply religious woman—daily mass, observance of the holy days—and she passed along the love of her faith to her children. Following her example they gave up things of importance during Lent, said their daily prayers, attended mass on Sundays, learned their catechism. To Rose Kennedy her Catholic faith meant far more than religious formality. It was something she could turn to when things did not go well, a constant and reliable haven where she might find solace in time of woe.

Rose gave her children a perspective that many in similarly affluent circumstances might have missed. "We tried to teach them never to waste an opportunity," she said. "We never gave them allowances that were any bigger than those of the neighborhood children. We never put a value on anything just because it was expensive." Her son Jack reflected this attitude during a European vacation with his friend Lem Billings. "I went over with very little money," Billings recalled, "because my father wasn't alive. He [Jack] was perfectly happy to live at places for forty cents a night, and we ate frightful food."

Rose had a theory about raising children. "The oldest boys usually take more responsibility than the others," she said. "Bring up the oldest ones the way you want them all to go. If the oldest ones come in and say goodnight to their parents and say their prayers in the morning, the younger ones think that's probably a good thing to do and they will do it."

The oldest boys. Joe Jr. and Jack. Yes, they were different. Their father would recall many

*Jack raced; Bobby learned.*

years later that, "Joe was altogether different from Jack—more dynamic, more sociable and easy going. Jack, in those days back when he was getting out of college, was rather shy, withdrawn and quiet. His mother and I couldn't picture him as a politician." (His mother, however, observed, "My son was rocked to political lullabys.")

Rose recalls her two oldest at a younger age:

"Joe was much stronger than Jack, and if there was a physical encounter, Joe really whacked him. So when they were young everybody was trying to protect Jack. But aside from that, of course, they did get along well, and they were interested in one another's experience, and in athletics, of course. They took part together a great deal when there were swimming races and boating races and all that sort of thing. Jack was a little different from Joe in that Jack always had a pal with him. I think Joe was more like me—he'd just as soon travel alone."

From all accounts Joe and Jack did have their share of brotherly scraps—and, as their mother noted, Jack, two years younger, usually got the worst of it. One can appreciate Jack's obvious glee, therefore, in a letter he wrote to his father, who was out of town when the boys came home during a Thanksgiving holiday, from prep school:

*When Joe came home he was telling me how strong he was and how tough. The first thing he did to show me how tough he was was to get sick so that he could not have any thanksgiving dinner. Manly Youth. He was then going to show me how to Indian wrestle. I then through him over on his neck. Did the sixth formers lick him. Oh Man he was all blisters. They almost paddled the life out of him. He was roughousing in the hall a sixth former caught him. He led him in and all the sixth formers had a swat or two. What I wouldn't have given to be a sixth former.*

Childhood scraps aside, Jack had only ut-

most admiration for his older brother. He admired how Joe spent long hours tossing a football with Bobby, swimming with Teddy, and teaching his sisters how to sail a boat. He admired his disdain of foul language, his sense of humor, his consideration for younger children which Jack felt his brother inherited from his mother, his drive and capacity for work which he felt came from his father. "I sincerely think," Jack wrote in 1945, "that of all the people I have ever met, Joe had truly the mark of greatness of him." And he added: "I think that if the Kennedy children amount to anything now or ever amount to anything, it will be due more to Joe's behavior and his constant example than to any other factor. He made the task of bringing up a large family immeasurably easier for my father and mother, for what they taught him, he passed on to us, and their teachings were not diluted through him, but rather strengthened."

Joe and Jack had parallel educations: both graduated from the Choate School in Wallingford, Connecticut, Joe in 1933, Jack in 1935; both went on to Harvard; both studied at the London School of Economics under socialist

professor Harold J. Laski (because, as their father explained, he wanted to expose his boys to a variety of viewpoints).

Despite their rigorous training in independent thought, learned not only at school but more importantly at the dinner table at home, neither Joe nor Jack engaged in any of the campus political ferment and rebellion that was a hallmark of the 1930s. While other students were picketing factories, attempting to unionize the Harvard janitorial staff, burning effigies of Hitler—and swallowing goldfish—both Joe and Jack Kennedy stuck to the books. Joe was the more serious scholar and, important in the Kennedy scale of accomplishment, the better athlete. "You take Joe," said their football coach at Choate. "He was a real athlete. But Jack made up for what he lacked in athletic ability with fight." (Later on, when Bobby took to school athletics, he would be remembered for the same qualities as Jack.) Joe was end on Choate's undefeated football team and played on the Harvard varsity three years. In his senior year, however, he did not get into the Yale game and so did not win his letter—a circumstance that some say contributed to

his father's embitterment against Harvard. After the game Joe Sr. stormed onto the field and dressed down the coach for not sending in his son at least as a last-minute sub.

Both Joe and Jack, with their thin, narrow faces, acquired the nickname "Rat Face" at Choate. All the boys, the headmaster explained, had nicknames, or at least the more popular boys did, and the more popular the boy the more derogatory the nickname. Its complimentary nature notwithstanding, both boys disliked the name intensely.

Jack was, indeed, extremely popular. Even as a preschooler he turned his winning ways on the family cook and got away with breaches of discipline his mother likely wouldn't have tolerated in another. She recalled trips to a beach club near Hyannis Port:

"The children were all supposed to be ready to go home at one o'clock. Jack was invariably late, so we would get into the car and drive off without him. We would start lunch, and the rule was that if someone was late for lunch he would just be served the course or second vegetable which was being served at that moment; he couldn't start from the beginning. Jack would arrive in somebody else's car, perfectly happy, and then after lunch he would go in the kitchen and the cook would give him everything he wanted to eat. I knew this was going on. Perhaps it was poor discipline, but he was apt to be rather thin, and I didn't think it was too serious a habit, so I used to let it go."

At Choate, Jack was the despair of his masters. He and Lem Billings, his roommate, formed a group which they call the Muckers Club, and their room was its meetingplace. The school's headmaster recalled that "mucker" was a popular word at the time to describe one who was anti-Establishment, anti-adult world. The headmaster said the faculty was rather amused at the club. Other groups had

rebelled against authority, he said, but the Muckers Club "had a quality of imagination of it, and particular daring, that few have had."

Imaginative Jack Kennedy and his pals were not wicked boys, said another master, "but they were a nuisance." He said it came to a point where he was spending about equal time running the school and running Jack Kennedy and his friends. At length he summoned Jack's father, and the three of them had a discussion.

"Well," the master reflected, "we reduced Jack's conceit, if it was conceit, and childishness, to considerable sorrow. And we said just what we thought, held nothing back, and Mr. Kennedy was supporting the school completely. I've always been very grateful to him. Jack's father didn't hold back. In fact, he spoke very, very strongly, and also with some Irish wit. You know, in dealing with Jack you needed a little wit as well as a little seriousness. Jack didn't like to be too serious; he had a delightful sense of humor, always."

A sense of humor and a spark of mischief, two highly developed characteristics of young John F. Kennedy. "Jack was a very naughty boy when he was home," wrote his little sister Jean to their father one Christmas holiday. "He kissed Betty Young under the mistletoe down in the front hall. He had a temperature of 102 one night, too, and Miss Cahill [the governness] couldn't make him mind."

Jack played on Choate's athletic teams and took on a few other extracurricular activities (the Dramatic Club, for one; not that he enjoyed acting—he didn't—but he disliked public speaking more, and members of the Dramatic Club didn't have to take public speaking), but he could never match the record of his brother Joe who was a stellar athlete, editor of the yearbook, superb scholar. Jack, on the other hand, was sixty-fourth in his

*Harvard '40: Swimming, Hasty Pudding; Honors*

graduating class of 112. Partly to get out from the shadow of his brother, Jack chose to go to Princeton rather than Harvard. But a recurrence of jaundice, which he first contracted at the London School of Economics, cut short his Princeton career before the first semester was over. He took the rest of the year off, toured Europe with his friend Lem Billings. They climbed Mt. Vesuvius, had an audience with the Pope, and Jack won $1.20 at Monte Carlo. On his return Jack decided to enter Harvard after all.

Joe, too, traveled abroad during his college days—to Russia, to Czechoslovakia at the time of the Munich Pact, carrying diplomatic messages to Spain during the civil war—so while he and Jack were at Harvard together they had much to discuss. They lunched

together often, daily if possible, becoming even closer to each other as they matured. Both enjoyed breaking the campus monotony with visits to the homes of friends. "Joe's idea of a real big evening," recalled his roommate, Ted Reardon, "was to get me to bring him to my family's house in Somerville, which was not fancy I assure you, so that he could sit in our kitchen and eat bacon and eggs and fried potatoes that my father cooked for him."

Jack, in turn, found relaxation at the home of Bennie Jacobson, a campus personality who ran the Gold Coast Valeteria in Harvard Square. Bennie had watched class after class of Harvard students pass through Cambridge, and Jack regarded him not only as a friend, but as sort of a homespun philosopher. He used to drop into Bennie's shop and chat about life, politics and other matters.

"Is Joe popular with the girls, Bennie?" Jack would ask. Bennie would demur; Jack would press on: "Aw, c'mon, Bennie, you know." Or he would ask, as though to confirm his own esteem of his brother, "Do you think Joe is a good football player?"

Once when he asked that, Bennie replied: "I ran track at high school, and I'd lose my wind. Then I'd lose my second wind. It seems," said Bennie, "that a Kennedy has three winds."

Bennie was amused by Jack's unpretentiousness. One evening Jack went to Bennie's house for supper and Bennie, a tailor, was horrified to discover the lining of the overcoat of this millionaire's son hanging out and the sleeve all but falling off. He also was dismayed by Jack's habit of never carrying money. Once Jack dropped into the tailor shop and asked Bennie to join him for a frappe. When they were ready to leave the soda fountain, Bennie said he'd take care of the check if Jack would get the tip.

"Bennie, I haven't . . . you know, I must

have left it in my other pants pocket," Jack stammered.

"Jack," Bennie said firmly, "really, Jack, what you should do is carry at least thirty-five cents with you when you leave the dormitory. You might need it."

Sometimes Bennie joined Jack and Joe for lunch at Schrafft's in Harvard Square. As at their table at home, conversation was never light and always animated. After one particularly spirited luncheon discussion of world affairs, Joe turned to Bennie and winked. "Jack's coming at me fast, isn't he, Bennie?" he said.

Another Kennedy who came on fast was Joe's and Jack's younger brother, Bobby, eight years Jack's junior. When Bobby got to Harvard, the captain of the football team,

Kenny O'Donnell, a rugged Irishman who would remain a lifelong friend, remarked: "I can't think of anyone who had less right to make the varsity squad than Bobby when he first came out for practice. The war was over, and we had plenty of manpower, all of it bigger, faster and more experienced than he was. But every afternoon he would be down on their field an hour early, and he always stayed an hour later. He just made himself better." As it turned out, the "runt of the litter" was the first of Joe Kennedy's sons to bring home a Harvard "H" to match his own. "He didn't attend school, he attacked it," a classmate said of Bobby, though his grades were never terribly impressive. He was a determined fellow, no question. Joe Kennedy required each of his sons to work

*Ted and Bob at the London Zoo*

*Robert Kennedy, 1939*

two weeks during summer vacation in P. J. Kennedy's old bank for experience. Bobby worked four.

But Bobby had another side. "Bobby is soft, soft on people," his father once said. "He has the capacity to be emotionally involved, to feel things deeply, as compared with Jack and that amazing detachment of his." This apparently was true from boyhood. Once Bobby asked his governness, Elizabeth Dunn, for an advance on his allowance. He did not tell her why he wanted it: to buy her a birthday present. She said no, so instead he gave her a hand-drawn card, and in a childish scrawl between ink blotches he wrote, "Sorry it aint better." That night Bobby wrote in his diary, "Just wait until she finds out"—why she didn't receive a gift.

Bobby's mother recalled that, unlike her other sons, he did not read much. He collected stamps (and, when he was ten, received a written invitation from President Roosevelt to stop by the White House next time he was in Washington and look over the Chief Executive's collection); he bred rabbits for profit; he sold magazines—and delivered them in the family's chauffeured Rolls.

Joe Kennedy used to say that Bobby was more like him than his other sons. "Bobby has always had a lot of moxie and guts," Joe told a reporter. "I doubt if Jack ever makes any enemies. But Bobby might make some. He's tough. Not that Jack isn't just as courageous, but Bobby feels more strongly for or against people than Jack does—just as I do."

Of all the Kennedy brood Bobby, Bobby and perhaps Eunice, absorbed more than the others their mother's deep attachment to the Catholic faith. "Sometimes when you talked to him alone," said his old friend Dave Powers, "you know, you felt you were talking to a priest." Indeed, Bobby once considered joining the priesthood. In his early teens he attended the Portsmouth Priory School in Rhode Island and followed the rigorous academic and religious regimen of the Benedictine monks who taught there. Bobby's devotion to his faith mirrored his mother's throughout his life.

Rose Kennedy sent her daughters to Catholic schools, but her husband preferred that the boys attend secular schools, as he had done. He felt it would be more broadening for them, and that they could get their religious instruction at home and at church. Jack, who attended the Canterbury School in New Milford, Connecticut, for a year when he was thirteen, was the only Kennedy boy besides Bobby to attend Catholic school.

Perhaps one reason the Kennedys cherished so deeply their moments together as a family was because, with one or the other away at school or vacationing abroad much of the time, it was almost a rarity when all eleven could gather in one spot. When they managed it, observers often were fascinated not only by their numbers, but by their activities. Never was this more true than during Joe Kennedy's ambassadorship in London. The Kennedys caused a mild sensation, with photographs and anecdotes appearing in the papers regularly.

The Ambassador himself was always good for a few lines of a non-diplomatic sort. Such as when he shot a hole-in-one on the first round of golf he played in England and, when asked to comment, quipped: "I'm much happier being the father of nine children and making a hole in one than I would be as the father of one child making a hole in nine." The British loved it. They also snickered when he jibed playfully at their suit styles: "A man went to the tailor," Joe deadpanned, "and complained that his suit was too tight under the arms. 'That's how we make coats,' said the tailor. 'I'm talking about the pants,' said the man." The staid Britishers were rather taken aback, however, when Joe refused to wear the traditional silk knee breeches when he appeared at court. "Not Mrs. Kennedy's little boy," growled the first Irish Catholic ambassador from America to the Court of St. James. He and four waiters were the only ones in long pants.

While their father kept the Britons agog with his relaxed unorthodoxies—feet on his desk at press conferences, English instead of French menus at formal dinners—his children enjoyed a swirl of sightseeing and gaiety. Rose and her two oldest daughters,

Rosemary and Kathleen, were presented at Court in dazzling gowns; the entire family jaunted off on trips to the Riviera, to the coronation of Pope Pius XII in Rome, to the Irish countryside of their ancestors; and sparkling parties brightened the staid old Embassy in Prince's Gate, where three chauffeurs and a staff of twenty-three struggled to keep pace.

"This is a hell of a long way from East Boston, isn't it, Rose?" Joe remarked one evening while they were dressing for dinner at Windsor Castle. It was. Joseph P. Kennedy, as ambassador, had found an acceptance in Great Britain that he had never experienced in his own homeland. Those were happy times.

With his family scattered on both sides of the Atlantic in that last summer of 1939, the Ambassador decided to gather them all together for a month on the French Riviera at a villa near Cannes called the Domain de Ranguin. The pallet of the Riviera with the dazzling blue Mediterannean, the pastels of the old buildings, the dull hues of the mountains that rise from the sea, the sky above reflecting the blue of the water, and the roses blooming about the villa in the summer warmth: it was a time to remember in later years. The roses, the sun, the sea, golfing with father Joe, swimming, boating.

It was a smiling interlude and family photographs caught the mood. The tanned Kennedys grinning back at the lens: Joe Sr., Joe Jr., Rose, Jack. Little Teddy . . . Rosemary. But behind her smile there was shadow.

Rosemary's mental condition had steadily worsened. It was heartbreaking for her parents and her brothers and sisters to watch what was happening. They gave her all they could, that affectionate girl whose mind did not keep pace with her years. She loved music and her mother played the piano and sang to her —and in private wept. Rosemary loved the

*The new ambassador*

sea, and her brothers and sisters took her sailing—and had to tell her, gently, "No, Rosie," when she asked to take the boat out alone. She learned to dance, and her brothers danced with her and took her to parties—and felt anguish when she said, "Why don't other boys ask me to dance?" If love or familial devotion could have helped Rosemary, there would have been no problem. The cruel and unalterable fact was that she was mentally retarded. Consultations at length with dozens of doctors convinced her parents that Rosemary's condition would never improve, only grow worse. This became painfully evident in London. It was impossible to watch her every moment, and her mother worried constantly that she might get lost or meet with an accident. The doctors suggested that she be placed in an institution, but her father said "What can they do for her that her family can't do better?" Finally, sorrowfully, he became convinced that the doctors were right. He and his wife consulted their friend, Richard Cardinal Cushing, the archbishop of Boston, and together they selected St. Coletta's School, a Catholic institution in Jefferson, Wisconsin. And in her twenty-third year Rosemary Kennedy went there to live. There was a vacancy at Joseph Kennedy's table.

*In London*

*From New Ross to Buckingham Palace in three generations.*

# War: Hostages to Fate

The roses of Domain de Ranguin. The sunny summer of 1939, the last Europe would know for many years. A final summer, too, for the Kennedys. The whole clan together for a month in southern France. But summer is only a season and there was work to be done. The Ambassador took his family back to trembling London. Jack did not go with them. He went instead to Berlin, a city he would return to in another time, but one that was in that summer about to sow the whirlwind.

On August 23, 1939 the impossible had happened. In Moscow, the Soviet Union and Hitler's Germany signed a mutual nonaggression pact. Between these two land-hungry giants stood Poland, hesitantly backed by Britain's pledge to fight for her independence. Hitler had been clear: he wanted the port of Danzig. But, as Jack reported to his father after a trip there, the Poles would not give up Danzig without a fight.

Berlin, too, was a frenzied city. Jack, driving there with two friends, Torbert Macdonald and Byron R. "Whizzer" White, had become engaged in a shouting match with some "stormtrooper types." The Nazis had thrown bricks at the car, which bore British license plates.

Now, on his last night in Berlin, Jack was given another message for his father by the United States chargé d'affaires, Alex Kirk. It said, flatly, there would be war in a week. That was the end of August.

When the sun rose over Poland on September 1, so did the Stukas of Nazi Germany. For more than thirty-six hours, while the German blitzkrieg battered Poland, Prime Minister Neville Chamberlain tried to escape the inevitable. He could not. On the morning of September 3 he called in Joseph Kennedy and read him the speech he would deliver at 11 A.M. declaring war. It said: "Everything I have worked for, everything I have hoped for, everything I have believed in my public life has crashed in ruins." Kennedy could have said the same words. He wept.

The Ambassador contacted Washington immediately and by phone told the President of the United States at 4 A.M. (Washington time) the news and emotionally repeated again and again, "It's the end of the world, the end of everything."

A few hours later 22-year-old Jack Kennedy stood in the gallery of Parliament to hear the Prime Minister of Britain declare war on Nazi Germany.

If the U.S. ambassador, the friend of Chamberlain, had been shaken by the onset of war, Joe Kennedy, the father of nine, the realist, was ready for it. Shortly after their return from France, Kennedy moved his family out of London to a secret home in the country nearby. When war did come, he put the embassy on a twenty-four-hour basis, and set his eldest son to work finding room for the 9,000 Americans in Britain on the packed ships heading home.

There wasn't much time. Before dawn on September 4, the day-old war touched Joe Kennedy himself. A German submarine had sunk the 13,500-ton British liner *Athenia.* Of the 1,400 passengers aboard, there were 300 Americans. Of the 112 who went down with the unarmed ship, 12 were Americans. Germany immediately blamed the sinking on the British, calling it an attempt to stir up anti-German sentiment. Joe Kennedy woke up Jack, and sent him dashing to Glasgow, where survivors of the sinking were brought. With Jack went Joe's aide and friend, Eddie Moore. Their job was to get the facts and care for the Americans brought ashore.

The survivors quickly established that the German sub had attacked without warning. But they also demanded angrily of the young, thin lad from the Embassy that the United States convoy them home. Jack checked back

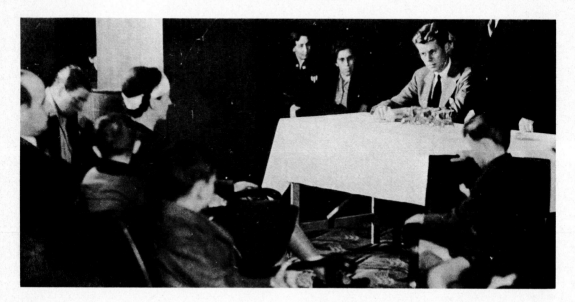

*At twenty-two the Ambassador's son interviews* Athenia *survivors.*

with his father, but the possibility of a U.S. Navy escort had already been precluded by President Roosevelt's neutrality ruling the week before against escorts for refugee ships. Their government too far away, the irate passengers took out their anger on the junior from Harvard, who was the closest representative at hand. Joe said later, "I sent him up to Glasgow to handle the whole job of taking care of the survivors and finding out from them what had happened. And he handled it well, too."

It spoke for the Kennedy family that when one of them needed help he turned, as the Ambassador did, to one of his own.

Joe Kennedy Sr. now found himself in the dénouement of his ambassadorship. He believed Europe should keep peace at almost any price, but Europe had gone to war. He believed that the United States should stay out of European wars, but now he saw his nation pulled inexorably toward it. He wanted—as would any father—to keep his sons out of war, but now Joe Kennedy saw that this hope, too, would fail. Yet his refrain remained: "I am pro-peace. I pray, hope and work for peace."

In everything else he had undertaken, Joe Kennedy had played the loner, the emotionally uninvolved operator who found the handle on power and knew how to wield it. But when he finally achieved the job he wanted, the ambassadorship, he found himself heavy with prestige, light with power. And he had ceased to be a loner. He befriended Chamberlain and the views of the pacifist clique at Cliveden, the estate of the Astors. With his heart and mind, he tied himself to a falling star, and he could not let go.

The temper of his telephone calls and cables to Washington had shaken Roosevelt's confidence in him. His enemies at home pointed to him as an Irish maverick who had been captured by the British. Kennedy stuck to his job long after he lost his taste for it. He kept paying the bills out of his own pocket and hoping for miracles.

The red-brick, seven-story apartment house that was the Embassy, the plain blue room with its three telephones and two radios,

*As he predicted, war.*

the two windows behind the desk that looked out on London preparing for assault—the barrage balloons, antiaircraft guns, sandbags—what had been his beautiful world was now his prison.

Whalen in his biography quotes Kennedy as telling a friend in that first week of war: "My days as a diplomat ended Sunday morning at eleven o'clock. Now I'm just running a business—an officer of a company. I'm back where I was ten years ago. Instead of going up, I've gone down."

He still tried. He proposed that President Roosevelt act as intermediary to halt the war. He was rebuffed. He could see the waves of change affecting the British people, could hear the strident tones of Winston Churchill, and could feel the shakiness of the Chamberlain government. He wrote the President that he was convinced England would go down fighting. "Unfortunately," he added, "I am one who does not believe that is going to do the slightest bit of good in this case."

This would be the theme of his last year as Ambassador, a theme Roosevelt tolerated, but did not believe. Indeed, the President of the United States set up an unusual communications link through Kennedy with the new First Lord of the Admiralty, Churchill, which, in a sense, made Churchill another of Roosevelt's diplomatic observers, and one who disagreed strongly with Kennedy on Britain's future.

It was Churchill who initiated a request for U.S. destroyers to protect British shipping lanes. His argument to Kennedy was simple and compelling. If Britain should fall and her fleet were taken by Germany, the Nazis would rule the waves and stand off America's shores. Kennedy acceded to the British request for the ships, and even gave tacit approval when the deal was completed almost a year later. He tended to look upon it as hardware-for-real-estate transaction, overage destroyers for 99-year leases on British land in the Western hemisphere for United States bases, a shrewd bargain for the United States. Announced on the first anniversary of the war, it was far more than that. It heartened embattled Britain, shocked the isolationist ranks in America and took the United States one step closer to Britain's side in the war.

On an extended visit home, Kennedy broadcast his noninterventionist views, and it made him the object of criticism when he returned to London. His one-time rapport with Roosevelt grew weaker. He wanted to resign, but Roosevelt prevailed on him to stay. Some said it was to keep Kennedy out of the 1940 election campaign. During his trip home, an abortive "Kennedy for President" campaign was started in Massachusetts until he squelched it. "Appreciating as I must the great honor implied in this step," he said, "nevertheless I must with positiveness state that I am not a candidate." Kennedy was embarrassed when it was discovered that a code clerk in

his Embassy was taking home classified documents, including some of the secret Churchill-Roosevelt correspondence, and some of them may have found their way to Nazi Germany. Bothered by Kennedy's pessimism about Britain's future, Roosevelt sent his own fact-finders to Britain, bypassing Kennedy and making him feel all the more alone. There were more hints he would quit. "I still insist," he said once, "that, whenever I leave England, whatever my record is, I shall still be known as the father of nine children."

If Kennedy's fortunes were at low ebb, his family's were not. Rose had brought the children back to the United States, and the family moved with the holidays along their accustomed orbit—Hyannis Port summers, Christmas holidays at Palm Beach and home base in Bronxville. That summer the Kennedy children swept a dozen trophies for sailing victories at the yacht club. Kennedy yearned to be out of England, and back to the hub of his life, especially to see his sons.

Both Joe Jr. and Jack shared their father's views on the war. Making up for his European sabbatical, Jack redoubled his scholastic efforts at Harvard, and, drawing on his father's cables and letters, wrote his senior thesis. It ran at twice the customary length of a college thesis, and was titled "Appeasement at Munich: The Inevitable Result of the Slowness of the British Democracy to Change from a Disarmament Policy."

The appeasement policy that let Hitler gobble up much of Europe without a fight was necessary to buy time for Britain to rearm, Jack Kennedy wrote. He defended Chamberlain, his father's friend, as being the scapegoat for what was actually the failing of the nation. Chamberlain, he said, "could not have fought, even if he had wanted to."

Jack had shown a copy of the thesis to Arthur Krock, the *New York Times* columnist and close friend of his father's. Jack's professors had suggested publishing it as a book, and Krock suggested the title, *Why England Slept*. Joe Sr. wrote his son, "You would be surprised how a book that really makes the grade with high-class people stands you in good stead for years to come."

*Why England Slept* did indeed make the grade. Joe Sr. prevailed on Henry R. Luce of Time, Inc., to write the foreword and sent copies to the Queen of England and Winston Churchill. The book was a best-seller and a Book-of-the-Month Club selection. It sold 80,000 copies. It was praised for its dispassionate examination of the Munich debacle, and earned $40,000 in royalties for Jack, who bought himself a car and donated all of the British royalties to the bombed-out town of Plymouth. Awarded the honor of magna cum laude, the thesis enabled Jack to graduate cum laude. Joe Sr. had reason to be proud of his 23-year-old second born.

Meanwhile, Joe Jr. was in Harvard Law School, active in a student peace group and vocally anti-interventionist, after his father's pattern. Law school had been Joe Sr.'s idea as a proper foundation for a political career. In 1940, Joe Jr. also took his first political steps,

## "I am pro peace. I pray, hope and work for peace."

JOSEPH P. KENNEDY

being elected delegate to the Democratic National Convention. He actively supported Jim Farley's challenge to Franklin Roosevelt's third-term candidacy. At the convention in Chicago that July, the Roosevelt forces built up steam, and the smart politicians shifted from Farley to the Roosevelt bandwagon. But not Joe Jr. Persistent political pressure was brought to bear on the son of the Ambassador. He was reminded of what Roosevelt had done for his father, and the political professionals even called his father in London to get him to change his son's vote. But Joe Sr. refused. "I wouldn't think of telling him what to do," he said. When Roosevelt finally won the nomination with over 900 votes, Farley's 72½ included the vote of the young Massachusetts delegate.

The Ambassador's own political fortunes were very nearly bankrupt. He felt undermined and isolated in London, amazed at the resilience of the British under the pounding of German bombs, but just as sure that the island could not survive. He felt his usefulness was over in Britain. But his requests to the State Department for permission to leave went unanswered. Finally he notified State that he was coming home, whether he had permission or not, and edged the statement, saying he had prepared a memorandum on his views of the war, and unless he was back in the United States before election, he would release it to the press. With the political campaign pivoting on the neutrality issue, Roosevelt could not take chances on what his outspoken ambassador might say. Kennedy was given permission to come home. Roosevelt told newsmen that Kennedy was not returning for good, but somehow most newspapers got the word he was.

The air trip home via Lisbon and Bermuda took nearly five days, and at each step Kennedy found messages from the President telling

him not to make any statements to the press until they had met in the White House. Senator James F. Byrnes, a close Roosevelt aide, was waiting for Kennedy's plane when it landed, and asked the Ambassador immediately if he would make a radio broadcast supporting the President. Kennedy declined. As Byrnes remembered the meeting in his book, *All in One Lifetime,* the President listened patiently that night at dinner while his embittered ambassador complained about the undercutting by the State Department, how his views were ignored and he was bypassed. When Kennedy had finished, Roosevelt shocked him by agreeing with his complaints and promising he would clean up the State Department after the election. And then the President asked his now mollified ambassador again: would he make the radio broadcast urging the President's reelection. This time Kennedy agreed, and the words were barely out of his mouth when Roosevelt's aides were on the telephone arranging the radio time. Roosevelt had captured Kennedy again.

The speech was effective. Roosevelt, he said, would keep America out of the war. The time was too critical to bring in a new, untrained, untried President. It was no time to change horses. Then he said:

"My wife and I have given nine hostages to fortune. Our children and your children are more important than anything else in the world. The kind of America that they and their children will inherit is of grave concern to us all."

Nine hostages to fortune . . . That was Joe Kennedy's stake in peace. "People call me a pessimist," he said in a disputed newspaper interview that he thought was off the record. "What is there to be gay about? Democracy is all done." The interview brought renewed criticism on Kennedy even though he had resigned his ambassadorial post after Roose-

velt's election victory over Wendell Willkie.

Joe Kennedy had seen war firsthand. He had gone through 244 air raids in London and only had been in a bomb shelter twice. He wanted his nation—and his children—out of war. It was not to be and fortune would, indeed, call its hostages.

As their father believed, so did his sons. They, too, were against intervention. But they, too, believed America should prepare. Joe Jr. acted first. He would leave Harvard Law School where he was a high-ranking member of his second-year class.

On July 24, 1941—only weeks before his twenty-sixth birthday; four and a half months before Pearl Harbor—the eldest son of the Kennedy family, enlisted in the United States Naval Reserve. He said his good-byes at Hyannis Port and reported to the Squantum Naval Air Station outside of Boston for primary training. On October 15, he began his flight training at the Naval Air Station, Jacksonville, Florida. He was there when the Japanese attacked Pearl Harbor. Four months later he was commissioned an ensign and a pilot. His father proudly presented him the Cutler Wings, a gold trophy to the top cadet in the class. He was assigned to the Atlantic Fleet.

For young Joe Kennedy decisions and responsibilities had always been clear. As the eldest son, he bore the full weight of his father's thinking and ambitions. He was brought up as a substitute parent, the one who set the example, the most competitive in a competitive family. Jack Kennedy lived in his brother's shadow. But this had its blessings. If he was shielded from the full blast of parental warmth, he was also shielded from the blinding light of Joe Kennedy's parental fire.

When he graduated from Harvard in June, 1940, Jack Kennedy was clearly groping for his path. He thought of enrolling at Yale Law School, in part following his brother's example,

*Ambassador Kennedy calls on the King.*

in part avoiding it. But as the summer faded, so did his law ambitions. He went instead to Stanford University's business school, but six months later he quit this, too. He wandered through Latin America for a few months, returning in the spring. By now the family council knew Joe's plans to enlist in the Navy. Jack tried to enlist in the Army.

When he was turned down because of his back, hurt on the football field at Harvard, he tried the Navy. No luck again. Every day for five months he exercised to shore up his weakened back with more muscle. Finally in September 1941, he passed the Navy fitness test. In October he was made an ensign in the Naval Reserve and was ordered to active duty in Washington where he wrote a daily news digest for the Navy Chief of Staff. To fill the time, he took correspondence courses in foreign intelligence, navy regulations and customs.

He was returning to his billet after a Washington Redskin-Philadelphia Eagle football game when he heard the news that the Japanese had attacked Pearl Harbor. He asked for sea duty, but the Navy sent him instead to Charleston, South Carolina, to work over plans to protect war plants from bombing. It was a dull job and he wanted action. To his distaste he now knew where he wanted to go, but he couldn't get there.

At Northwestern University in an officer-training program, Jack had become interested in the roaring PT boats, had met Medal of Honor winner John Bulkeley, the PT boat hero of the Philippines who carried General Douglas MacArthur to safety before the islands fell. Bulkeley and John Harllee, senior instructor, recommended the young ensign for the eight-week training course at the Motor Torpedo Boat Squadron Training Center, Melville, Rhode Island, on Narragansett Bay.

When the Japanese struck Pearl Harbor, Joe Kennedy Sr. sat in shock at his home in Palm Beach. By telegram he offered President Roosevelt his services. He received no answer. For the next months, he appealed several times, and tried to reach the ear of the President. At length he was offered some vague and ill-defined duties with shipyards, but felt the offer so weak that he could be of no real service. The enemies he made in his long years of government service blocked his way now.

In the years ahead, this man who fought so hard to keep the United States out of war would be given no part in it now that it had come. This father whose two sons had enlisted before Pearl Harbor would have to satisfy himself in the critical days ahead with minor hobbies, puny conquests, backing a Broadway show, and buying part interest in a race track. He, too, wanted action, but could not get it. Joe Kennedy, who had angered some of his Harvard classmates by not enlisting in World War I, would also sit out World War II.

Ensign Jack Kennedy was now in his element, again in familiar waters. His sailing and swimming were assets again. In October, 1942, he made lieutenant junior grade. When he graduated in November he was kept on to train others, much to his annoyance. He wanted action.

For the young officer there were echoes of the past and foreshadowings of the future. His bunkmate in the quonset hut billet at Melville was Torbert Macdonald, the Harvard roommate who had endured the stormtrooper stoning with Jack in Berlin. In 1961, he would be a Democratic representative from Massachusetts. The man who kept Kennedy on at Melville as a training officer was Harllee. In 1961, Rear Admiral Harllee would be nominated to the Maritime Commission. And there was Ensign Paul B. Fay Jr. who one day

would remember those days and many to come in a book called *The Pleasure of His Company.*

With his fellow officers at Melville, Kennedy organized touch football games and expeditions to Hyannis Port. The first time Fay saw Kennedy was in a touch football game at the base. Fay thought the skinny youngster was an officer's son. Before the game was five minutes old, Jack Kennedy argued about the rules. "I wanted to brain him," Fay said. The next day the skinny kid turned out to be his instructor. Fay once missed a training cruise on Kennedy's boat *PT 101,* and when the cruise was over Lieutenant Kennedy read the ensign out, but good, and even threatened him with dismissal. In 1961, Paul Fay would be Undersecretary of the Navy.

Orders finally came through for Kennedy's flotilla to head south, first to Jacksonville, Florida, under its own power, then by freighter to Panama for Canal Zone duty. One of the boats ran aground on the trip south. Kennedy brought his boat to its aid, but a tow line tangled in Kennedy's own propellers. Kennedy himself jumped into the icy water to clear the line and nearly froze. By the time he reached Jacksonville, he was hospitalized with a high fever. He phoned Macdonald, who was always complaining of the frigid waters of Maine. "It's colder in North Carolina," Kennedy said.

In Jacksonville, Kennedy learned his boat would be held in Panama for extended duty. Jack Kennedy phoned his father who made a personal plea on his son's behalf with an old Wall Street friend, Secretary of the Navy James Forrestal. The young officer was reassigned forthwith as a replacement officer to the Solomon Islands.

On March 6, 1943, at sunset, Jack Kennedy sailed aboard the converted French liner *Marshal Joffre,* renamed *Rochambeau.* Destination: Espiritu Santo in the New Hebrides,

PT 109, *the crew* . . .

1,000 miles northeast of Australia. It was an uneventful voyage, luckily, since most of the time the laden transport was without escort.

At Espiritu Santo, Kennedy transferred to *LST 449*, bound for Guadalcanal and Tulagi. On April 7, 1943, nearing Guadalcanal, the ship was told Japanese planes were on the way. Kennedy was below, wrapped up in a book, rolling around in his bunk from the ship's maneuvers, and unaware of the coming attack. The destroyer *Aaron Ward* and *sub chaser 521* joined the LST as a screen and the tiny convoy headed back toward Espiritu Santo. But, by midafternoon, nearly three hours after the first alert, the Japanese bombers found them. Besides its passengers, *LST 449* was carrying a load of bombs. The LST began evasive tactics as the planes approached. Aroused by the strange motion, Kennedy made for the deck. Just then, a Japanese plane flashed by, and a 500-pound bomb sliced into the water

ten feet off the port bow. The explosion racked the ship. Kennedy was nearly thrown to the deck. He had found the action he came for.

Nine Japanese planes kept after the LST and her destroyer escort. The transport escaped serious damage, but a bomb found the protecting *Aaron Ward* and blew her engine room apart. She sank while under tow. The crew of the LST, with Kennedy watching from the rail, tried to recover a downed Japanese flier. But as they approached, the Japanese drew a gun and fired wildly twice at the LST crew. Before he could shoot again, he was cut apart by small-arms fire from the ship. "Welcome to the South Pacific," murmured Jack Kennedy.

Five days later, the replacement lieutenant reached his new post at Tulagi in the Solomons. There they met for the first time; Jack Kennedy and a nine-month-old plywood eighty-footer, dirty, dark green and battered by war: *PT 109*.

On April 25, 1943, at 1100 hours, the log

*. . . and the skipper*

of *PT 109* was signed in a barely legible hand: "Lt. (jg.) J. F. Kennedy assumed command of the boat." At 11:45: "Moored at usual berth in the bushes."

Lieutenant Kennedy picked his crew from replacements, some of them new men fresh from the training base at Melville. While he pushed repairs on *PT 109*, he tried to get the crew in shape, too. Then began the long, monotonous rounds of night patrols. The PTs were infested with rats and cockroaches that left the jungle to find a home in the Navy. The crews of the PTs were limited, and Kennedy insisted that each man be able to perform any job on the boat. On an errand to Guadalcanal, Kennedy asked one of the men to plot the course and give him an arrival time. The seaman locked himself up in the charthouse and sweated over his computations. Finally he emerged with an answer: "About two o'clock."

"About?" Kennedy said. "I don't want any 'about.' I want the earliest time we can get there." Back in the charthouse, the chastened crewman pored over his figures again and came back with a precise answer: "Two-ten." "Good man," the skipper replied.

If the young lieutenant was grade A in seamanship, he was considerably below that in naval bearing and neatness. While *PT 109* was stationed at Rendova and making sorties against Japanese barges, the lieutenant and his men lived a miserable life, yellow with the antimalaria drug, atabrine, cursing the hordes of black flies and the constant diet of canned meat. It was hot, so hot the uniform of the crew became scantier as the mercury rose. Mostly Kennedy overlooked it. But some of the men started coming to meals with no clothes on at all. That was too much. The skipper posted a rule: no one at mess without at least a pair of undershorts.

The competitive skipper's spirit lifted with the throb of the roaring engines of *PT 109*. The boats raced to see which one could make it to the fueling dock first after a mission. First in, first off duty.

The skippers would dash for the berth at full speed, ramming the engines into reverse at the last possible moment. One day, racing another PT, Kennedy drove *PT 109* too fast and slammed into the fueling dock, slicing off part of it and dumping men and tools into the water. He and his crew escaped a chewing-out when two other PT boats nearby broke loose from their moorings. In the confusion, Kennedy moved his boat away.

*PT 109* kept up her night patrols, returning at dawn. The grueling routine and the lack of fresh food grated on morale. The crew took some casualties in an air attack in July 1943, but the real test came in August.

The Japanese were intent on reinforcing and resupplying their troops on the island of Munda. They assigned four destroyers, the *Amagiri, Arashi, Hagikaze* and *Shigure* to land 900 men and 70 tons of supplies. The convoy left on the moonless night of August first. That very day, at Rendova, Kennedy installed a 37-millimeter antitank gun on a plank platform on the foredeck to make *PT 109* more effective against enemy barges. Naval Intelligence learned the Japanese were coming, and six U.S. destroyers and all available PT boats were ordered out into the straits to block their way. In the same order headquarters warned that Japanese planes were out to get the PT boats. No sooner had the message been seen at Rendova, than the Japanese planes hit. Twenty-five dive bombers left only fifteen boats in operating condition for the big move that night against the "Japanese Express." One of them was Kennedy's *PT 109*.

Ordered out at dusk, *PT 109* stood station with three other boats, one of which had a primitive radar set aboard. As the night progressed, the boats became scattered. The Japanese ships meanwhile reached their destination and unloaded. Then they re-formed and headed back. In their path, although no one realized it, was Kennedy and *PT 109*, several miles distant. In the darkness, lookouts on Kennedy's boat and on the lead destroyer, the *Amagiri*, made their sightings simultaneously. "Sound General Quarters," Kennedy said, and the alarm rang through the boat.

They were so close that the destroyer could not depress its deck guns to fire at *PT 109*, and *PT 109* couldn't fire its torpedoes. The Japanese captain decided to ram and aimed the *Amagiri's* steel prow at the plywood hull of Kennedy's boat. One of the *PT 109* seamen saw the destroyer coming, grasped a medal of the Virgin Mary, and began to pray, "Mary, conceived without sin. . . ."

One hundred yards . . . fifty . . . twenty-five. . . .

In seconds it was all over. The destroyer sliced the eighty-foot hull in half, spilling flaming fuel all over the stern. Kennedy was thrown back in the cockpit, ramming his back against a steel frame. The impact crushed one crew member. His body was never found. Another in the engine room was badly burned. Several were thrown overboard, and driven beneath the water by the churning propellers of the destroyer. The stern of *PT 109* sank. Fearing the fuel in the still-floating bow section would explode, Kennedy ordered the remaining crew members into the water.

Two of the men were dead. Kennedy and the ten others bobbed in the water, choking on gasoline fumes. One seaman from Kennedy's hometown told the skipper he couldn't go on. Kennedy fired back: "For a guy from Boston, you're putting up a great exhibition out here."

When the flames abated, Kennedy brought his crew back on board the bow section. He asked them if they wanted to fight or give up.

"There's nothing in the book about a situation like this," Kennedy told them. "A lot of you men have families and some of you have children. What do you want to do? I have nothing to lose."

They voted to fight, or at least to survive. They waved to passing planes the next morning, but Kennedy, fearful an enemy plane would discover them, ordered it stopped. The bow of *PT 109* was losing buoyancy. Kennedy ordered nine of the survivors to group around a plank to avoid being separated, and to swim together to Plum Pudding Island. He took the badly burned sailor with him, gripping in his teeth a strap from the sailor's lifejacket and swimming the breast stroke three-and-a-half miles to the island. Someone asked if they'd ever get out alive. Kennedy replied: "It can be done. We'll do it."

The exhausted men reached the island and hid in the jungle. Japanese were all around the area. But there was also an Australian coastwatcher, Lt. Arthur Reginald Evans, spying on Japanese bases from a vantage point high up on the other side of Blackett Strait. He had seen the fire of *PT 109* the night before, and had seen the hulk floating the next day, but was too far away to tell for sure what it was.

At the PT base at Lumberi, thirty-eight miles away, Paul Fay, who knew both Kennedy and Ensign George Ross had been aboard *PT 109*, wrote to his sister:

*George Ross has lost his life for a cause that he believed in stronger than any one of us, because he was an idealist in the purist sense. Jack Kennedy, the Ambassador's son, was on the same boat and also lost his life. The man who said that the dream of a nation is lost in war can never be accused of making an overstatement of a very cruel fact.*

But Fay was wrong. Kennedy and Ross were very much alive and thinking of how they could save their crew. They decided to try to intercept one of the patrolling PT boats at night. Kennedy swam out into the straits with a battle lantern bobbing in the water, hoping to find a friendly boat. The currents of the straits were erratic. By morning he washed up on a small island called Leorava. When he finally swam back to his men, he was exhausted, vomiting sea water and nearly unconscious. He woke long enough to tell Ross to try it the next night. Profitting by Kennedy's experience, Ross followed the same route but had an easier time. But he found no PT boats. Kennedy decided to move his men to neighboring Olasana Island. He and Ross then went exploring nearby Naru Island. From there they could see the mountain that rose over their home base. But all they could do was see it.

Later, two scouts working for coastwatcher Evans saw Kennedy and Ross from a distance. Each group thought the other was Japanese. The scouts fled but luckily ran into the rest of Kennedy's men on Olasana. "Americans, Americans," said one of them, Ensign Leonard Thom. The natives headed for the PT base at Rendova carrying a message Kennedy cut into a coconut with his sheath knife:

NATIVE KNOWS POSIT

HE CAN PILOT 11 ALIVE NEED

SMALL BOAT

KENNEDY

Evans got the word and sent out more scouts with food and a note which began: "On His Majesty's Service." Kennedy grinned. "You've got to hand it to the British," he told Ross. The crew was picked up by PTs at night and finally arrived back at Rendova August 8. It had been a week since *PT 109* had gone down.

At Hyannis Port, a friend who had heard of the rescue telephoned Rose.

"Jack's been saved," she said.

"Saved from what?" asked his mother.

Joe Kennedy had heard several days earlier that *PT 109* had gone down, but didn't want to upset his wife by telling her. Rose located him at the riding stable and told him the news. Saved!

Safe Jack Kennedy was, but hurt. A fellow Bostonian was in the base hospital when Jack Kennedy was brought in. Ed McLaughlin, who would one day become president of the Boston City Council, saw that the young officer was badly mangled by coral cuts. "He didn't talk about it too much," McLaughlin recalled. (And Kennedy didn't ever talk about it much. In later years when McLaughlin introduced John F. Kennedy at a political rally and began mentioning his war record, Kennedy kicked him under the table).

Some of Kennedy's crewmen, ill and injured by their experience, were rotated to rear areas for rest but not their skipper. He refused to leave the base. As his squadron commander, Al Cluster, said: "He got to be more determined—and he was very determined before."

Kennedy was given a new boat, *PT 59*, which had been converted into a gun ship with the addition of heavier weapons. That made her a more potent attacking vessel but also more cumbersome to handle. *PT 59* hunted barges along the coasts of the many jungled islands in the area.

"That was really perilous and terribly exposed fighting, but Jack kept at it," said Cluster. "It got so the crew didn't like to go out with him because he took so many chances."

At one point, Kennedy and some of the other more ventursome PT skippers planned a bold daylight raid on a heavily defended Japanese upriver barge base. Some of the base crewmen were skeptical of the endeavor and one told Cluster: "This Kennedy has to go. He's *too* brave. He'll get us all killed."

As Cluster later remembered he approached Kennedy "who said something like 'I've

got a job to do. I'm going to finish the job I came out to do.' It was a serious, teeth-gritting answer."

The patrol never came off, however. But Kennedy kept on patrolling up into November. One time he ran into Whizzer White at the base and took him out on a night patrol. White later would serve Kennedy in other ways. Kennedy's last major action was the rescue of eighty-seven surrounded Marines. By now Kennedy was suffering from malaria and the aggravated back injury. His weight was down to 125 pounds. Finally, on November 18 Kennedy gave in. The ship's log for that date read Lt. Kennedy "left the boat as directed by Dr. at Lambu Lambu."

He had been in the South Pacific nine months and been awarded the Navy and Marine Corps Medal for his heroism on *PT 109*, had suffered disease and injury, but his wit was still intact. On November 14, 1943, he wrote a letter to his younger brother, Bobby, who had just enlisted in the Navy:

*Dear Robert:*

*The folks sent me a clipping of you taking the oath. The sight of you up there, just as a boy, was really moving particularly as a close examination showed that you had my checked London coat on. I'd like to know what the hell I'm doing out here while you go stroking around in my drape coat, but I suppose that's what we are out here for, or so they tell us, is so that our sisters and younger brothers will be safe and secure—frankly, I don't see it quite that way—at least, if you're going to be safe and secure, that's fine with me, but not in my coat, brother, not in my coat. . . . I gathered that cold vicious look in your eye was due to the thought of that big blocking back from Groton. I understand that you are going to be there till Feb. 1, which is very nice because it is on the playing fields of Milton and Groton, and maybe Choate, that the seeds will be sown that in later years, and on other fields, will cause you to*

*Aboard the destroyer* Joseph P. Kennedy Jr.

*turn in to sick bay with a bad back or a football knee.*

*Well, black Robert, give those Grotties hell and keep in contact with your old broken down brother. I just took the physical examination for promotion to full Looie. I coughed hollowly, rolled my eyes, croaked a couple of times, but all to no avail. Out here, if you can breathe, you're one-A. and good for active duty anywhere, and by anywhere, they don't mean El Morocco or the Bath and Tennis Club, they mean right where you are. See you soon, I hope.*

*Jack*

Three days later, Lt. John F. Kennedy turned over command of *PT 59* and headed home.

Time had made its changes, and the world inherited war as Joe Kennedy feared. His second son Jack was returning home for medical treatment. His third son Bobby was entering the service. His eldest son Joe Jr. was still flying hazardous missions in the lumbering planes of the antisubmarine patrol in Europe. His third child Rosemary was in a Catholic home. And his fourth child, Kathleen, the toast of London when they lived there, was back in the British capital, destined to bring more hurt to Joe Kennedy's heart.

Kathleen, the Kennedy they called "Kick," had quit her job as a reporter for the Washington *Times-Herald,* joined the American Red Cross and gone back to London. She was a hostess at the Hans Crescent Club in Knightsbridge, dispensing coffee, doughnuts and Kennedy ebullience to an endless procession of servicemen lonesome for home. There she met some old friends from the ambassadorial days. One of them was Billy Hartington. He had taken her out in that other London. Since then he had been mentioned as an eligible suitor for Crown Princess Elizabeth. Handsome and dashing, William John Robert Cavendish, the Marquess of Hartington, was now a captain in the Coldstream Guards.

His family background was in sharp contrast to the Kennedys. One ancestor, the first Duke of Devonshire, withdrew from the Privy Council of Charles II in a protest over Catholic influence in the government. His father was Grand Master of the Craft of Freemasons, a fraternal group with a long history of anti-Catholicism. Hartington's family was as Protestant as the Kennedys were Catholic. Yet, somehow, Billy and Kathleen were in love, Capulet and Montagu in bomb-torn London. Kick helped Hartington in his unsuccessful bid for a seat in Parliament in 1944. He was devoted to her, and she to him. They became engaged. But the plans for their marriage caught on the snags of their religious upbringing. In disagreement on how to rear any future children, they finally compromised and were married in May 1944, in a civil ceremony. Joe, Kathleen's devoted big brother, gave the bride away. Her parents, in America, sent no messages of good wishes as had Billy's father and mother. From across the Atlantic there was only silence.

Kathleen would never forget Joe's strength in what she called "those difficult days before my marriage."

As she wrote in tribute to him.

*From the beginning, he gave me wise, helpful advice. When he felt that I had made up my mind, he stood by me always. He constantly reassured me and gave me renewed confidence in my own decision. Moral courage he had in abundance and once he felt that a step was right for me, he never faltered, although he might be held largely responsible for my decision. He could not have been more helpful and in every way he was the perfect brother, doing, according to his own light, the best for his sister with the hope that in the end it would be the best for the family. How right he was!*

The newlyweds had a month together in London. She returned to her family in Hyannis Port when he rejoined his regiment. The con-

voys were gathering for the D-Day landings in France. Something more than two months later, Billy Hartington was leading a patrol, backed by tanks, on a battlefield in France. Cap in hand, he was walking calmly and casually as if on a stroll, saying almost offhandedly to his men, "Come on you fellows. Buck up." Death came quickly. Later Kathleen would write a friend, "I guess God has taken care of the problem in His own way, hasn't He?"

But that summer at Hyannis Port, the only son missing from the family was young Joe. The son who had joined peace groups at Harvard, the boy with his eye on the Presidency, the Kennedy who said "England is not fighting our battle, this is not our war," now had his war.

After winning his wings, he patrolled the Caribbean, helped organize a new squadron of four-engine Liberator bombers for anti-submarine duties, and then flew to England to join in the long hunt for subs over the Bay of Biscay. His squadron, VB-110, was stationed at the Royal Air Force field at Dunkeswell, Devonshire. When they first arrived it was a total mire, billets heated only by small coke stoves, and cold showers a muddy half mile away. The squadron flew 173 missions before the end of 1943. By April 1944, the squadron had lost half its planes. Joe Jr. won promotion to lieutenant, and by May was due for rotation to the States. But he refused, and prevailed on his crew to remain on duty with him to join thirty-six other patrol bomber squadrons harrying Nazi submarines away from the massing invasion fleet, the fleet that would carry Kick's new husband to France.

After D-Day, Lieutenant Kennedy felt he could no longer ask his crew to stay with him, and they returned to the United States. His own luggage was already packed for shipment home when this flier who had flown so many missions volunteered for one more: Project Anvil.

The invasion of France coincided with Hitler's desperate buzz-bomb attacks on London. The V-1 bombs could be intercepted in the air, but they still gave the British a bad pummeling. Bombing of V-1 and V-2 plants and launching pads was not effective enough, and was tremendously costly as well. Almost 3,000 fliers lost their lives trying to stop the robot bombs. The Allied command concocted another plan: to create a drone airplane, load it with explosives, guide it by radio to the buzz-bomb sites. This joint Army-Navy operation converted Liberator bombers so that they could be flown electronically from mother planes. Liberator PB4Y No. 32271 was out-fitted for one mission. The Liberators could not take off by themselves. Two pilots were needed at the controls of the heavily-laden, cumbersome bombers. They would hand the drone off to mother planes near the coast, and bail out. Lt. Joseph P. Kennedy Jr. volunteered, as did Lt. Wilford J. Willy, regular Navy, and the father of three children.

For two weeks, they pored over the plane, testing the equipment, trying it out with a dummy load, rehearsing the mission. The target was a V-2 rocket site across the English Channel in Normandy.

Shortly before 6 P.M., August 12, 1944, Ensign James Simpson was in the Liberator drone checking equipment. He shook hands with young Joe Kennedy and said, "So long and good luck, Joe. I only wish I were going with you." Joe Kennedy turned and thanked him. "Don't forget," he said, "you're going to make the next one with me. Say, by the way, if I don't come back, you fellows can have the rest of my fresh eggs." It was three minutes to takeoff time.

At 5:52 P.M., Kennedy gunned the engines of the big B-24 and moved it down the field, nudging it and its load of nearly 22,000 pounds of explosives into the air for its last flight.

*When Kathleen married, Joe Jr. gave the bride away.*

*In flight training, Joe Jr. led his class.*

At an altitude of several thousand feet, Kennedy rendezvoused with the escorts and the mother planes and headed to checkpoint "Able" over Framlingham. Kennedy began his first radio control checklist. The formation wheeled over checkpoint "Able" and headed for "Baker," and the tower at the city of Beccles. It was 6:15 P.M., the North Sea to starboard, the sun settling in the west, the towns and rivers of England below. Then, at 6:20 P.M., for reasons never known, the plane exploded like a star.

Two blasts, a second apart. Searchers later found nothing big enough to pick up, no sign, nothing. Nothing . . .

At Hyannis Port, it was almost like summers before the war. Everyone but Joe and Rosemary was home. Kathleen, back from England . . . Jack, ailing, but under treatment at Chelsea Naval Hospital, withered by war, but home for weekends . . . Bobby, Teddy, the girls. They had all come home.

The day the two priests came, Joe Sr., Rose and the children were sitting together, talking. Joe met the priests in another room. He returned to his family in silence, then spoke a few words, horrible words, unremembered words, his face the ghost of his hope.

Then he turned and went up that long staircase to his bedroom and locked the door. For the next months, he remained there mostly, the only voice of his grief, the melancholy strains of recorded symphony music echoing in the rambling home.

Jack collected a number of tributes written by family and friends, and the family had them privately printed in a book. It was called *As We Remember Joe*. Years later, when peace of a kind had returned to the world, someone mentioned the book to Joe Sr. "You know," he said, "I was never able to read that book."

# 1946: The First Hurrah

It has been often said—and often believed—that Jack Kennedy was destined by his father's ambition to be President of the United States from the moment Joe Jr. was killed. He was the heir apparent become heir in fact, surrogate by accident, but surrogate nonetheless. That has the simplicity of legend.

But John Fitzgerald Kennedy went into politics because he wanted to go into politics; because he was wealthy enough to afford to go into politics; because he came from a family that for two generations had gone into politics and, certainly not least, but perhaps not first, because he had a father who saw politics as a source of power and as an entry for family into history.

Jack Kennedy, in 1945, when peace finally came, was one of millions of Americans returning to an uncertain nation, as uncertain of its future as they were of theirs. Kennedy returned a legitimate war hero. He was bone-thin from malaria, yellowed from the drugs taken to combat the disease.

While in the Chelsea hospital he edited the family's book of remembrances about his dead brother. Writing had always interested him and on his release he eventually took a job with the old International News Service, an outpost of his father's friend, William Randolph Hearst. Young Kennedy covered the founding of the United Nations in San Francisco, reporting the events from a G.I.'s point of view. His editors thought his writing a bit stiff, and Kennedy himself was not too at ease in the work. "I felt that it was too passive. Instead of doing things, you were writing about people who were doing things."

Well, if not journalism, what? Teaching? Perhaps. Politics? Maybe. Yes, just maybe.

"I think Jack thought while he was in the hospital recovering from his war injuries that he wanted to do something for his country," said William Sutton, who would be a close aide to Kennedy during his early Congressional years. "Instead of just being a guy with an ailment I believe he was thinking then about what he was to say later, about ask not what your country can do for you . . ."

Yes. Ask what you could do for it. The extent that he asked his father or was told by him what he might do for his country—and the family—has almost as many accounts as tellers.

Certainly, his brother's death was a factor. A father with as strong a sense of continuity as Joe Sr. would not forget the oft-stated ambitions of his lost son. There was the grief—many years later he told a columnist who was asking about his children: "Ask her [Rose] about that one. She can talk about him. I can't." And, certainly, there was the desire to bring some lasting good out of the loss this man of great wealth could least afford.

"It is the realization that the future held the promise of great accomplishments for Joe that has made his death so particularly hard for those who knew him," Jack wrote. "His worldly success was so assured and inevitable that his death seems to have cut into the natural order of things."

A Boston legend says that young Jack Kennedy—still suffering from war injury and malaria—was summoned to his father's presence. He was commanded, the story goes, to pick up the torch from Joe and he agreed without question. It is a fascinating tale, but some who were with Jack in those crucial years of his developing life said it didn't happen exactly that way.

As Joe Sr. himself put it: "I told him Joe was dead and that it was his responsibility to run for Congress. He didn't want to. He felt he didn't have the ability. But I told him he had to."

Jack agreed with this version. "It was like being drafted," he said. "My father wanted his

The New Generation Offers A Leader
JOHN F.
KENNEDY
FOR
CONGRESS
11th DISTRICT
PRIMARIES: TUESDAY, JUNE 18

*No one climbed more stairs.*

eldest son in politics. 'Wanted' isn't the right word. He demanded it.''

But his friends say that he did not immediately accept the order. Young Joe, who had wanted with all his heart to be the family's champion, had been set on a firm course, enthusiastically backing the beliefs of his father. But Jack, until then, had drifted. He was still looking at a war-torn world and its titanic problems with inquisitive gray eyes.

To his friends, Jack admitted readily that he had no real political philosophies, no program of his own. He had met many conservatives, he said, and felt that he had nothing in common with them. And he believed that devotees of both the left and the right were too doggedly set in their views, too blindly willing to follow their leaders without careful consideration.

Kennedy had seen much of a world on the brink of war. He had seen the war itself. He had some thoughts on disarmament, but they were vague. To feel, to think, was one thing. To act was another.

James MacGregor Burns, a Williams College political science professor, wrote in his book, *John F. Kennedy, A Political Profile,* that Jack was "not at all sure that he would like politics at the level where he would have to start. He was still shy with people outside his social circle, a bit withdrawn and unassertive. Nor was he convinced of his own talents as a speaker or as a mixer."

Jack hated the blarney, the backslapping, the intrigue, the election promises broken the day after, the breezy ward-boss antics of the dear old days of the Dearos. He was too much an idealist. But nonetheless, that was the way one got into the game. He decided to try.

Lem Billings said most people thought he made the decision "to prove himself to his father, to outdo his brother Joe, or to be an implement of Irish revenge. But, really, after

he had considered journalism and teaching, he decided that politics offered a better way to express his ideals."

But a politician needs a base, and Jack Kennedy had none. He had spent his youth in New York, Massachusetts, Connecticut, Florida and abroad. Where, really, was home —or even a home address?

Fate in the unlikely form of James Michael Curley, the nemesis of Honey Fitz, set Jack Kennedy on his course for Congress. The wily old politician, his gilded oratory somewhat tarnished, nonetheless was elected to Congress in 1942, but abandoned his seat in 1945 when he won the mayoralty of Boston. (He was subsequently jailed while still mayor for wartime fraud, despite his appearance at sentencing in a shirt two sizes too big in order to accentuate his plea that he was suffering from nine different ailments, all serious, including an imminent cerebral hemorrhage.) Kennedy decided to run for Curley's empty seat in the House.

First he moved into the Bellevue Hotel, the roost for Boston politicians, to establish residency. He later moved to a third-floor apartment in a far-from-elegant building down the street. Kennedy's apartment—above a barber shop, tailor shop and shoe repair shop—overlooked a parking lot at the side of the State House, had two small bedrooms, a living room and a tiny kitchen.

Joe Murphy, the building superintendent, would carry up a breakfast of orange juice and soft-boiled eggs from the basement when Jack was in residence. Mrs. Murphy saw to it that there were always towels in the bathroom and the bed was made. The living room had a broken-down divan and a couple of easy chairs almost as far gone as Curley later said he was. One newsman had a chair arm give way under him while interviewing the young candidate.

"You have to watch those chairs," Jack Kennedy laughed.

His mother paid a visit to the place one day. The next morning a truck appeared and carted everything in the apartment away. She had it refurnished, put in wall-to-wall carpeting and hung sailing scenes on the wall. This apartment, at 122 Bowdoin Street, was Jack Kennedy's voting residence for the rest of his life.

Rose might be able to tidy up her son's rumpled dwelling, but there wasn't much she could do about the candidate himself. "He looked like he combed his hair with a brick," said Ed McLaughlin, the acquaintance from South Pacific days who had gone to work in the campaign.

His clothes were expensive, but one would have had to have looked at the labels to determine it. Once he went to mass with John Galvin, a campaign aide. "I saw the back of his pants were ripped. I told him it was going to look awfully funny up there at the communion rail with those pants. He said, 'Well, I like the suit and I'll keep the coat down.' I sweated through the whole thing."

The district John Kennedy had chosen to begin his career in was no better dressed than he. The Eleventh Congressional of Massachusetts stretched across East Boston, across the Charles River into Somerville, Charlestown and Cambridge.

Its people, mostly, were poor. They were immigrants or sons or grandsons of immigrants. Slavs. Italians. And, of course, Irish. Their homes were tenements, thousands of them, clustered block after block like dingy red boxes crammed and forgotten in a cupboard, clustered so tightly they seemed to shut out the air. These were the homes of the Kellys on the first floor with their brood. A tight stairway led up to the Hennesseys on the second floor and the O'Briens on the

third. Irish country. A couple of blocks away it would be the Ionellas, Guglielmos and Rizzos tiered one over the other. Italian country. And everywhere kids. These were people who could warm to a mother who had raised a flock, who would give some extra understanding to a son of such a mother who had made good no matter what his background. If he could, maybe one of theirs could.

If the district was a frowzy warren, its blocks of tenements broken by dumps, ancient factories, some abandoned by industry's flight to greener and less expensive fields in the South, it also was one of the historic places of the nation. Bunker Hill. The Old North Church where Paul Revere saw his signal. And Harvard University, mother of so many who stood high in American history, her stately brick buildings and elm-shaded Yard a world away from most of the Eleventh Congressional. (But the people of the district remember Harvard and its sons. A few years ago one of its housewives waved an interviewer, who had made his way to her upstairs tenement flat, towards a hassock in her parlor. "Sit there," she said. "That's where John Kennedy sat in 1946. Oh, no. That's not the one. It's just like it. We keep the real one in storage.")

John Kennedy, who would climb more stairways in the Eleventh than perhaps any man in its history, perhaps more than his grandfather, P. J., whose territory it was, once was passing the blight and the history on his way with Dave Powers to make a speech. They passed the monument of Bunker Hill, Old North Church, the faceless tenements remembered only by those who called them home. "This," he said, "is the kind of district I want to represent."

Jim Curley said that anyone with the name Kennedy might as well go directly to Washington without bothering to campaign. But Jack

Kennedy—and Joe—didn't see it that way. Kennedys don't take risks without covering all eventualities. Or almost all. There was one brief flurry when all seemed to have been in vain: John F. Kennedy, it was learned at the very last minute, had not registered as a Democrat. This necessity was hurriedly corrected at the last minute before the deadline.

Kennedy faced nine other candidates in the primary, victory in which was tantamount to election. One campaigner was Mike Neville, a popular figure in the district. Another was Catherine Falvey, a former WAC major who liked to campaign in her dress white uniform and call Jack "that poor little rich kid."

Others called him an "interloper" and a "Johnny-come-lately." Mike Neville didn't see it as having much difference in the campaign. "How the hell do you beat a million dollars?" he said.

Joe saw to it that this campaign would not have any overtones of the freewheeling era of the Dearos. "The New Generation Offers a Leader—Jack Kennedy" was the campaign slogan.

To help educate the leader, father Joe borrowed someone from the old generation, a cousin, Joe Kane, who was a veteran of Boston politics.

One of Kane's headaches was Honey Fitz, then eighty-three. The old war horse was forever popping up to help his grandson, but Kane didn't want any "Sweet Adeline" in his chorus. It has been reported several times that Kane once spotted Honey Fitz walking into a strategy meeting and hollered:

"Get that sonofabitch out of here!"

Jack looked up in surprise: "Who? Grampa?"

There were those, however, who wondered if Honey Fitz might not have been a more welcome association to the voters of the Eleventh than this 28-year-old millionaire who spoke with a Harvard accent. The world in which

he had moved could not have been more alien to the people of his district if he had lived on another planet.

The political veterans complained that Kennedy did not start at the bottom in the traditional way, perhaps in the legislature. They grumbled that he was not true Irish like most of them but "Harvard Irish." They said Joe Kennedy had boasted that, with all his money, he could elect his chauffeur to Congress. One of them told Jack bluntly: "You're a damned carpetbagger!"

And their tempers rose still higher when young Kennedy smiled at their gabbing and paid no attention to them. "One handicap Jack recognized and accepted," Sutton said, "was that almost everyone in public life was going to be opposed to him."

Shunning the old pros entirely, Kennedy began months before the June primaries to put together a large personal organization. For its nucleus, he chose friends from Choate, Harvard and the Navy—Democrats, Republi-

EPH P. KENNEDY JR.
NS OF FOREIGN WARS

POST NO. 5880

cans, liberals and conservatives. He wanted young men who were energetic, politically inexperienced and ideologically uncommitted. These were people, most of them just back from the war, who were weary of the old faces, the corrupt politics. As the captains were picked, they fanned out and recruited scores of volunteers.

"Jack came along at a time," John Droney, campaign treasurer, said, "when the rabble rousers were finished and didn't know it. He was the antithesis of all the politicians around at the time. He was the beginning of an end, the beginning of a new era."

John Galvin, who was to become his press agent, said Kennedy "was 180 degrees different from the typical pro politician. He avoided everything that he considered political doctrine or political bible. There was no blarney with him. Right from the first day, his campaign was a test of new methods, new ideas and new ways of campaigning."

Pasty-faced and gaunt to the point of ema-

ciation, Kennedy was in appearance "not a very attractive candidate," said Joe Lahey, a Navy shipyard worker and charter member of what Kennedy called his "Little Brain Trust."

"As he talked to me," Lahey said, "I could not help thinking, 'Gee, this guy needs something to eat.' I introduced him to my mother, and she asked him, 'My God, don't you ever get a haircut?' But Jack had a million-dollar smile that captured people."

In political circles, Lahey said the opposition to Kennedy was so bitter that "I started to lose friends. They couldn't understand how I could be associated with a young millionaire they said had never lived in the district. Mike Neville told me in no uncertain terms that I was an undemocratic traitor."

While Jack was setting up campaign headquarters at the Bellevue Hotel, his father was establishing a command post at the Ritz-Carlton, from which he recruited several battle-hardened pros to work behind the scenes. Jack's young crowd, sometimes called the

*So thin they wanted to mother him.*

Bunker Hill Gang, was all well and good, but the father decided the youngsters could use some old-fashioned, hard-nosed, practical, political know-how from such as Joe Kane. It was Kane who drafted the campaign slogan.

David Powers had just returned from the China-Burma-India theater and was living with his widowed sister and her eight children when he heard a knock on his door in the Charlestown section. He opened it and "this tall, thin, handsome young man reached out his hand and said, 'My name is Jack Kennedy. I am a candidate for Congress. Will you help me?' "

Sutton, who had sold newspapers with Powers in the Charlestown Navy yard, had sent Kennedy to him.

"Just that day down at the local tavern, they were talking about a Charlestown boy named John Cotter who was going to run," Powers said. "Charlestown people have a reputation for sticking together, and I told Kennedy, 'Gosh, if I help anyone, it should be John Cotter.'

"He smiled and told me he was speaking to a group of Gold Star mothers that day and asked me if I would go with him. I did."

Several hundred women were there and Powers listened as Kennedy spoke to them, sincerely, honestly—and awkwardly. Instead of coming to a rousing finish, as an accomplished speaker would, Powers said he "sort of stuttered and stammered for a while.

"Then he looked out at them and—right

from the heart, you could sense it—he said, I think I know how you mothers feel, because my mother is a Gold Star mother, too.'

"Well, those wonderful Charlestown mothers swarmed around him then, and in the background I could hear them saying that he reminded them of their own Mike or John or Dan. It took him a half hour to get out of there."

Afterward, they walked together down the street and Kennedy asked, "How do you think I did?"

"I never saw anything like it," Powers replied.

"Then you'll help me?"

"I've already started."

They shook hands and it marked the begining of a friendship that was to endure until the day Powers rode in a car behind John Kennedy in Dallas, Texas.

Droney, who had passed the Massachusetts bar examination before the war, had just returned from service when a friend asked him to support Kennedy.

"I went to see him," Droney said, "but I was determined not to get into any political fights. I told Jack I knew little of politics and I was anxious to get started in law practice."

"Well," Kennedy said, "I wanted to be a newspaperman, but my brother was killed in the war, and my dad thinks I'm best fitted to carry on for him. You want to be a lawyer, and I want to be a newspaperman, but if we're going to change things the way they should be changed, we have to do things we don't want to do."

"That little speech," Droney said, "changed my mind in ten seconds. He asked me to round up a few of my friends. I got about forty or fifty young veterans together, and he won them all over."

When Kennedy asked Droney to be his campaign treasurer Droney objected that he was no good at arithmetic. "You don't have to be disturbed about that," Kennedy replied. "My dad has all the accountants we will need. I want somebody I can trust, but dad has to approve."

Dad had to approve everybody. Every key worker lined up by his son was brought in for a personal interview. All campaign arrangements were subject to change at his order. But his father was concerned only with campaign tactics, never with substance. On most matters of policy, Jack disagreed with him sharply, telling him, "We speak for different generations."

Colbert said he once heard Kennedy tell his father, "I'm running, not you, and I'll campaign my way, not your way."

"Another time," Colbert said, "I heard him in polite but firm language ask his father to leave the room when they got into too vigorous an argument. The old man put up a show of anger, but you got the impression that he was pleased because his son had the guts to tangle with him."

Joe's influence was not as great as he let people think nor as little as many suspected.

"The father let Jack make his own decisions," Droney said, "but he was always there when he was needed, and this was dreadfully important.

"We were all green as grass and we could have made many mistakes. Against opponents of great experience, you have to be very careful that you are not knocked off the ballot, or, if you win, that the election is not taken away from you on a technicality. Joe Kennedy said that if Jack won that election, nobody was ever going to take it away from him."

Joe Sr. selected the John C. Dowd Agency of Boston, to which he had once thrown lucrative advertising business, to handle the publicity. Mark Dalton, a Harvard law graduate who was to be one of Kennedy's key advisors

for six years, became campaign manager. Jack recruited his war buddy, "Red" Fay, as another member of the team.

The reservations the head of the family had felt when he told Jack to take Joe's place began to dissipate the first day Jack took to the streets of Boston.

Kennedy was standing in Maverick Square in East Boston, Pat Kennedy's old stronghold which had changed through the years into a tough Italian neighborhood. He watched as Jack walked up to a group of men on a corner with hands jammed in their pockets, swarthy men suspicious of the skinny, shock-haired kid. Jack grinned broadly, stuck out his hand and asked for their votes, and in a few moments they were smiling and talking to him.

"I would have given odds of 5,000-to-one that this could never have happened," the father said. "I never thought Jack had it in him."

Jack's first speeches were hesitant. He lacked poise. He was pale and thin and sometimes at the end of a long day his face was twisted with the pain of his back.

"Jack wasn't too nervous," Dalton said. "It was more of a tiredness and tension, from the pain and the long schedule. He drove himself as few human beings ever drove themselves."

"He could walk with humble people and understand them as if he had been with them all his life," said McLaughlin. "He talked to people who were not educated, but had a real instinct for politics—the feel for it—and he listened to them. Jack represented to the poor something that they aspired to be themselves, somebody they wanted in their family. He could walk in and get along with them and understand them as well as if he had been brought up among them. You either have this or you don't. He had it in great abundance."

Tramping the dark stairwells of the tenements and talking his way into the small,

*Listening to the New Generation: Rose Kennedy, Mrs. Fitzgerald, Honey Fitz, Mayor Curley.*

crowded apartments was distasteful to him at first. "If Joe had lived," he once told a friend, "I would never have done anything like this." But he never gave a hint of his shyness to people he approached. And few seemed to resent the fact that Kennedy came from the lap of luxury. They laughed appreciatively when he told them with a grin, "I'm the one who didn't come up the hard way."

Probably, his wealth became a factor in his favor. "The poor people realized," Droney explained, "that if he was going to get into public life and pay the price that you must pay, that he wasn't going to do it for money. He wasn't going to steal anything. I heard that comment many times."

Slowly, Kennedy developed a simple, informal style that people, tired of the old bombast, found new and refreshing. Ignoring all his opponents as if they did not exist, he talked of the need for jobs and housing for those who were coming back from the war, and for low rents and medical care. These were the real bread-and-butter, vote-getting issues in the poor Eleventh District.

And there was the pain from his back. Always.

"Many times," Sutton said, "he came in exhausted, his face drawn, after some energetic young guy had broken his back running along streets and up and down stairs. We knew he was suffering, but he had a will to go on that overcame it. Sometimes the pain made him cranky, and he would jump on me about something. But he always came back later to apologize and say, 'Billy, you know it's nothing personal.' We couldn't bring in big, expensive cars because the people of the district were extremely poor, and this would keep pointing up the fact that he was rich. So he was a foot man. He would walk, walk, walk."

Walking up narrow alleys. Walking along the docks, talking to longshoremen. Walking

to factory and saloon. Walking up musty stairs of tenements. Always walking. But not alone. Before going into a neighborhood Kennedy would recruit a captain to guide him around. It was a tactic that was not forgotten in later years.

And he recruited his family. As the campaign got under way, the Kennedy clan surrounded Boston like a Comanche war party.

Bobby, just out of the Navy, came in his uniform and plunged into the tenement districts of Boston. He was fresh from duty as an able-bodied seaman aboard the U.S.S. *Joseph P. Kennedy Jr.*, a destroyer launched in the fall of 1945.

"Bobby always took the toughest jobs," Dave Powers said. "In the history of American politics, I can't think of another case where one man was so dedicated to the success of a brother as Bobby was to Jack. No one ever worked so hard, no man ever displayed such courage or made as many sacrifices to have his brother elected as Bobby Kennedy did."

Opening a campaign office in East Cambridge, where Jack thought he would do well to lose by five-to-one to the local favorite, Mike Neville, Bobby shook hands and ate spaghetti and talked about his brother. He would leave his office to play softball with the kids in a park across the street. When the votes were counted in that ward, Neville just squeezed past Kennedy.

Rose Kennedy jumped into the fight for her son with all the vigor of the younger members of the clan. She knocked on doors, and housewives hurried back into their bedrooms and change into their better dresses in honor of the occasion. She told the Italians, in a few words of their own language, how she grew up in North End. In Dorchester, she reminisced on her years at Dorchester High School. She talked about the Kennedy kids and showed them her carefully kept records of their vaccinations, dental work, childhood diseases.

When she talked to upper-class women, she told them a little bit about Jack and what a fine congressman he was going to be. Then she would say, "Now, let me tell you about the new dresses I saw in Paris last month!" That did it. Those women weren't going to vote for Jack; they were going to vote for Rose. But either way the Kennedy name got the vote.

"Mrs. Kennedy used to come into our hotel suite, kick her shoes off and just flop on the bed," Galvin said. "She would be worn out after hours of shaking hands and talking to people."

Only Jack wandered in and out of more homes than his mother. It was traditional to hold "house parties" in the district. Workers would line up housewives to ask the neighbors over for tea and cookies—and a chat with the candidate. Jack would amble in, stroll out to the kitchen, take a badly needed glass of milk, ask about relatives over in the Old Country and then slouch in the parlor, one leg thrown over the arm of a chair, and make small talk.

The Kennedy girls, wearing black felt skirts with the family name printed all over them, rang doorbells throughout the district. Eunice loved it; Pat and Jean did not. Helen Keyes, an old friend of the family, said the girls "were awfully cute in their outfits, but Jean and Pat felt like jackasses in them."

The younger girls made a great game out of ducking their father. As long as they were with Mrs. Keyes, Joe Sr. thought they were out working for the cause. "They'd walk out the door," Mrs. Keyes said, "and Joe would say, 'Where are you going?' They would reply, 'We're going with Helen, Dad,' and he'd say, 'That's fine.' Of course, we were going swimming or something like that, but he thought as long as they were with me, they were campaigning."

"Pat and Jean were really shy girls. When they were supposed to ring doorbells in a housing project, they'd sneak into a movie for the afternoon. I'd catch them, and they'd plead, 'Please don't tell dad.'"

On rare occasions, a sorehead would show resentment at the mass invasion of Boston by the Kennedys. At the armory on Bunker Hill Street, a man in the audience tried to question Jack about the family. Kennedy turned on the man, his eyes blazing. "I don't ever have to apologize for any Kennedy," he said. "I'm running for Congress, and let's stick to that. If you want to talk about families, I will meet you outside."

Memories of young Joe Kennedy were always with them. "Jack rarely showed sentiment," Dalton said. "But one morning we went to mass together and as we were getting up to leave he said to me, 'Would you wait a moment? I want to light a candle for Joe.' It was totally unlike him, and I was amazed."

At another time, they were in a car and Dalton was talking, when he suddenly realized that Jack's thoughts were far away. "He turned to me and said, 'I'm sorry. I wasn't listening. I was thinking of Joe.'"

As the campaigners and the campaign ground on, Kennedy picked up increasing acceptance.

"Jack was something new in Boston politics," Sutton said. "He was like a ray of sunshine coming in the window on a rainy day. He was winning voters who looked on politics as an odious business dominated by crooks and windbags."

Kennedy may have been a sunbeam coming through the window, but he was also a tireless candidate knocking at the doors. There were Kennedys all over the Eleventh District, Kennedy relatives, Kennedy classmates, Kennedy war buddies.

"He didn't need a press secretary," said

one volunteer. "He had 125 guys on the street. They were his real press secretaries."

Later watchers of the Kennedys on campaign talked often, if not inventively, of "juggernauts" and "well-oiled machines." Not really, although the years did develop a most efficient expertise that both borrowed and innovated. What John Kennedy showed in 1946 was the secret of all his successes: hard work. Organizational skills developed by trial and error, but his breakthrough was to replace person-to-person politics of the *Last Hurrah* variety with personality-to-person. Kennedy won friends because they liked him, not because he owed them anything or bought their loyalty. "He was playing to the young guys who were just back from the service and to the families who had someone in the service. To them all, he had the image of the war hero, not the politician. People who

wouldn't vote for a millionaire would accept the skipper of *PT 109.* The boys came back from the war with a dream. They were tired of being poor and living under those conditions. He was the rich boy who came along and gave them a gleam of hope, a goal they could work toward."

But probably, most of all, Kennedy appealed to the women. Warren McCully, Grand Knight of the Bunker Hill Council, Knights of Columbus, sponsored Jack as a member and helped expose him to the people of Charlestown. "He was thin and scrawny and apparently didn't care about his appearance," McCully said. "His hair was always sticking up in the middle of his head, and he had a nervous habit of brushing it off his forehead. But his careless appearance didn't hurt him. I sat behind two older women at one of his speeches, and they felt sorry for him because

he looked so thin and his clothes needed pressing. He was the kind of boy you wanted to do things for. We took him to the people, but we didn't get him the votes. He got his own votes."

Although millions of dollars were at his disposal, Kennedy, as always, never seemed to have any cash in his pockets. Once, when Rose Kennedy asked a cab driver what he thought about the Congressional race, he replied: "I'm going to vote for a young war hero by the name of John F. Kennedy. His grandfather came from the North Side and was a personal friend of mine."

"I'm glad to hear that," Mrs. Kennedy said. "I'm his mother."

"I'm glad to meet you," the driver said. "Remind him when you see him that he owes me $1.85 fare from yesterday."

Colbert once went to lunch with Kennedy and wasn't surprised when the candidate fished through his pockets and couldn't come up with $1.95 to pay the check. Colbert laughed and reached into his own pocket. Empty.

" 'Don't worry,' Kennedy said, 'I'll take care of it.' He called the waitress and told her, I'm John F. Kennedy, the son of Ambassador Joseph P. Kennedy, and I'd like to open a charge account and charge this lunch.'

" 'Yeah, I'm Greta Garbo,' the waitress replied. 'Pay the check.'

"He was asked for identification, and he didn't have that, either. Finally, I identified myself, and they let him charge the lunch— $1.95."

Meanwhile, for the Ritz-Carlton headquarters, money flowed into the campaign. "Winning takes three things," Kane said. "The first is money. The second is money. The third is money."

No Congressional campaign in Massachusetts was ever so elaborately advertised.

Billboards, posters, car stickers and leaflets papered the city. Jack loved to see cars bearing his campaign stickers. Sometimes he followed the cars and thanked the drivers. Galvin was with him once when he followed a car for several miles before he was able to pull up alongside at a traffic light. He leaned out to tell the driver, "I want to thank you for wearing my sticker." "The man was stunned," Galvin said. "When he recovered, he said, 'I'm honored to have your sticker, Mr. Kennedy.' Jack turned to me and said, 'These are the people who will win for me.'"

As Kennedy's name blanketed the district, invitations to the house parties became sought after. "The people would gather, and when Jack would come in, it was like a movie star making an entrance. You could hear the women sigh," said McLaughlin. "Each night we'd wind up at the Ritz at one o'clock in the morning having scrambled eggs. This went on for the entire spring. The parties broke the backs of his opponents."

If house parties were such a success, why not try a tea party for women only? Droney thought the idea crazy. Tea parties were effeminate, and this was a rough district.

"I was dead wrong, as usual," said Droney.

Hand-engraved invitations were sent to every woman on the voting list. "Before that tea the hair stylists were working twenty-four hours a day. Every unmarried woman had that hope and dream that lightning would strike."

Hundreds of women, all in their best gowns, showed up, forming a line that extended from the lobby of the Commander Hotel in Cambridge, across the street and into a nearby park. The women walked one by one into the ballroom and up on the stage to shake hands with the candidate. And at the head of the receiving line, in white tie and tails, was the former Ambassador to the Court of St.

James and his wife. It was Joe Sr.'s one and only public appearance for his son.

One old politician who saw the crowd exclaimed, "I never would have believed it, but this kid will walk in easily."

"Several times," Droney said, "I heard women tell Jack he was going to be President. It was fantastic."

A poll by the Boston *Post* showed that Kennedy would receive almost as many votes as the combined opposition, but the father wanted confirmation. He borrowed the New York *Daily News* straw poll crew and had his own count made. The *News* men canvassed the district as thoroughly as if they were assessing the chances of a Presidential hopeful. They confirmed the first poll. Kennedy was far out in front.

There were several days to go before the election and Joe Sr. suggested that this son could relax and coast home. But Jack never slowed down. "He followed Franklin's advice, 'Early to bed and early to rise,' only when he could not otherwise arrange his schedule," one aide said.

It was a runaway. Kennedy nearly doubled the vote of Neville, his nearest opponent, and scored heavily in every district but Ward Two in Charlestown, home of the third-place candidate, John Cotter. For the newly elected Congressman from the Eleventh District it was an auspicious beginning.

The Kennedy headquarters was a joyful uproar as a new era in Boston politics raised its glass in a first hurrah of victory. The old times were not forgotten—Honey Fitz climbed on a table, danced a jig and sang "Sweet Adeline"—but John Kennedy's triumph was not just another Irish march to office, it was not the triumph of the man who sat quietly in a corner watching his son's followers celebrate. It was the triumph of John F. Kennedy who won not on issues or vote

*Kathleen: May 13, 1948*

trading or empty promises. He won because this young aristocrat went to a tired and unprivileged district and asked its poor to entrust in him their votes for an uncharted future none of them could predict. This they gave him.

"They're saying that many people were close to Kennedy and made him," said Joe Lahey, watching the party. "I'm going to differ and say that Kennedy not only made himself, he made them."

There was one Kennedy who had been away from the tumult and triumph of young Jack Kennedy's campaign. His sister, Kathleen. She had made England her adopted land, the family of her late husband her adopted family. Friends said she had become more Cavendish than Kennedy.

Had her husband survived the war, Kathleen most likely would have been chief Lady-In-Waiting to Queen Elizabeth because of his titled position. As his widow she moved in high circles in British society, a contrast to the dedicated, simple piety of her widowhood. While guests at the weekend parties of the British manor houses were sleeping late on Sunday mornings, Kathleen Kennedy Hartington was regularly getting up with the Catholic servants to attend six o'clock mass. She had forgotten neither her family nor her faith.

It wasn't that Kick was estranged from her people in the States. In 1948, for instance, she and her father planned to meet on the Riviera for a joint holiday. Joe Sr. was in Paris. Kathleen was to fly down from London.

A friend of hers, Lord Fitzwilliam, at thirty-eight one of the richest peers in Britain, offered to fly Kathleen to the Riviera in a twin-engine DeHavilland Dove to meet her father. Lord Fitzwilliam had chartered the aircraft from Skyways Ltd. in London. Capt. P. A.

Townsend was at the controls as the plane took off and headed south. It was May 13.

There were reports of bad weather in central France and a thunderstorm had been rattling the hills around Valence all day. About 6 P.M. a farmer saw a plane suddenly come out of the clouds. A wing fell off. "The plane then plunged straight into the ground behind a hill," the farmer said. It took him and his father an hour to find the wreckage.

Captain Townsend and his radio operator were thrown against the instrument panel. Lord Fitzwilliam was still in the cabin. But Kathleen was thrown from the wreckage. She was lying on the ground as if asleep, the farmer said. But she was dead. They all were dead. Kathleen was identified by her passport. Joe Kennedy was reached in Paris. His voice broke as he told a reporter, "I have no plans, I have no plans."

He rushed to the village of Privas near the mountain of Le Coran where the crash occurred. He watched as an ox-drawn cart slowly made its way down the slope bearing the body of his daughter.

# A Brahmin Called Kennedy

The winter winds blow chill from the west, always with the promise of snow. They climb the white-starred hill of Arlington, cross the Potomac, embrace the Lincoln Memorial, crisp the reflecting pool, whip past the Washington Monument, the White House, along the old path to the heart of the Union, the towering dome, the Capitol, its wings spread as if to catch the breath of the nation.

The freshman congressman from Massachusetts's Eleventh District, hatless, his tousled hair blown, deeply tanned, grinning, wearing a black cashmere coat over a gray flannel suit against the wind, striding briskly to the steps, already late. This January 3, 1947, the first day of the Eightieth Congress, Jack Kennedy came to the Capitol.

A few hours earlier his aides waited impatiently in the lobby of the Statler Hotel, promising House Minority Leader John McCormack on the telephone that their new congressman would be there shortly, in time for a Democratic Party caucus.

Then he blew in the door, fresh from Palm Beach and hungry. "We are going to have some eggs," he said. His aides protested. The Minority Leader was phoning every hour. Breakfast could come later. He should go upstairs and get dressed.

"Well, let's just go and get one egg in the drugstore," Kennedy compromised. They tried to rush him through breakfast. Especially Billy Sutton.

"Why don't you take your time, Billy?" he said. "The thing you don't know is that it is going to be a great year. . . . By the way, how many years would you say Mr. McCormack has been down here in Washington?"

"About twenty-eight."

"Well," Kennedy said, "I was wondering if Mr. McCormack would mind waiting another fifteen minutes for me after being down here for so many years without me."

The events of the day piled one on another: the caucus, the oath as one of 435 representatives of the United States. At the end, the day found him with his aides at the National Press Club. There he recognized another new congressman. They shook hands cordially, kidding each other. Jack Kennedy of Massachusetts had met Richard Nixon of California.

Great expectations. Jack Kennedy, only twenty-nine, still his father's son, not yet committed to any particular path, so young-looking. Once, stepping off an elevator to meet a friend, he said, "Well how do you like that? Some people got in and asked me for the fourth floor."

Another time, watching a high school football team practice, he asked to borrow a uniform and joined the workout. "Hey kid," a halfback yelled to him, "come on over here and snag some passes." Kennedy did. A few minutes later the coach asked the high school halfback; "How's the Congressman doing?"

"Is that what they call him?" the halfback asked. "He needs a lot of work, coach. What year's he in?"

From London, before the war, Joe Kennedy Sr. once sent an angry telegram to movie censors protesting the James Stewart comedy, *Mr. Smith Goes to Washington,* because it would give foreigners the idea that outrageous things happen in the United States Senate. Now, in Washington, people were comparing his son, Jack, to the young freshman senator played by Stewart: shy, sincere, introverted.

"He was not that Jimmy Stewart type of guy all the time," said Billy Sutton. "He was a wise, tough guy, and he let us know that we were in a fight, and godammit, let's get going."

Yet in those early days in Congress, Jack was noticeable by his casual, if not sloppy dress. He arrived in town in a yellow sweater, carrying his extra shoes in his hand and a

briefcase that held three shirts, three pairs of socks, two pairs of underwear. He sometimes appeared on the floor of the House in khaki pants and an old jacket, his shirttail out. Sutton remembers the first time Kennedy spoke to the assembled House.

He called, "Mr. Speaker," and was recognized by House Speaker Joe Martin, a Republican in a heavily Republican Congress. Then Jack Kennedy reached into his jacket pocket for his speech. He couldn't find it. While he searched for it, he looked pleadingly up at Sutton in the gallery, but Sutton indicated he didn't know where it was either.

Speaker Martin, noticing the plight of the freshman Democrat from his own state, informed the House that Mr. Kennedy was looking for his speech. Jack Kennedy found it in his back pocket, pulled it out. Finally, he read the speech, more like a bumbling teen-ager than an elected representative.

Walking with Sutton later, he said, "I don't remember your giving me this speech."

"I don't think these guys will remember the speech you gave them either," Sutton gibed.

The young congressman set up house in Georgetown, hiring a housekeeper and a valet he inherited from his father's friend, Arthur Krock. Domestically he was in better shape than he was legislatively. Freshmen in the House don't have the time to accumulate the power, the seniority, the debts, that make representatives effective. He inherited his father's pride and prejudice on many matters and had yet to grow out of them. Through his years in the House the most that could be said of his legislative record was that it reflected the sentiments of his tenement constituency. He did not favor farm aid because his people didn't need it. He voted conservatively on foreign policy after his father's fashion, but he favored foreign aid with the pro-

vision that the receiving nation contribute as well. He voted strongly for legislation to boost housing and to aid labor and laboring people. Overall, he was neither liberal nor conservative in those early days. He defied categorization. He was, if anything, a pragmatist.

But there was one early incident that indicated the hero of the South Pacific might be more than just another deckhand in Congress. When Mayor Curley, his pleas of ill health unavailing, was sentenced to prison, he asked his political friends to bail him out with a petition of clemency to President Truman. All Congressional members of the Massachusetts delegation signed it except one: Jack Kennedy. It wasn't that Honey Fitz's grandson was repaying any old scores. He just did not believe Curley's claims of illness.

And it was typical of Joe Sr. that he resisted any effort to have him put pressure on his son.

In those first days Jack was put on the Labor Committee, then considering the Hartley Bill which was to become the Taft-Hartley Labor Act. He called down Mark Dalton and some other Boston aides to help him.

"The thing I always loved about John Kennedy," Dalton recalls, "was no matter how audacious the idea was, he liked it. The more audacious, the more he liked it. About three or four months after he was in Congress, we wrote a separate dissenting opinion on the Hartley Bill . . . As we were typing out the dissenting report, the word got out that Kennedy was filing a separate report, and you can imagine the reaction of the old time men in Congress: Who is this character with the gall to file a separate report? Senator Taft knew that this was going on in Kennedy's office, and I think he was quite amused that this young fellow should be trying to remake the whole of government."

Kennedy also carried his dissent to the

Rules Committee, and Dalton went with him to the hearing room. "There was a young fellow up talking to the committee and there were two or three seats right in back of this speaker, and John and I sat down. John said to me, 'Listen to this fellow, Mark, listen to this fellow. He's going places.' So I listened to him and he was quite impressive. And he finished within a minute or two, and turned around to take his seat, and John stood up and I stood, and John said, 'Mark, I would like you to meet Richard Nixon of California.'"

Nixon's suite was across the hall from John Kennedy's in the House Office Building. Once in the coming weeks, the two traveled to Pennsylvania to debate the Taft-Hartley Bill. Few showed up to hear a debate between two obscure congressmen.

As did other eastern representatives, Kennedy developed an impressive absentee record. He frequently returned to Massachusetts to keep in touch with his constituents. In a sense, as the Irish politicians of his family's past, he never quit campaigning. But his method and motive were different.

One old-time Boston ward leader of the day put it this way: "In this town a politician is a man who comes to the police station in the middle of the night with a topcoat thrown over his pajamas to get a drunk constituent out of jail in time to go to work. Kennedy doesn't do that. As far as I know Kennedy doesn't pay for anybody's funeral, seldom goes to wakes, and he never seems to get anybody a job."

A freshman congressman doesn't have many jobs to pass out. But it was part of the Kennedy mode to look after people who helped you, or who voted for you, or who might.

Bill Sutton's sister taught school in a run-down area of Boston and once told Jack she had been describing circuses to her class and asked them how many had ever been to one. None of the forty pupils raised his hand. Kennedy took the teacher aside and told her that when the circus came to town she was to take the entire class, buy them everything they wanted and send him the bill. She didn't think he would remember, but she did it anyway. She received a check for the full amount with a note from Jack Kennedy asking her please not to mention the whole affair since he'd learned that the school was in Rep. John McCormack's district.

Joe Kennedy Sr. still had his doubts about whether his son would make it politically. He worried, too, about the ailing back that caused Jack so much pain. So he considered other things. Once he thought of buying the New York *Sun*, and another time put in a bid for the Boston *Post* with the idea of making Jack editor. He needn't have worried about Jack's future. His son ran unopposed in 1948, and was building up a solid background of votes in the state.

If his own voting record seemed without pattern, it did not lack courage. In 1949, Jack Kennedy, a Catholic, introduced a bill for federal aid to parochial schools for items like buses, books and health services. It was knocked out in committee. Jack Kennedy, the millionaire's son, sided with budget slashers and asked: "How long can we continue deficit financing on such a large scale with a national debt of over $258 billions?" Jack Kennedy, the poor man's representative, offered a housing bill and when the American Legion attacked it, shot back: "The leadership of the American Legion has not had a constructive thought for the benefit of the country since 1918."

In 1950, running for reelection again, Jack Kennedy devastated five primary contenders, building up a five-to-one margin over their combined votes. Then he turned his attention to his Republican opponent, Vincent J. Celeste, a young Boston lawyer. Celeste had watched the 1946 Kennedy campaign in amazement. Among other things, he was impressed by the number of placards Kennedy had printed. Celeste gathered up the old placards in 1950 and had his own slogans printed on the reverse side. Unfortunately, when the wind blew the signs down, the public could read VINCENT CELESTE FOR CONGRESS on one side and THE NEW GENERATION OFFERS A LEADER—JACK KENNEDY on the other.

Celeste did his best, but, as he observed, "Campaigning against John Kennedy, even for Congress, was like fighting the phantom. He's everywhere, and he's nowhere. His publicists are working day and night, his hired hands, so to speak . . . did a magnificent job."

He felt, Celeste said, as if he were running "against the father rather than the candidate, and I say this with all due respect. Joe was a tremendously able politician, a very able man behind the man."

"Mr. Kennedy," recalls Mark Dalton, "was very, very close to the picture and key decisions would certainly be made by Mr. Kennedy. He sought our views, gave great latitude to our thoughts and decisions, but he was always a key man in the picture in every good sense. Very helpful. He would call on the phone and talk at some length as to how the campaign was developing . . . That was one of my problems, he'd talk for two hours on the phone, wanting to know every facet of what was happening."

Celeste felt he was running against Kennedy money, and said so. But Jack Kennedy retorted he hadn't spent a penny on his 1950 campaign. He beat Celeste by almost a five-to-one margin. It was, after all, a Democratic district.

By now Jack Kennedy was campaigning all over the state—not just in his Eleventh District—under the banner: "Kennedy Will Do More for Massachusetts." Obviously the young congressman had something larger in mind. "I think the pros wait too long to start," he said of that time. "I began running for the Senate four and a half years ahead of time. My opponent, Henry Cabot Lodge Jr., didn't go into action until two months before election day."

While he was in Washington, Frank Morrissey ran Jack's Boston office at 122 Bowdoin Street, his old apartment, now a headquarters. But Thursdays Jack Kennedy flew home to make speeches in one or more of the 351 Massachusetts cities and towns. He was always on the go. He flew or drove at all hours, in all weather, grabbing a quick hamburger, bedding down for the night in inexpensive countryside hotels.

A Boston friend described the pace: "You're driving with Jack eighty miles an hour, and he keeps asking you to go faster because he's already ten minutes late at the next town. A motorcycle cop starts chasing you, so you stop and get out, and, miraculously, you fast-talk the cop into letting you go on. Naturally, you're feeling rather proud of yourself for accomplishing such a feat. A few miles farther on, you come to a railroad crossing where the red light is flashing and the bell is ringing. Jack says, 'Come on, we've got to beat that train.' So you step on it and race to the crossing, but the locomotive gets there a couple of inches ahead of you, and you just miss hitting it. Jack grits his teeth in disgust. 'If you hadn't wasted so much time back there talking to that cop, we would have made it,' he says."

Aide John Galvin recalls one weekend trip to Danville in a rented car. The planes were fogged in. Jack Kennedy drove, and he "drove

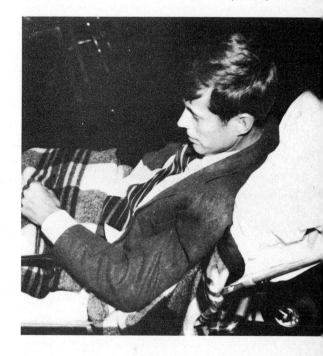

*He knew pain half his life.*

very fast." When they arrived, Kennedy rubbed his chin and decided he needed a shave. Galvin ran into a drugstore and bought shaving cream and razor blades. They ducked into a bowling alley and found the men's room. There was only a cold water tap. Standing at the mirror, still wearing his topcoat, Congressman Kennedy shaved. Galvin remembered: "The guys would come in from bowling and there was this guy shaving, and sometimes they forgot what they went in there for."

Jack was becoming bored in Congress. "We were just worms over in the House," he said. "Nobody pays much attention to us nationally." The hazards were many, the rewards few.

If Jack's was a little-heard public voice, his father's could be loud and clear—and controversial. The possibilities began to arise that he could embarrass his son in the public arena.

In December 1950, he was invited to speak at the Student Forum of the University of Virginia where son Bob, a law student, was Forum president. Bobby introduced his father to the audience. Joe Kennedy chose as his topic United States foreign policy. He took his accustomed isolationist stance on the war in Korea. He said the United States was over-committed. He called for getting out of Korea, and "every point in Asia which we do not plan realistically to hold in our own defense," a statement that would include French Indochina. Nor could the United States, he said, hold off Soviet Russia if it moved into Western Europe. Nor should it try. "Our policy is politically and morally a bankrupt policy," he said.

Three months later, back from a six-week, personally paid tour of Europe and the North Atlantic Treaty Organization, Jack Kennedy was asked to testify before the Senate com-

mittees on foreign relations and armed forces. Both were considering whether to build up U.S. military strength in Europe. Jack Kennedy insisted that industrialized Europe could not be abandoned. It was too important to the United States. United States troop strength there should be kept sufficient.

After his testimony, Senator Walter George asked if he had read his father's Virginia speech, and if he disagreed with it. Jack Kennedy said he could understand his father's viewpoint. He added: "To him and to a lot of other Americans it looks like almost a hopeless job and that we are committing troops to be lost." Nevertheless, he said, his own dispassionate view was that Europe must be held, was worth the troops and the risk. "That is my position," he said. "I think you should ask my father directly as to his position."

It was a nice compromise, as long as it

held up. One family friend put the difficulty this way:

"Joe Sr. was opposed to World War II, he had split with Roosevelt, he had ultra-conservative views in the eyes of many. All of these factors, he realized, could have been detrimental to the future of his son, and as much as I think he would have liked to have been out in the forefront, he put his own desires into the background for the benefit of his son. But I honestly believe that without his advice—even though at times there would be sharp disagreements—it never would have been done, as brilliant as Jack himself was, and as able."

One of the soldiers sent to Germany to bolster the U.S. presence there was a Kennedy. Edward was a freshman at Harvard in 1951. He was heading for a C-minus grade in Spanish, so he asked a classmate to take the examination for him. Both students were expelled, and the shame was borne by others in the family as well. Edward joined the Army

and was sent to Germany to serve, and allowed to return to Harvard when his hitch ended. For Joe Sr., his son's behavior was a severe disappointment, but he was not a man without compassion. Not long after the incident he helped West Point cadets, thrown out of the academy for cribbing, by paying their tuitions at other schools. Said one of Joe's classmates: "Joe was as tough as they come, but he never did anything I would consider dishonest or unethical. Teddy's cheating was a great shock to me."

In the postwar years Joe Sr. turned a sizeable fortune into a massive one. He dealt in real estate where 400 percent profits were not unusual, and where mortgages could be bought for fifty cents on the dollar. Partly because of increasing taxes, he went into oil, where the tax benefits from depletion allowances let him keep more and more of the enormous sums he was making. He lived an easy life in Palm Beach, conducting his business from poolside by telephone. As he told a friend: "I really began to make money when I came down here to sit on my butt and think."

(Joe Kennedy's lexicon of inelegant expression was extensive, and not above reproof. Once a well-bred daughter-in-law, Jacqueline Kennedy, told him: "You ought to write a series of grandfather stories for children, like 'The Duck with Moxie,' and 'The Donkey Who Couldn't Fight His Way Out of a Telephone Booth.'" Taken aback, Joe froze in momentary silence, then roared with laughter.)

Joe Kennedy's passion for politics was too great to avoid. When Jack's campaigns came up in turn, he would move in to direct much of the action from the wings. By 1952 Jack Kennedy had been campaigning for higher office for nearly four years. The only remaining question was, which office? For a time he had considered running for governor of Massachusets. Yet again, the rewards of the state's top executive office had to be weighed against the possibility of doing anything for the state's worsening economic condition from the State House. The other target was the Senate seat held by Republican Henry Cabot Lodge. Not one Democrat in the state felt strong enough to tackle the popular Lodge, the scion of Boston Brahmins, the polished product of old money and old family. When Democratic Governor Paul Dever decided it wasn't worth the risk in 1952, the three-term representative from the tenements of the Eleventh District decided this was his chance. Jack Kennedy, thirty-four, declared his candidacy. This time the Irish did apply.

Old-line Democrats thought he was crazy. Lodge passed on a message to Joe Sr. through Arthur Krock, telling him "not to waste his money on Jack because he can't win."

"I'm going to win by 300,000 votes," Lodge boasted. Nearly everyone believed him. *Nearly* everyone.

The pessimism was reasoned. It was all right to have an Irish mayor, an Irish representative, as it was all right to have an Irish cook or an Irish nanny. But a Senate seat from Massachusetts was like a seat in the House of Lords. Only aristocrats need apply.

After all, Honey Fitz battled with the first Senator Lodge in 1916 and lost. Honey Fitz fought the battle Irish style, personally attacking his distinguished opponent: "The robber baron is still his highest ideal and his dearest friend." But this appeal to the Irish was futile in the face of the Lodge name and Lodge money. As Joe Kennedy put it: "All I ever heard when I was growing up in Boston was how Lodge's grandfather had helped to put the stained glass windows into the Gate of Heaven Church in South Boston, and they were still talking about those same stained glass windows in 1952."

Now Joe counseled his son: "When you've beaten him, you've beaten the best. Why try for something else?"

Why indeed, for, as Dever himself said, Jack Kennedy had become the first Irish Brahmin.

But to the dispassionate eye of Jack Kennedy, the pessimism and the old reasoning were only rhetoric. This would not really be a battle between the Brahmins and the Irish. This would be Jack Kennedy against Henry Cabot Lodge, both the sons of millionaires, both Harvard graduates, both already tested in Congress, both equal in a way their grandfathers never could be equal. The only differences now were Democrat and Republican, and the failing fortunes of Massachusetts under Democratic control seemed to favor the Republican. Besides, Republican Lodge had beaten the Irish before by swinging Democratic votes into his column. Only this time Jack Kennedy had done his homework, and Joe Kennedy had measured the effect. He had polls taken. Lodge would be easier to beat than the state's other Republican Senator, Leverett Saltonstall.

Jack called again on Mark Dalton, the young lawyer, to handle his campaign, this time on a paid basis. But the campaign autocrat was still Joe Kennedy. Joe confronted Dalton one day, early in the campaign, and told him that he'd spent $10,000 of Kennedy money and "you haven't accomplished a damn thing." Dalton never returned. He was replaced by a 26-year-old, fresh from the University of Virginia law school. Bobby Kennedy.

Bobby whet his teeth in his brother's 1946 campaign. Now, in 1952, he brought vigor and sharp direction to this most crucial campaign yet, the one that could open the door to national prominence for Jack Kennedy—and maybe himself.

Up until now Bob had been catching up with the memory of his first brother, the life of his second. After Jack's first campaign, Bob entered Harvard where he won his letter in football, something neither of his elder brothers had been able to do. Kenny O'Donnell, his roommate, remembers that in one scrimmage Bobby tried to throw a block and crashed into an equipment cart on the sidelines. He came back to scrimmage at end for three more plays, then collapsed. They carried him off on a stretcher. He had broken his leg.

At the University of Virginia, Bobby was responsible for bringing in speakers like his father to the Student Forum. He also arranged for Senator Joseph McCarthy, and for Ralph Bunche, who would become the first Negro winner of the Nobel Peace Prize. Bunche's proposed visit gave the young law student a complex legal problem. Virginia law forbade the mixing of races in public places such as movie theaters. The United States Supreme Court had already ruled that such statutes could not apply to institutions of higher learn-

ing. Bunche refused to come if the audience was segregated. Bobby tried to circulate a resolution affirming that there would be a mixed audience, but southern students balked at signing it because it might cause them trouble when they went home. Bobby Kennedy got angry. He and two other students drew up a long brief citing the Supreme Court decision to show that the Virginia statutes could not apply to university functions. The President of the University affirmed that the meeting could be mixed. Bunche came. Robert Kennedy had won his first racial battle.

His career at U.Va. was not particularly notable. "He didn't make too many friends," said a girl who knew him. "He had no obvious leadership qualities." But the young student may have had other things on his mind than books.

In 1944, when he was nineteen, he had met Ethel Skakel on a skiing trip at Mont Tremblant in Canada. She was a roommate of Bob's sister, Jean, at Manhattanville College of the Sacred Heart, something of the Harvard of Catholic girls of the Kennedy's social status.

She had been born in Chicago and raised in New Jersey and Westchester county's prosperous New York suburbs. She was as extroverted as Bobby was introverted. She had to work hard for her grades and did, harder than Bobby, but once got an A on a paper written on *Why England Slept*.

But she was athletic—and rich. Her father owned Great Lakes Carbon Corp., a private company. Ethel took an immediate liking to Bobby. "I thought he was divine," she said, a definition among well-raised girls that covers everything from an ice cream soda to a $500 Dior gown. "Bob went around with me for a few weeks, then fell in love with my sister, Pat." But Pat later married someone else, and "Bobby came back to me, thank God."

On Saturday, June 17, 1950, Ethel Skakel

and Robert Kennedy, his hair smoothed back, were married by the Rev. Terence L. Connolly of Boston College, one of the few occasions when a Cardinal did not perform the nuptial rites of a Kennedy child. Jack Kennedy was best man.

The young couple moved into a rented, three-bedroom house near the school after a Hawaiian honeymoon. They worked hard all week and usually gave a party Saturday night. People at the school had widely divided opinions about Bobby. They all thought Ethel was wonderful.

"Outside [of class] he was very brash," said a professor. "He seemed to think most people weren't worth his time. He didn't want to waste time and was thinking ahead. I don't think he had any thought of just being a lawyer."

He graduated 56th in a class of 124, then took a $4,200-a-year job with the government investigating cases in Brooklyn against former members of the Truman administration. He was twenty-five when Jack called from Massachusetts asking him to run his campaign. Robert Kennedy didn't want to go. But his brother had asked. He went.

As a campaign manager, he would be tops in his class. His father summed him up this way: "Bobby is more direct than Jack. Jack has always been one to persuade people to do things. Bobby tends to tell people what to do. He resembles me much more than any of the other children. I make up my mind quickly and go ahead and get it done. Bobby is the same way."

Bobby came in early, and there wasn't much central organization when he arrived. Said campaign aide John Droney: "Actually, until Bobby moved in, there seemed to be chaos . . . He quit his job in Washington. I guess there was a little compulsion involved, and he came here and took over, and we started to move on in."

Dave Powers was in Boston, too, when Bobby entered the campaign. "I never saw anything like it," Powers remembers. "He'd be the first one there in the morning and the last one to leave at night. And I think what made the campaign such a great success was that he did the toughest work.

"Bobby sort of set the tone of it. I remember one incident involving the bridge coming from Boston to Charlestown and the fellow who was handling the Charlestown campaign. Bobby told him, 'I want a big sign—one of our signs—on that bridge.' It was a marvelous spot, and, where Bobby wanted it, the ladder didn't quite reach. And Bobby drove over there in the car, and he stood on top of that ladder, on the very top rung, and the only support he had was the hammer and the nails. And he put up his brother's sign."

Jack, for one, would never forget his brother's devoted labors and his ability. "Bobby works at high tempo," Jack said. "I remember in [the Senate campaign] when some politicians came into our headquarters and stood around gabbing. Finally Bobby told them: 'Here are some envelopes. You want to address them? Fine. Otherwise, wait outside. They addressed the envelopes."

"Every politician in Massachusetts was mad at Bobby," Jack Kennedy said. "But we had the best organization in history. You can't make an omelet without breaking the eggs."

"Those politicians," Bobby commented, "just wanted to sit around and talk about it and have their pictures taken at rallies."

Larry O'Brien, a lifelong politician, plotted strategy.

Bobby was the organization man, the one who was on the telephone checking with the Kennedy campaign people in every town in the state, the master planner. But once, in the absence of any available Kennedy, he emerged from behind the scenes to make a speech. In its entirety it went:

"My brother Jack couldn't be here. My mother couldn't be here. My sister Eunice couldn't be here. My sister Pat couldn't be here. My sister Jean couldn't be here. But if my brother Jack were here, he'd tell you Lodge has a very bad voting record. Thank you."

That's the kind of campaign it would be, the Kennedy clan covering the state from Boston to Pittsfield, from Haverhill to Fall River. Rose enlisted for the duration. Jack's mother was the gentle, graceful focus of the distaff campaign. At first her husband objected, but later yielded to the good sense of having a Gold Star mother in the campaign. Then Rose herself explained that she hadn't made formal speeches and didn't know how. Johnny Powers, a Kennedy adviser, convinced her. "Now, you're the daughter of a congressman and a mayor," he reminded. "You're the mother of a congressman. You're the wife of an ambassador. So you've got to say something."

She agreed. Her political remarks were few. But her feminine appeal was great. She was a symbol of what women in the audience wanted to be. It was not done without effort. Rose would begin her day of campaigning in a basic black dress. In fashionable Chestnut Hill of suburban Boston, she would add at least three strands of pearls, some tasteful but expensive rings, a fur stole and a stylish matching hat. Before these affluent groups, she would be introduced as the wife of the Ambassador to the Court of St. James.

Back in the car, heading this time for Dorchester or West Roxbury and the "wall-to-wall Irish," she would make subtle changes in costume, removing a strand of pearls and one or two rings, donning a less modish hat. There she would be introduced as the daughter of the late John F. Fitzgerald, former mayor of Boston and member of Congress.

Back in the car again to a reception in the tenements of South Boston, or the Italian section of the North End. This time a single strand of pearls, a plain wedding band, a small black hat befitting a Gold Star mother.

If Rose was the heroine and the Kennedy girls her chorus, then the tea party was her stage. The tea party, or reception, was an accepted political tactic in the Boston area—but no one had done it the way the Kennedys did it. One of the largest held was at Lowell. The planning took almost eight weeks. It began with lists of the most prominent people socially, grew with the addition of women members of prominent organizations, finished with those politically active. For this one tea, the Kennedy people addressed 6,000 announcements, borrowed fifty silver serving trays, mobilized the local faithful to decorate the auditorium. The halls were never large. Why have a big hall with a crowd lost in it? "That was our great rule," said a woman worker. "Small halls, large crowds."

The plan was simple, the Kennedy women in the reception line, Jack's speech never more than ten minutes long, never partisan, just something simple about himself, an invitation for people to join him, the invitation followed up by the attractive women of the tea party committee approaching guests, asking them to hold coffee parties in their homes to bring in more people.

The effect was not surprising. Said one Kennedy worker: "You [send] a nice, engraved invitation from Mrs. Joseph P. Kennedy to attend a tea in honor of the Congressman, and they'd break the doors down to get in. They'd go out and buy new dresses. It was utterly fantastic, unbelievable." Jack put it best: "In

the first place, for some strange reason, there are more women than men in Massachusetts, and they live longer. Secondly, my grandfather, the late John F. Fitzgerald, ran for the United States Senate thirty-six years ago against my opponent's grandfather, Henry Cabot Lodge, and he lost by only 30,000 votes in an election where women were not allowed to vote. I hope that by impressing the female electorate that I can more than take up the slack."

It was short, honest, flattering, and women loved it. And the ultimate return with the R.S.V.P.'s was woman power. Said Bobby, "We had twenty-three teas, to which 65,000 to 70,000 women came. We concentrated on women because they do the work in campaigns. Men just talk." Women formed the arms and legs of the Kennedy organization.

They were captured by Jack's style. "This man," said a close aide, "was a totally political animal . . . John Kennedy turned many sides to many people. And everyone who claims to have known him well knew him in one or two sides." A professor of Jack's at Harvard, Arthur Holcombe, said: "You can pick some crusaders out of a class while they're still undergraduates. They have that commitment to act upon an idea, which to them is the decisive factor controlling their behavior . . . To my mind he was a great politician, a very great politician."

The truth was Kennedy needed all the help he could get. The campaign was basically constructed on Congressman Kennedy moving around the state, seeing as many people as possible. The primary contact in a community was called a "secretary," so that the regular local party "chairman" would not take offense. Still the state party, under Governor Dever, resented the newcomers, and their single-minded objective of getting Jack elected. Democrats all over the state could sense they

were in trouble. The Eisenhower momentum was building. The Democrats in power were edgy and wanted to ride the coattails of Kennedy's campaign. The governor wanted his handbills included with Jack's and distributed by Kennedy campaigners. Kennedy's people wanted no part of Dever's. They finally compromised but still argued as to whose handbill should be on the outside, whose on the inside. It all got so tense Dever said he would deal with the Kennedy organization only through Joe Sr., which suited Jack Kennedy fine. Said a Kennedy aide: "We knew his father would tell Dever, 'They're just a bunch of fresh kids and I can't do anything with them either, but I'll call them up and give them the devil.'"

It was obvious Joe Kennedy was not about to give his son the devil, but neither was his son, by now, just a dutiful harkener to his father's voice. Joseph Kennedy was still considered a wise counselor—at one point in the campaign he criticized the guest list for a tea party in Worcester saying it looked like a "lace curtain Irish picnic" and should include other national groups. But one of the reasons Bobby had been named campaign manager was to place him between the father and his brother as a buffer. It took a Kennedy to deal with a Kennedy.

The elder Kennedy, himself, said: "If Jack ever feels he has anything to ask me, he knows where he can find me, and I'll tell him what I think. But I feel very strongly about older people keeping their noses out of the businesses of their children." That didn't preclude his keeping his hand in.

As the Kennedy campaign excited the hamlets and towns of the state, the Republicans met in national convention to choose a Presidential candidate. Who? Senator Robert A. Taft, the darling of the conservatives? Or General Dwight David Eisenhower, war hero and moderate? Whoever it would be, someone was going to be in trouble, Joe Kennedy reasoned, and the somebody would be a Republican. Since Lodge was managing Eisenhower's campaign, he might be a moderate champion nationally, but to Taft supporters in Massachusetts, he would be the goat. Joe Kennedy went to some noted Taft men and reaped the fruits of disappointment. "Independents for Kennedy" was organized, which started a letter campaign among the Taft faithful.

There was another area where some work had to be done: religion. Joe Kennedy had a whispered reputation as an anti-Semite. At least he had made some statements that had been interpreted as such. In defense, he could point to his audacious scheme before World War II to rescue the persecuted Jews of Germany, and he boasted that he was about the only Christian in his Palm Beach golf club. Still, among the postwar Jews in America, his father's image on Jewry was an emotional presupposition, which Jack Kennedy could not ignore. He went into the Jewish districts to face it down. At one private dinner meeting, attended by several hundred Jewish leaders in Boston, Kennedy listed his qualifications and cited his 1951 visit to Israel. When he was done, he could see in their faces that they felt the question had not been answered, and he finally put it to them: "What more do you want? Remember, *I'm* running for the Senate, not my father."

Nonetheless, some of Lodge's people tried to stop the Kennedy swing developing among Boston's Jews with a handbill which headlined, GERMAN DOCUMENTS ALLEGE KENNEDY HELD ANTI-SEMITIC VIEWS. It was based on secondhand information. The Kennedy headquarters printed up a speedy reply, headlined SHAME ON YOU MR. LODGE, which also accused the incumbent senator of supporting Senator Joe

McCarthy in Wisconsin and McCarthy tactics in Massachusetts.

The implication was that Jack Kennedy was opposed to his father's old friend in Wisconsin, a fact little in evidence until then.

The Kennedy campaign was an odd assembly. There were the intellectuals from Harvard, Princeton and Choate. There were the varied flags of Boston's tenements. There were the well-to-do, doing something. There were the ladies holding their teas, and the ordinary housewives holding coffee hours. There were the Kennedy Serenaders, touring the state, singing "Heart of My Heart," because Jack Kennedy liked the tune. There was the Kennedy family, and there was Jack, on crutches toward the end, to spare his aching back. As one friend said, "He gave it everything he had, you know. But even then, even in the final week of the campaign . . . he kept a sort of gaiety about him."

Everyone was in constant motion. And everything they did, they did in a big way. Jack Kennedy needed 2,500 signatures on his nominating petition. They got him one hun-

dred times that—262,324. When Bobby discovered the lists of registered Democrats were short, he set his staff to poring over the records. They found 100,000 missing voters, most of whom would vote for Jack. When someone suggested more be made of Jack's war record, his staff printed up an eight-page tabloid with pictures of Joe Jr. and Jack and a reprint of a magazine story of PT 109. They sent 900,000 copies to homes all over the state. When Jack asked his mother and sisters to go out and shake hands with the state of Massachusetts to make him friends, they turned out for him, Rose from her busy home, Eunice from her social work, Jean from the Kennedy-owned Merchandise Mart in Chicago, Pat from her New York job in television. Before it was over, some two million Bay Staters met a Kennedy.

Even Ethel Skakel Kennedy provided some happy publicity for the campaign. On September 23, she campaigned for Jack in Fall River. On September 24, she gave birth to her second child, a son, and named him Joseph Patrick after his grandfather. Said a Lodge supporter: "When Archbishop [later Cardinal] Cushing baptized the baby of Bobby and Ethel in a special weekday celebration just before the election, that cut our hearts out."

Election day, 1952, in Massachusetts was brisk and windy. In Kennedy headquarters on Kilby Street in Boston and in Lodge headquarters across the way, the waiting began. As the votes started their slow march into totals, they seemed to chant Eisenhower, Eisenhower, Eisenhower. The magic of the name, the hope of his ending the war in Korea as he had the one in Europe—all of these things were pouring huge pluralities into the ballot boxes of the nation. Presumably this would be a blessing for Henry Cabot Lodge, the man who had persuaded Eisenhower to run.

But, remarkably, the Lodge-Kennedy contest was close. Too close. Jack Kennedy, alone, it seemed, was confident. He stood among his supporters and kept his first campaign promise to sing "Heart of My Heart." A listener remembered: "Of course he couldn't sing at all. He had a very flat voice. Then Bobby sang it after him, and he was worse."

Occasionally, to release the pressure, Jack and Bobby stepped into the street to take a quick walk. At one point, Jack Kennedy stretched out on his desk to rest his back. At another, he ignored the unfavorable vote and mused, "I wonder what job Eisenhower's going to give Lodge."

Bobby stook on the desk top to read the latest returns to the crowd. Still close. Eleven o'clock. Midnight. Still close.

"About one o'clock that night, or rather the following morning," said Bobby, "everybody thought he was going to lose: votes were falling off, and it appeared that all the Democrats were going to lose. Many people left the headquarters then. Only a handful remained between one and four in the morning.

Then about five o'clock, people started to come back in."

At 7:25 A.M. a number of people came out of the Lodge offices across the street. The one hundred or so Kennedy supporters spotted Lodge himself and rushed to the windows. The cry went up: "There goes Lodge . . . There he goes . . . He's getting into his car . . . There goes your opponent, Jack. . . ."

Ten minutes later the telephone rang. A telegram:

I EXTEND MY CONGRATULATIONS AND EXPRESS THE HOPE THAT YOU WILL DERIVE FROM YOUR TERM IN THE SENATE ALL THE SATISFACTION THAT COMES FROM COURAGEOUS AND SINCERE EFFORTS IN PUBLIC SERVICE

HENRY CABOT LODGE

Jack Kennedy defeated Lodge 1,211,984 votes to 1,141,247, a tremendous victory considering that Eisenhower carried Massachusetts over Adlai Stevenson by 208,000 votes.

John Kennedy was now the highest elected Democrat in his state, and only the third ever to win a Senate seat from Massachusetts. Lodge grumbled: "It was those damned tea parties," and John Kennedy would be introduced as "the man who drowned Henry Cabot Lodge in 75,000 cups of tea."

Said Rose: "At last the Fitzgeralds have evened the score with the Lodges."

With flashbulbs popping in his face, John Kennedy shook a hundred hands, and someone put on a record of "Heart of My Heart." and Jack said quietly to someone, "I'm very pleased and happy." They read the Lodge telegram, and John Kennedy climbed up on the desk, stood above the crowd, and said to the jubilant people: "I want to thank all of you for staying through this long night. But I think we're all glad we stayed. Now, I'm going home to bed."

# 1956: Almost

*"John, do you take Jacqueline, here present, for your lawful wife . . .?"*

They met as they lived, as stars in separate orbits whirl near each other in some predestined way that only seems like chance. Once before they had almost met, at a wedding party on Long Island in 1948. They were at opposite ends of a crowded room. A friend of his tried to bring them together, but she fell into conversation with Gene Tunney, "a fascinating man," and before she was free again, John had driven away. They met finally two years later, when the same friend, Charles Bartlett, brought them together for dinner at his Georgetown home. "I leaned across the asparagus and asked for a date," Jack said.

*"Jacqueline, do you take John, here present, for your lawful wedded husband . . .?"*

"It was in early spring," Bartlett remembered, "and John Kennedy was just gearing up for his race in Massachusetts and Jackie was just about to leave for Europe; and I must say, it happened there. We sat around and chatted. . . .

". . . they left at the same time—and I was seeing Jackie to her car, which was parked across the street, Jack came over rather shyly and said, 'Shall we go somewhere for a drink?' Jackie was about to reply when her eye fell, as mine already had fallen, on the back of her car.

"A young man, who apparently had walked along the street and recognized Jackie's car, had decided to wait for her to come out . . . Seeing this, Jackie had really very little option except to say she couldn't go on for a drink. So John Kennedy went off to Massachusetts to campaign, and she went to Europe."

*"I call upon all of you here present to be witnesses to this holy union which I have now blessed. 'Man must not separate what God has joined together.'"*

Jacqueline remembered, "It was a very spasmodic courtship. We didn't see each other for six months, because I went to Europe again, and Jack began his summer and fall campaigning in Massachusetts. Then came six months when we were both back. Jack was in Congress, and I was in my last year at George Washington University. But it was still spasmodic, because he spent half of each week in Massachusetts. He'd call me from some oyster bar up there, with a great clinking of coins, to ask me out to the movies the following Wednesday in Washington. He loved Westerns and Civil War pictures. He was not the candy-and-flowers type, so every now and then he'd give me a book. He gave me *The Raven*, which is the life of Sam Houston, and also *Pilgrim's Way* by John Buchan."

Jack Kennedy's old Navy buddy and campaign companion Paul Fay came for the wedding and the bachelor dinner that Jacqueline's stepfather Hugh Auchincloss gave for Jack at Newport's Clambake Club.

"About eighteen of us sat down," Fay recalled, "and I sat next to the then Senator. Since I have five sisters and have been through many bachelor dinners, he said, 'Well, now, why don't you just see that this thing runs according to protocol?'

"I said, 'The first thing you have to do is toast the bride—you've got to throw that glass in the fireplace.' Well, there were these beautiful crystal glasses. The . . . Senator stood up, and he said, 'To my future bride, Jacqueline Bouvier,' and drank his toast down and said, 'Everybody throw your glasses in the fireplace.' All eighteen crystal glasses went flying into the fireplace and were destroyed. Mr. Auchincloss was an ashen gray. He called in an almost broken voice to the waiter for more glasses. And no sooner had they been brought and refilled with wine, than the Senator stood up and said, 'I realize that this is not the custom, but the love that I hold for

*September 12, 1953*

# "I leaned across the asparagus and asked for a date."

Jacqueline Bouvier overcomes me. A second toast to Jacqueline Bouvier.'

"Everybody drank down the wine, and he said, 'And into the fireplace with the glasses!' As a result of that second toast, the third set of glasses to come to the table were the kind you get at Healey's ten-cent store."

The wedding. The old brownstone Gothic spires of St. Mary's Roman Catholic Church in Newport. The crowd of 3,000 that broke police lines and nearly crushed the bride. The most exciting wedding in that old seaport in almost twenty years. Senator John Kennedy grinning. Jacqueline, a little apprehensive, as the crowd pressed forward. Eight hundred guests including Senators Green of Rhode Island, Paine of Maine, Purcell of Connecticut, Saltonstall of Massachusetts; Governor Roberts of Rhode Island; Congressmen Keough and McConnell of New York; Garrahan of Pennsylvania; the Ambassador from Peru; old family friends like Morton Downey, Arthur Krock, Bernard Gimble and Arthur Vanderbilt.

The bride. A product of the exclusive Miss Porter's School and the Chapin School, an A-minus student at Vassar, the Sorbonne, George Washington University; of late, an inquiring photographer for the Washington *Times-Herald.* Her father, handsome, rich, Republican and Catholic John Bouvier III, a stockbroker with a year-round suntan, a man they called "Black Jack" or "The Black Orchid" or "The Sheik." He and his wife, Janet, were divorced when Jacqueline was eleven. She remarried, this time to Auchincloss. Bouvier never remarried and was too ill to give his daughter away at the wedding. (He would die in 1957.)

Jacqueline, who grew up on Park Avenue, summered at East Hampton, toured Europe with three friends and a chaperone, was presented to Newport society at eighteen and named Deb Queen of the Year. Now she was twenty-one, wearing a gown of ivory silk taffeta, fitted bodice, portrait neckline, bouffant skirt, a veil of rosepoint lace worn by her grandmother, a lace tiara and orange blossoms extending in a long train, a bouquet of pink and white spray orchids, holding gently the arm of her stepfather as they walked slowly down the aisle.

The bride's attendants all wore pink taffeta gowns. The matron of honor was the bride's sister, then Mrs. Michael T. Canfield, one day to be a princess of Poland's royalty in exile. The maid of honor, Miss Nina G. Auchincloss of Newport and McLean, Virginia. Both wore pink cummerbunds and matching Tudor caps. The bridesmaids were Ethel and Jean Kennedy; Martha Bartlett who served that dinner in Georgetown and other friends like Miss Nancy Tuckerman who was a roommate at Miss Porter's School, all with red cummerbunds and matching Tudor hats.

The groom. A scratch on his face from falling into rose bushes in a touch football game the day before. Bobby, the best man. Ushers drawn from the events of his life: George A. Smathers from the Senate, Charlie Bartlett who introduced Jack to Jackie, Torbert Macdonald and James Reed from the Navy and Harvard, "Red" Fay, Lem Billings, Charlie Spalding, Teddy, members of Jackie's family, all in cutaways and striped trousers.

Luigi Vena of Boston, a tenor, sang "Ave Maria" and "Panis Angelicus" at the mass, his voice a gentle contrast to the singular, stentorian near-monotone of Archbishop Cushing, the old family friend who guided Kennedys in happy times and sad. Earlier his rough, almost nasal voice sounded the exhortation through the great church, full of portent for the young couple standing before him:

"That future with its hopes and disappointments, its successes and its failures, its pleasures and its pains, its joys and its sorrows, is hidden from your eyes. You know that these elements are mingled in every life and are to be expected in your own. And so, not knowing what is before you, you take each other for better or for worse, for richer or for poorer, in sickness and in health, until death.

"Truly, then, these words are most serious . . . And because these words involve such solemn obligations, it is most fitting that you rest the security of your wedded life upon the great principle of self-sacrifice . . . Henceforth you belong entirely to each other; you will be one in mind, one in heart, and one in affections. And whatever sacrifices you may hereafter be required to make to preserve this common life, always make them generously. Sacrifice is usually difficult and irksome. Only love can make it easy; and perfect love can make it a joy. We are willing to give in proportion as we love. And when love is perfect, the sacrifice is complete. God so loved the world that He gave His only begotten Son, and the Son so loved us that He gave Himself for our salvation. 'Greater love than this no one has, that one lay down his life for his friends.' "

Just before the last blessing, he turned his back again to the great stained-glass window that covered nearly all of the rear wall of the church—a jeweled tableau of the Crucifixion and the life of Christ—and the Archbishop said to the couple and their witnesses:

*Ite, missa est.* Go, the mass is ended. Go in peace.

The service ended, the great oak doors opened and the happy people spilled out onto Spring Street. Later, 1,200 guests attended a reception at Hammersmith Farm, the 300-acre Auchincloss estate overlooking Narragansett Bay. Cars lined up for half a

*Robert worked at the right hand of Senator Joseph McCarthy.*

mile as they arrived. Jackie and Jack, with his painful spine, stood in the reception line for nearly two hours. Then they joined the guests at tables under parasols on the lawn and on the canopied terrace. Joe Kennedy, his friends say, beamed, "Thank God, at last we have someone in the family who made it."

There was another relationship that was not to prove so harmonious for the Kennedy family. This was the family tie with Sen. Joseph McCarthy, a friend of the father, employer of one son and colleague with another. All three would come under considerable criticism because of their association with one of the most controversial men ever to sit in the United States Senate.

It was Joe Kennedy Sr. who invited Joe McCarthy out to Hyannis Port, who hosted him at Palm Beach, who visited him in Washington. McCarthy, the Communist-hunter, the chairman of the Permanent Subcommittee on Investigations of the Government Operations Committee of the United States Senate, played shortstop for the Barefoots on Joe Kennedy's lawn. McCarthy, a Republican many feared and hated, was a guest on Democrat Kennedy's boat, and almost drowned once swimming behind it. To Joe Kennedy, McCarthy "was always pleasant; he was never a crab. If somebody was against him, he never tried to cut his heart out. He never said that anybody was a stinker. He was a pleasant fellow."

As his sons inherited some of his political views, so did they inherit his friends and his allegiances. McCarthy was godfather to Bobby Kennedy's oldest daughter. Once at a Louisville Junior Chamber of Commerce banquet honoring him as one of the nation's ten outstanding young men, Bobby walked out when he heard that television commentator Edward Murrow would speak in criticism of McCarthy.

Ultimately, when McCarthy died, Bobby was at the funeral.

So it was, his job of helping his brother to the Senate ended, that Bobby went back to his job at the Department of Justice. The Senate's Investigations subcommittee needed "a young attorney, one you can get cheap," said Francis Flanagan, the subcommittee's general counsel. "What I need is a smart attorney who can work for nothing."

"I got just the fellow for you," a friend said. The name didn't mean anything to Flanagan, who remembered:

"An hour or two later, in comes Bob Kennedy, hat in hand. 'You must be related to Jack Kennedy,' I said. 'Yes,' Bob replied. 'He's my brother.' We talked an hour or so. It was a Wednesday. I asked him to come to work Monday. 'I can't,' he said. 'At Justice we have to give two weeks notice.'

" 'That's okay,' I said. 'I'm sure I can fix it.' 'No, I don't want to do it that way,' Bob said. He came to work two weeks later. That shows you the kind of guy he was."

On the sixth paragraph of a news release from the McCarthy subcommittee it was noted that 27-year-old Robert Kennedy, Jack's brother, had been hired.

McCarthy was the new chairman of the committee, and his subject was shipping interests carrying goods for Communist countries. Through pipelines to intelligence sources, the subcommittee received detailed listings of ships of other nations that carried on trade between Eastern Europe and Red China. Bob Kennedy, the young investigator-lawyer, was the witness from whom McCarthy elicited the evidence. It seems that the same ships that were involved in Red trade were at other times hired to carry United States aid materials. Sample from the record:

"THE CHAIRMAN: Bob, I think you said there were four French vessels carrying goods to Red China.

"MR. KENNEDY: Senator McCarthy, since the outbreak of the Korean War, there have been four French vessels that have gone into China. Three out of the four vessels are owned by the French Government. Two of those vessels went into China in 1952, and one went in intrabloc trade from Constantsa into China, Constanta in Rumania.

"THE CHAIRMAN: Were those ships purchased from us, do you know?

"MR. KENNEDY: Yes. The three owned by the French Government were purchased from us. The French Government purchased four, I believe, all together, and three of the four ended up in the trade with China . . .

"THE CHAIRMAN: May I ask you a question here, Mr. Kennedy? Has the staff established and confirmed the fact that British-owned vessels have been transporting Communist troops?

"MR. KENNEDY: That is right, Senator."

With the report of the subcommittee on trade with the Soviet bloc filed, Bobby Kennedy wrote out his resignation, to begin work with the Hoover Commission studying government efficiency, although the reason he gave was a decision to enter the private practice of law. His major reason, although it was not pubicly stated, was his dislike for McCarthy's chief aide, Roy Cohn.

Bobby wrote McCarthy:

*I have enjoyed my work and association on the Subcommittee, and I wish to express to you my appreciation for the opportunity of having served with your group.*

*Please accept my sincere thanks for the many courtesies and kindnesses you have extended to me during this past seven months.*

McCarthy replied:

*I know it is needless to tell you that I very much*

One of the Barefoots

regret seeing you leave the Committee. In accordance with our conversation, I sincerely hope that you will consider coming back later on in the summer to complete the project with Mr. Flanagan and the full Committee.

The letter was dated July 31, 1953. Bobby Kennedy was a free agent again.

Senator Jack Kennedy was sensing the difficulties that his family's connections with McCarthy could cause. Yet he was not at all unsure that McCarthy's pursuit of the Communists wasn't a good thing. He wrote a woman constituent:

*I have always believed that we must be alert to the menace of Communism within our country as well as its advances on the international front. In so doing, however, we must be careful we maintain our traditional concern that in punishing the guilty we protect the innocent.*

In the Senate, Kennedy consistently voted against issues with the McCarthyism tag. He was opposed to liberalized wiretap laws, against the requirement of loyalty oaths for students and union leaders, against a bill to compel waiver of a witness's rights under the Fifth Amendment. He was for the confirmation of James Conant as ambassador to West Germany although McCarthy opposed him, for the confirmation of Charles Bohlen as ambassador to the Soviet Union although McCarthy attacked him.

The Kennedys were realistic enough about their controversial friend from Wisconsin. McCarthy never came to Massachusetts to help Lodge in his Senate race with Jack Kennedy. He did not even vocally support Lodge. There were many supposed reasons why he stayed away. Some thought Joe Kennedy's fine Irish hand stiff-armed him. Long after the election, John Fox, owner of the conservative Republican Boston *Post* testified during hearings on the relationship between Eisenhower aide Sherman Adams and Boston textile manufacturer Bernard Goldfine. In the course of the hearings, Fox testified that he had received a loan of a half million dollars from Joe Kennedy after the paper had switched its support from Lodge to Jack Kennedy in 1952. Both Fox and Kennedy denied there had been a deal. Fox still later said he would have endorsed Lodge had either McCarthy or Robert Taft asked him to. He said he even called McCarthy, but could not get him to come to the telephone.

Whatever the circumstances, Bobby's role as a McCarthy investigator, Joe's long friendship with McCarthy and Jack's persistent silence on McCarthy the man, was a source of grievance for the liberal voices in the Senate and in the nation. Wrote Richard Rovere: "Paul Douglas of Illinois, the possessor of the most cultivated mind in the Senate and a man whose courage and integrity will compare favorably with any other American, went through the last Truman years and the first Eisenhower years without ever addressing himself to the problem of McCarthy. Senator John Kennedy of Massachusetts, the author of *Profiles in Courage* . . . did likewise."

Eleanor Roosevelt, the hub about which the liberals of the day revolved, said she would hesitate to place Presidential decisions in the hands of someone who understood what courage was and admired it, but didn't quite have the independence to possess it.

As another liberal put it, Jack Kennedy "should show less profile and more courage." When Harvard professor Arthur Schlesinger later asked Kennedy if he hadn't paid a great price for the name of his book, Jack answered wryly, "Yes, but I didn't have a chapter in it on myself."

As Jack Kennedy's experience grew, so did his political rationale. He became, some

said, less a patron of politics and more a statesman. About his role, or non-role, in the McCarthy drama, Jack Kennedy said, "Most members [of the Senate] are reluctant to judge personally the conduct of another. Perhaps that was wrong in McCarthy's case— perhaps we were not as sensitive as some and should have acted sooner. That is a reasonable indictment that falls on me as well."

In 1954, Bobby Kennedy went back to work for the Investigations subcommittee as chief counsel for the Democratic minority and Sen. John L. McClellan of Arkansas. It was in time for the Army-McCarthy hearings, and the dénouement of the Wisconsin senator. The Democrats on the subcommittee were now open in their criticism of "The Chairman" and his methods. McCarthy's aides, Roy Cohn and G. David Schine, were the real powers before the television cameras and behind the scenes. Bobby Kennedy kept out of sight. Cohn and Kennedy were almost natural antagonists.

Once, as Cohn sought to tie Mrs. Annie Moss, an Army Signal Corps clerk, to a known Communist, Robert Hall, Kennedy faced him down and won the point. The Robert Hall Mrs. Moss knew, Kennedy said, was a Negro. The Robert Hall Cohn cited was white.

Another time Cohn and Kennedy got into a shoving match, punctuated with Cohn's threats and screams, outside the hearing room. Cohn shouted that Kennedy was not qualified for the job, and Kennedy stalked off, his eyes burning with anger. When he had taken the job, Cohn had objected that he had no right to it because of his animosity to Cohn. "If I have any dislike," Bobby snapped back, "it's well justified."

Both Jack and Bobby Kennedy were faced with difficult decisions as the McCarthy episode continued. As Jack remembered it, "The Joe McCarthy thing? I was caught in a bad situation. My brother was working for Joe. I was against it . . . How could I get up there and denounce Joe? . . . It wasn't so much a thing of political liability as it was a personal problem." Old Joe Kennedy observed some years later with sadness in his eyes, "I thought he [McCarthy] would be a sensation. He was smart. But he went off the deep end."

Jack Kennedy, plagued by his worsening back pains, said he would vote for censure of McCarthy because the Senator had attacked the reputation of the Senate itself, but for no other reason. He felt that McCarthy should be given a hearing as a matter of due process. But the freshman senator from Massachusetts was still seeking a rapport with the liberals in his own party. Ted Sorensen wrote, "Most of the professional liberals were slow to warm to him. But I found he was the truest and oldest kind of liberal: The free man with a free mind. Kennedy entered Congress, he freely admitted, with little or no political philosophy." As Kennedy himself said, "Some people have their liberalism 'made' by the time they reach their late twenties. I didn't. I was caught in cross currents and eddies. It was only later that I got into the stream of things."

As it turned out, Jack Kennedy never faced Joe McCarthy with a censure vote. He was in the hospital at the time.

*In sickness and in health until death.* The Archbishop's exhortation, those "serious words" to Jack and Jackie Kennedy, echoed through the early years of their married life. The ache of his back was to become nearly fatal. But that came later.

Married life was not an easy adjustment for Jacqueline, accustomed to the genteel life and now linked to the political tempo of a vigorous family. When the newlyweds stayed at their Hyannis Port home in what had become a family compound of houses, she ob-

jected to dinner every night at Joe Kennedy's. "Once a week is great," she said. "Not every night."

At Palm Beach, she was late for a lunch, and Joe Kennedy's sarcasm was met with her own. Joe was a complex man, a man who avoided drink or tobacco yet liked a good time, who could use all the Anglo-Saxon words without blushing, words he could intertwine with his cultural tastes as when some friends back in the SEC Washington days once asked him to stop playing symphonies on his phonograph and put on some upbeat music. "You dumb bastards don't appreciate culture," said Joe Kennedy.

Jacqueline was her own woman among her many new in-laws. She created her own home in Georgetown. "I have filled the Georgetown house with eighteenth-century furniture, which I love," she said, "and my pictures— the drawings I collect. Jack has been very nice about letting me do the inside, but I haven't made it completely all my own because I never want a house where you have to say to your children, 'Don't touch,' or where your husband isn't comfortable. And though there are lots of little things around, there are also big comfortable chairs and the tables that every politician needs next to his chair, where he can put papers, coffee cups, ashtrays. So it's a little bit of everything."

Including a little bit of Jack. He was so often on the road, dashing up to Massachusetts to talk to his constituents, running all over the country on political missions. And even when he was home, she once complained, he was so involved in his work she felt she "might as well be in Alaska." She interested him somewhat in painting, framing his better pictures, and he interested her somewhat in the art of politics. When they found free time, they played Monopoly or indifferent bridge with the Bartletts or with Bobby and Ethel.

"He always wanted to win," Bartlett remembered, "as he was a good competitor, he fought hard to win. But he was always a very gracious loser. He was not a bitter ender, and it didn't undo him to lose a game of Monopoly, or a game of tennis or golf. Actually he was rather casual at golf and rather casual at tennis. He loved golf, but I think he liked the sunlight and the grass and the gaiety of it."

Jackie was a competitor in her own way. The wild Irish football games were not for her. Once in a touch football huddle she turned to a teammate and said, "Just tell me one thing. When I get the ball, which way do I run?" After she broke her ankle in a game with some of Ted's Harvard teammates, she bowed out of football for good. "Just watching them," she said of the Kennedys, "wore me out." To her, it was less a matter of win or lose, but how she played the game. Once she made a deliberate error to cut short a Monopoly game because she was tired of playing. "Does Jack mind?" she was asked. "Not if I'm on the other side."

"It was a perfectly average kind of marriage in many respects," an old friend of those days recalled. "He would be complaining about the price of her clothes. I remember two, new, expensive rugs that she put in the Georgetown house she hid in her budget and paid a little bit each month. She didn't want him to know how much they had cost, because they'd been wild extravagances. He was crazy about them. Of course, eventually he found out how much they were. But there was that kind of little playback, of course."

Jack's political life filled the house as much as did Jackie's furniture. Once he brought in an economist to teach Bartlett and himself. The economist delivered hour-and-a-half lectures on economics after dinner. "He was very interesting," Bartlett said. "He was teach-ing us the details of the economic system about which none of us knew very much. One time, the fellow arrived before the Senator had finished dinner, and so he brought his dessert in—ice cream with chocolate sauce—while the fellow was discussing the Federal Reserve Board. Suddenly he was interrupted by Jack, who called the butler, George, and said, 'George, isn't this yesterday's chocolate sauce?' This undid the economist."

Reminded years later of the incident, someone asked Jack Kennedy what had happend to the economist. He thought a minute and said, "I don't know. He probably committed suicide."

Of all the elements of these crowded days, McCarthy and the Senate, Jackie and the new household, none was as critical as the convergence of ailments that had plagued him all his life. He was almost in constant pain with his back. He carried a metal disc that replaced a vertebra in the Navy operation of 1944. Now, ten years later, he hobbled on crutches much of the time. His weight fell to 140 pounds, scant for his six-foot-one frame. The stresses on his life powers, the interludes of jaundice and malaria, left his adrenal glands weakened, and gave him symtoms such as discolored skin that resembled Addison's disease. He required doses of cortisone to replace the hormones the adrenals failed to produce. For years he took injections to counteract his allergy to dogs, which he loved. He took three warm baths a day to relax the cramped back muscles. He tried a number of treatments with little effect. He bought a rocking chair and a couch for his office, to rest his back. His brother Bob said that Jack was in pain "at least one-half of the days he spent on this earth." Yet he seldom showed it.

Kay Halle, the Washington hostess, recalled, "Once, when he was at a dance talking to me, sitting on half of a chair, the girl who was sitting on the other half got up without his knowing it, and the chair collapsed. He went smack on the floor . . . and he hit on the bottom of his spine. I saw his face go absolutely white, and I was terrified. I made him get up, holding on to both my hands—get up straight instead of twisting. You could just see the perspiration coming off his forehead but never a word came out of him. I said, 'Are you hurt, Jack?' 'No,' he said, 'no, no, everything is all right.' "

In the first year of his marriage, Jack Kennedy was involved in a silent, personal debate. Doctors told him that the only hope for his back was an operation to fuse the vertebrae. The operation held grave risks, heightened by the weakened adrenal glands that left him vulnerable to shock and infection. Only in occasional outbursts were the underlying feelings shown. A friend recalled him striking his crutches with his fist and saying, "I'd rather die than spend the rest of my life on these things."

About this time, he was asked for his feelings about prayer, and he wrote: ". . . I believe that man is created by God with an immortal soul. I believe that those who follow His teaching will be rewarded by eternal life with him in Heaven. On the long and difficult road of life it is quite natural we should turn to Him, our Master, for guidance and for relief from troubles that beset us. It is unfortunate that too often we are prone to turn to Him only in moments of difficulty, but He never permits prayer to go unanswered."

That fall he made his decision. On October 21, 1954, doctors at New York's Hospital for Special Surgery attempted the operation. As they feared, an infection set in, racing through his weakened body. He was near death. Doctors twice brought Jackie and his

parents to the hospital, where they prayed for him. The last rites were administered. But he grew stronger. But for two weeks he lay in a darkened room, while nurses tested his blood every half hour. An old family friend, Thomas Schriber, saw him several times in the hospital. "He had a frightful time during that period," Schriber said. "Again, it showed the guts the guy had. He knew he probably didn't have more than—maybe less than—a fifty percent chance of pulling through, but he was willing to take the chance. One thing all the Kennedys had was confidence. Good or bad, they had more guts than anything."

He showed improvement, but was slow in recuperating. Taken from the hospital on a stretcher, he was flown to the family home in Palm Beach. It was there that Jackie got him to paint. Joe Kennedy said, "Jack couldn't sleep for more than an hour or so at a time because his pain was so bad. So he'd study to get his mind off the pain. That's where the book came from."

The book was *Profiles in Courage*. Jack Kennedy sent for stacks of reference books from the Library of Congress, and with Jackie and Dave Powers to help, read them and compiled the biographical information for this portfolio of Americans, well known and little known, in moments that required personal and moral courage.

A young Nebraskan who had just come to work with the junior senator from Massachusetts, Theodore Sorensen, also helped with the research and outlining. Some later said Sorensen really wrote the book, which both he and Kennedy vehemently denied.

After Palm Beach, Jack and his wife went to the Auchincloss home in Virginia. Bartlett visited them there: "He was flat on his back, and I don't think he could use much of a pillow, but he had a board that he wrote on in longhand. His secretary would type up

the pages as he went along. We used to go out and talk to him about it, and talk to him about the political situation. Even when he was literally dying he was still fascinated by what was going on in Congress. His political interest didn't flicker for a moment."

He kept in touch with his office by telephone, and used a dictaphone to keep up on his senatorial mail. That done, he would return to the book, with the help of Sorenson and Jackie, especially Jackie. Dave Powers remembered, "She'd sit down at his bedside and read to him for hours from the material that was to become the book."

By February 1955, he was well enough to return to the Hospital for Special Surgery. Again he nearly died, and again was given the last rites. But the second operation had

been more successful and he recovered more rapidly, and, nearly whole again, walked out of the hospital, and recuperated in Palm Beach. On May 23, 1955, returned to his Senate office. Waiting for him, with the letters and telegrams, was a big basket of fruit with the message, "Welcome Home," signed "Dick Nixon." And when he walked into the Senate chamber, Lyndon Johnson of Texas met him. "We are glad to see you, Jack," he said.

For all the worry, these were busy, if not always happy, days for Joe Kennedy. One by one his children married. Bobby and Ethel, June 17, 1950; Eunice and Sargent Shriver, May 23, 1953; Jack and Jackie, September 12, 1953; Pat and Peter Lawford, April 24, 1954; Jean and Steve Smith, May 19, 1956.

Cardinal Spellman performed the ceremony for Eunice and Sargent Shriver. Shriver worked at one of Joe Kennedy's enterprises, the Merchandise Mart. At the reception, Pat caught the bridal bouquet. She had met Peter Lawford a year earlier. They saw each other from time to time, and when she was on a Far Eastern tour he telephoned her in Tokyo and proposed. Her father grumbled to Lawford: "If there's anything I'd hate as a son-in-law it's an actor, and if there's anything I'd hate worse than an actor as a son-in-law, it's an English actor." Lawford was both.

Bobby and Ethel were building their family, but even that didn't stop the touch football games. One Saturday they had been to a Maryland football game with two Justice Department friends, one of them a triple-threat quarterback from Columbia College. After the game, Bob and Ethel suggested a game of touch at their home. He picked his wife, then six or seven months pregnant, to oppose the two young lawyers. The grass was wet, and when Ethel broke loose for a touchdown, the young athlete chased her, slipped, and pulled a muscle. The young Kennedys would not let their two guests forget that they had been scored on by a pregnant woman.

The highest-ranking elected Democrat in his state: a senator at thirty-five, married at thirty-six, and now thirty-nine: Jack Kennedy faced some obvious facts of his political life. The 1956 National Convention of the Democratic Party seemed to hold no suspense. The Democrats would undoubtedly renominate Adlai Stevenson as their Presidential candidate. But what role was there in it for the freshman senator from Massachusetts? His own state party was in the hands of the defeated Old Guard. It was headed, for instance, by a man named William H. "Onions" Burke, an ally of Rep. John McCormack who by now was Majority Leader in the House of Representatives. Jack Kennedy returned to his state to do something about it. He campaigned among the eighty members of the state committee and told them he wanted to elect his own chairman. As one last effort on the day of the election of the new chairman, he lunched with those leaders he thought he could still convince. Then, he announced he was driving immediately for New York City and an appointment that couldn't be postponed.

Richard Donahue, a young lawyer from Lowell, Massachusetts, who had helped him in his campaign, watched Jack Kennedy's tactics develop: "There were a lot of humorous overtones to the meeting—people were knocked down—there were all kinds of threats and recriminations." And Jack Kennedy? He had not gone to New York. Instead he waited in an automobile some distance from the hotel where the election battle was going on. He stayed there until he got the word his man had won, and then he ordered the car on to New York. "And here," Donahue said, "in the industrial northeast, in the absence of a Democratic governor, a U.S. Senator had not only turned over the party machinery to himself, but he had turned over one of the great, known Democrats in the nation [John McCormack]." Now he would lead his state's delegation to the national convention.

Jack Kennedy had never been a truly influential member of the Senate. His first-term status, his long illness, his supposed softness on McCarthy, all had precluded that. But now the balance began to turn in his favor, weighted by the takeover in Massachusetts. The book he had written while ill, *Profiles in Courage,* became a best-seller—Kennedy's second—won the Pulitzer Prize in biography for 1967. He donated the $500 prize money to the United Negro College Fund. (In fact, he never accepted for himself any money for prizes or governmental service.) He was invited to narrate the party's campaign movie, *The Pursuit of Happiness,* at the convention in Chicago. When Kennedy was called on stage to take a bow, the prolonged applause surprised the Democratic leaders. They caucused offstage, and called Kennedy at one A.M. to ask him to deliver the nominating speech for Adlai Stevenson due twelve hours later. In spite of the short notice, Kennedy agreed. It put him in the spotlight of national television. Nevertheless, as Sorensen observed, "He had no illusions about himself as a serious presidential possibility in 1956. He was not even motivated by a serious interest in the vice Presidential nomination at that time." As Jack Kennedy told Sorensen, "I thought the matter was closed and was not especially unhappy."

But when Stevenson himself opened up the vice-presidential nomination to all takers, the Kennedy people began a wild, last-minute operation to win their man the nomination. They dashed around Chicago to get signs and flyers printed, to buy buttons and banners. Jack decided to make the try when the Georgia delegation came out for him. "The Senator's own interest in the nomination," Sorensen wrote, "was growing more out of a sense of competition than conviction."

When they came to Chicago, Kennedy's followers had no real organization. They were hardly known outside of the Massachusetts delegation. Said one Kennedy aide, "It would take me fifteen minutes to introduce myself to the average delegate." But the Kennedy family and friends spread through the convention seats, introducing themselves, talking up Jack Kennedy. Even Peter Lawford, in California, got in the act, calling friends in Las Vegas who promised nearly all of Nevada's fourteen votes.

Earlier that year Sorensen worked up an analysis that claimed to prove that a Catholic would be an asset to a Protestant presidential candidate by drawing in Catholic votes in the heavily populated states. The document was leaked to the press under the aegis of John Bailey, Connecticut State Chairman. It may have fooled most newsmen, but one professional politician called Kennedy's office to get copies, and Sorensen found himself "successively and unsuccessfully feigning ignorance, surprise, reluctance and the hope that I could 'get hold of some' for him." When the analysis got into several national magazines, supporters of Hubert Humphrey of Minnesota, also a vice-presidential bidder, put out a counter-study analyzing the anti-Catholic vote.

The Kennedys set up headquarters in the Stock Yard Inn outside of the Convention Hall. From there, they dispatched material to the delegates, arranged for spontaneous Kennedy cheers from the floor, delivered and received messages, and issued instructions to the convention orchestra. Joe Kennedy, who had been against any such bid by his son this early in his career, was in Europe vacationing. He had been forewarned that Stevenson might open the race by his son-in-law, Sargent Shriver. "I knew Adlai Stevenson was going to take a licking," Joe Kennedy said, "and I was afraid Jack might be blamed because he was a Catholic. That would have made it much more difficult for another Catholic in years to come."

When the balloting began, Jack Kennedy was a surprising second with 304 votes to 483½ for Tennessee's Senator Estes Kefauver. The remainder were split between Humphrey, Albert Gore of Tennessee, Robert Wagner of New York and a few others. Jack Kennedy listened to the results on his television set in his room, lying on his bed. His lieutenants, Abraham Ribicoff of Connecticut and Paul Dever of Massachusetts, were working hard on the New York delegation. Southern dissatisfaction with Kefauver moved more votes to Kennedy, including fifty-six from Texas which deserted Gore to block Kefauver.

While the fight on the convention floor was going on between ballots, Jack Kennedy stepped into the bathtub. He was still there when Torbert Macdonald shouted, "Sam Rayburn just swung Texas to you." Kennedy, dripping wet and wrapped in a towel, came out of the bathroom to watch the rest of the balloting. He heard Lyndon Johnson announcing the Texas switch on television. On the second ballot, Kefauver trailed Kennedy 618 to 551½. Kennedy needed only 686 for the nomination.

Now in his shorts, Kennedy watched the third ballot, saw Kentucky deliver him thirty votes. "Congratulations," said Sorensen, "that's it." "No," said Kennedy, "Not yet." He started to dress.

There was havoc on the convention floor. Kennedy signs flew all over and Kennedy people searched for the needed votes. In the fever of such moments, it is often he who seems to be winning who actually wins. Sam Rayburn, the convention chairman, was des-perately trying to obtain order and recognize delegates at the same time. Vote-switching was in earnest, but Kefauver's strength in the farm states remained stable. It was John McCormack of Massachusetts who called Rayburn's attention to the Missouri standard waving for recognition. Rayburn called on Missouri. The convention broke into a roar as Missouri announced its shift from Gore to Kefauver. It was just the momentum the Senator from Tennessee needed. In a few minutes it was all over. Kennedy, now dressed, turned to his companions and said, "That's it—let's go." Sorensen said: "He wanted to get out there fast and make his speech to give Kefauver unanimous support. He seemed to have no regrets. His idea was always to get on with the next thing."

Jack Kennedy strode quickly to the microphone, grinning and tired. He said, "Ladies and gentlemen of this convention. I want to take this opportunity to express my appreciation to Democrats from all parts of the country, north and south, east and west, who have been so kind to me this afternoon. . . ." The convention roared again. The band played "Tennessee Waltz," and it was all over.

Some of Jack Kennedy's people blamed the loss on the breakdown of the electric vote tabulator and the fact that delegates could not get a measure of the close race. But Sorensen hit on a more likely reason: "We had no plans, no facilities, no communications, or organization, little know-how and very few contacts." He doubted he could have lined up even a single delegate from his own state of Nebraska. The lack of preparedness turned up in the last-minute battles especially, when Chicago's Mayor Richard Daley and New York Tammany boss Carmine DeSapio tried to see Kennedy. Daley was turned away and DeSapio kept waiting half an hour because the inexperienced Kennedy

*If Joe had run, he would have won . . .*

aides didn't recognize them. It would not happen again.

Jack, Bobby, Eunice, and friends went out to a happy dinner after the close but losing battle. Then Jack Kennedy flew to Europe to join his vacationing father on the Riviera. He left, Sorensen said, "with no foolish claims, charges, tears or promises to retract or regret. He was content."

Joe Kennedy helped his son analyze what had happened. He told Jack that "God was still with him, that he could be President if he wanted to be and worked hard."

Later Jack measured the good fortune in his defeat: "Joe [Jr.] was the star of our family. He did everything better than the rest of us. If he had lived he would have gone on in politics and he would have been elected to the House and to the Senate, as I was. And, like me, he would have gone for the vice-presidential nomination at the 1956 convention. But, unlike me, he wouldn't have been beaten. Joe would have won the nomination. And then he and Stevenson would have been beaten by Eisenhower, and today Joe's political career would be in shambles, and he would be trying to pick up the pieces."

Joe Kennedy had written John and Jackie earlier that year: "God love you both and good luck on the coming event. Now you kids will have one of your own. Whatever it is, boy or girl, you'll love it like you never loved anything in your life."

During the convention, Jacqueline was in the final weeks of her pregnancy, staying with her parents at Newport. Jack, resting now from the long convention nights, was out sailing on the Mediterranean with his brother Teddy when the message reached the villa. It sent him flying home to her bedside in the Newport hospital. She had already lost the baby.

# Marching to Washington

Jack Kennedy did not retire disgruntled to the political sidelines when he failed to win the vice-presidential nomination in 1956. He stayed in the arena to campaign for Adlai Stevenson with all the vigor that was in him. In one five-week span, he contributed 150 speeches and 30,000 miles of travel across twenty-six states.

A friend suspected a personal motive behind the activity and, perhaps thinking so much barnstorming was unnecessary, assured Kennedy that he already had the inside track for nomination to the second spot in 1960. "I'm not running for vice-president any more," the campaigner replied. "I'm now running for President."

Recalling Jack's trip to Europe after the 1956 defeat, and their talk about the Presidency, Joe Kennedy said, "Jack had already made up his mind on the way over. He was already working on it." And as a close associate put it, Jack "was everybody's number-one choice for the number-two place. But hardly anyone . . . favored him for the only place he would take."

Another Kennedy had his eye on the Presidency in the 1956 campaign—although not on his own behalf. He was the quiet, slender, curious young man who invariably rode in the back of Stevenson's plane. He was supposed to be a liaison with campaign headquarters but, "nobody asked me anything, nobody asked me to do anything, nobody consulted me." So Robert F. Kennedy had time to watch and study, and he "filled notebooks with notes on how a Presidential campaign should be run."

Thus did the two brothers, grandsons of men who had been taught in a classic school of ward politics and bossism, lay the foundations of a campaign that would startle and confound old-line politicians, a campaign that would be innovative, marked with an appeal to youth, characterized by the thoroughness and hard-eyed calculation of its planning and execution.

The beginnings were modest. Jack Kennedy and Ted Sorensen, at thirty-one already a veteran of seven years of close association with the candidate-to-be, initiated a card file which quickly began to bulge with information about Democratic politicians, prospective delegates to the 1960 convention and party workers at every level, information about their work, their families, their loyalties. Every one of many trips around the country, beginning in December 1956, added to the store.

More than three years lay ahead before this bundle of seeming trivia would be put to practical use. In the minds of Kennedy and Sorensen, it was none too soon. Kennedy had learned the value of an early start when he began planning for his Senate race more than four years before he ran. Both of them had learned at Chicago that a political convention, however haphazard and spur-of-the-moment it might appear, was the fruit of careful preparation in the precincts, at the grass roots. Part of the job before them would be to meet and talk with and remember every one of the thousands who would have a hand in selecting the next Presidential candidate of the Democratic party. They would have to build an organization that would know more about the state of Democratic affairs than local leaders on the scene.

Another facet of the early industry would be exposure. Jack Kennedy would be the subject of a build-up designed to introduce the relatively unknown junior senator from Massachusetts to every household in the land. The primary aim would not be political; the focus would be on his youth, his personality, his good looks and—to a lesser degree—his family. There would be speeches, all he could

*James R. Hoffa: "I don't have any use for him."*

handle. Between 1956 and 1960, no Democrat would speak in more states, address more party dinners, help more party candidates, than John F. Kennedy. For the women's magazines, there were his wife, the personification of young grace and beauty, and his first child, Caroline, born November 27, 1957.

Interesting copy, some of it uncannily lucky. A *Saturday Evening Post* article in 1957 said, "Fervent admirers of the Kennedys . . . confidently look forward to the day when Jack will be in the White House, Bobby will serve in the Cabinet as Attorney General and Teddy will be the Senator from Massachusetts."

It would be an uphill fight. Kennedy's youth—forty-three at election time—would be raised as an objection; so would the corollaries of immaturity and inexperience. Liberals were suspicious of his liberalism. Labor leaders and Negro leaders had their points for dislike. First and last, though, Jack Kennedy was a Catholic. Democrats had nominated a Catholic once before—Al Smith, the Happy Warrior of 1928—and had been burned. All

the whispers against Smith would find fresh use against Kennedy. So ran the arguments.

Privately, friends said, Jack Kennedy resented that his religion should be held against him. Realistically, he accepted the fact. He came out of the 1956 convention defeat with certain proven axioms. The farm states that held on for Stevenson did so because Stevenson had voted for the farmer. Kennedy, representing industrial Massachusetts, had not. Leverett Saltonstall, Jack's fellow senator, noted that after 1956 Jack Kennedy's voting habits began to change in the Senate. "I was still looking at things from a Massachusetts point of view. But he was looking at things more broadly."

There were other lessons. Richard Donahue, the young Massachusetts lawyer drawn to Kennedy's side, said: "After 1956, the fat was in the fire . . . because he emerged as a national figure . . . he was not about to approach a convention again without a tremendously better organized front. So, starting almost immediately thereafter, the thoughts and directions of those of us who were active with him in Massachusetts looked to the 1958 reelection campaign for him and the 1960 campaign for the Presidency."

Jack Kennedy began to tour the nation as he used to tour the Eleventh District. "His memory," Donahue said, "was so remarkable that he could ride through his old district in Charlestown and talk about the 1946 campaign and recall those store owners who put his signs in their windows and those who had refused. It was not with a particular spirit of vengeance that he remembered, but he understood that politics ran by rewarding your friends and punishing your enemies— and it was his concern as he went around the country in 1956 to find out with whom alliances might properly be made, and what particular strength they had."

Jack Kennedy decided that in 1958, since he had no serious opposition for his Senate seat, "We would run a campaign which was really a dry run for the Presidency," a staff aide said. It would refine those techniques that were so successful in 1952 and would tailor them to a Presidential race. John Kennedy was now a speaker in demand around the country. Going into the 1958 Massachusetts campaign, Donahue remembered, "we had all of the organization and everything but the candidate. For during the entire campaign he spent only seventeen days within the Commonwealth."

The rest of the time, John Kennedy was on the go from coast to coast. The problem was how to get people out to see him. The solution drew on the experience of the 1952 campaign again when Bobby noted ruefully how Stevenson people in Massachusetts could not be counted on to organize anything for Jack Kennedy. Jack needed his own men, and it was from this concept that the "advance man" was born. The Kennedy people decided to avoid the big dinners and meetings as too time-consuming for their candidate. They decided to create their own crowds, as they had with the tea parties, drumming up interest before the candidate arrived.

Donahue said, "The basic system that's used in the national campaign was tried out, here. He would spend a full day in a geographic area. That would mean that he would hit all the surrounding towns for as little as ten minutes or as long as thirty-five minutes. Within each of the towns he would make sure that he made more than one stop, whether it be at a high school to address the students or the Town Hall or a public square or a tour of an industrial plant."

At night, he would end up in the principal city in the area, and would hold a reception to which everyone of note was invited. That was the pattern conceived in 1952, tested in 1958, and detailed for future use. No one would be more surprised than the people picked to drum up advance interest at how large the crowds would be.

There was a basic philosophy to the Kennedy campaign technique. In 1958, Jack's nominating petitions carried 256,000 signatures. In addition, some 1,800 volunteers signed up to help Jack campaign. There were obviously too many volunteers, but it would be bad manners and bad politics to disappoint them. The solution: Put the 1,800 to work writing thank-you notes to the 256,000.

Jack Kennedy's opponent in 1958 was Vincent J. Celeste, the lawyer he had swamped in 1950. Celeste picked up his campaign where he left it, eight years earlier, attacking Kennedy money. The result was never in doubt. Kennedy had a margin of 874,608 votes, the largest plurality in Massachusetts history.

One of Celeste's campaign attacks was, "What right do Kennedy and his brother Bobby have to sit in judgment on labor without ever doing a day's work in their whole lives?"

In a sense, Jack and Bobby Kennedy were sitting in judgment on labor, as member and counsel respectively of the Senate Select Committee on Improper Activities in the Labor and Management Field. It was also called the Labor Rackets Committee. One of its targets was the powerful Teamsters Union and its president Dave Beck. Beck wouldn't say, in response to Bobby's biting questions, what happened to some $320,000 in union money. When Kennedy asked if Beck thought the answer might incriminate him, Beck said, "It might." "I feel the same way," Kennedy said. Beck was jailed for income tax evasion and grand larceny. When James Hoffa, a tough, stocky career unionist, replaced Beck as Teamster president, Bobby Kennedy pur-

sued him as well. It was the dogged pursuit that was to fashion one of the adjectives that Bobby would face later. They called him "ruthless."

Jimmy Hoffa was indicted by the Justice Department for bribery in 1957, and was defended by Edward Bennett Williams. Bobby was sure Hoffa would be convicted. "There could be no doubt about it," he said. "I knew the evidence. I knew the chief witness. I knew the case." But Hoffa was acquitted, and Bobby, who said he would jump off the Capitol if Hoffa got off, received a sarcastic offer of a parachute from Williams.

Hoffa, who had met Bobby Kennedy socially, asked: "This is a lawyer? He's never even been in a courtroom except as a witness. You know how he got his job, don't you? His brother got it for him; nepotism." He called Bob "a spoiled young millionaire that never had to go out and find a way to live by his own efforts and cannot understand resistance to what he wants. . . . There is only one thing I like about Bobby Kennedy—his willingness to work and to fight to win. Now outside of that I don't have any use for him."

It would be a long contest, a ruthless pursuit. Hoffa had marked his man well. Bobby had just finished his book on racketeering in America, called *The Enemy Within*, which became a best-seller. But now, in 1959, Jack needed Bobby again. Nearly coincident with the birth of his seventh child, Bobby quit the Rackets Committee to host an unusual group

The committee counsel fought to win.

of men and women in his living room at Hyannis Port. They met on Wednesday morning, October 28.

Their subject was well-defined: to fix areas of responsibility, plan strategy and set up the lines of assault on the consciousness of the Democratic voters.

The center stage was held by Jack Kennedy, now the man *New York Times* columnist James Reston described as "on the make. He makes no pretense about it and he dismisses out of hand the suggestion that he is young enough to wait for some other Presidential campaign . . . He is swinging for the fences now."

Jack Kennedy didn't need to have anyone say it for him. "I suppose anybody in politics would like to be President," he admitted. "That is the center of action . . . at least you have an opportunity to do something about all the problems which I would be concerned about . . . as a father or as a citizen."

With Jack was Bobby, now thirty-three, and the familiar faces of earlier campaigns: Ted Sorensen; Kenny O'Donnell, thirty-five, Bobby's football teammate at Harvard; Steve Smith, thirty-one, the businessman-brother in law; Pierre Salinger, thirty-four, a former San Francisco newsman who came to help; Lou Harris, thirty-eight, the poll-taker; John Bailey, fifty-four, the Connecticut state chairman who had "handled" the analysis of the Catholic vote before the 1956 convention; and Larry O'Brien, forty-two, the organizer, the compiler of the "O'Brien Manual"—a 64-page black-bound political bible, the pattern of a Kennedy campaign based on the volunteer notion to make everyone feel he is part of the grand plan.

Of the sixteen persons present that day were also the youngest and oldest adult Kennedys, Teddy and Joe. Teddy, twenty-seven, was just thirty-two days from his first wedding

anniversary, about to get a look at national politics in the same states that had denied his brother the nomination in 1956. Joe Kennedy, now seventy-one, still outspoken, sitting in on the meeting that would launch his ultimate dream on its way to reality.

Memories of those present varied in detail on what happened but all remembered what Jack Kennedy did. For three hours, without map or notes, he surveyed the country, region by region, state by state. O'Brien recalled "his remarkable knowledge of every state, not just the party leaders, not just the senators in Washington, but he knew all the factions and the key people in all the factions." Sorensen added, "He knows . . . who likes him and who doesn't, he knows where he should go and where he shouldn't, he has this incredible memory of places, names, dates, who should be written to and who shouldn't."

The first target of strategy was the primaries, which ones should be contested and which ones should be passed. There was a lot of scorn for Presidential primaries in the country; Harry Truman had shrugged them off as "eyewash," and Senator Hubert Humphrey would say, in the light of experience, "you have to be crazy to enter a primary."

But, for Kennedy, running in the primaries was a practical matter of hard politics. He had to convince the party's powers that he, a Catholic, could get votes. It was not a matter of prejudice or outworn shibboleths but simple political arithmetic: by the best available figures, nearly three-fourths of the United States population was non-Catholic.

Among four rivals for the nomination, only one—Humphrey—saw a need to make the primaries a family fight. The Minnesota senator, hero of a civil rights fight at the 1948 convention, leader of the drive to nominate Adlai Stevenson in 1952, still was either unknown or regarded as a wild-eyed radical outside his own state. He, too, had to become known, show muscle at the polls, to make his case for the convention.

The other potentials took different approaches. Senator Stuart Symington of Missouri, favored by Truman, made his appeal to party leadership as a compromise candidate, a logical choice in case of the deadlock that seemed highly possible. To preserve his standing, he would have to avoid the fratricidal war of the primaries. Lyndon Baines Johnson of Texas had Congress as his power base, he, as Majority Leader, and "Mr. Sam" Rayburn, Speaker of the House, controlled the machinery and knew how to use it. Like Symington, Johnson saw his best chance in case of deadlock. The fifth man in the lists, the twice-defeated Stevenson, still was in the to-be-or-not-to-be phase of candidacy, but motions were being made in his behalf.

Eventually, Kennedy went into seven primaries and won them all, but all of the drama and excitement was wrapped up in two states—Wisconsin and West Virginia.

Wisconsin, the state that had invented the Presidential primary in 1903, came first on April 5. Kennedy's initial reception was as cold as the weather sweeping off windy Lake Michigan. As Theodore White related it, (in *The Making of a President, 1960*) Jack Kennedy traveled 185 miles into Wisconsin that first day and saw no more than 1,600 people, of whom 1,200 were probably too young to vote. (On one stop in Wisconsin a young tyke asked Kennedy how he became a war hero. "It was involuntary," he said. "They sank my boat.")

Faced with such small turnouts the Kennedy organization went to work. Manpower —and womanpower—streamed into the state: his sisters and brothers, his Harvard classmates, friends of the family, people drawn by nothing more than the candidate's own attraction. Kennedy set the pace with indefatigable campaigning, imparting the message that the nation needed to be revived and set on a new course and only a new President could do it. Gradually, the gloomy forecasts faded; Kennedy would carry six of the ten Congressional districts, he would carry eight, then nine, perhaps all ten.

Actually, he carried six and received 56 percent of the popular vote. But his margin came largely from four dominantly Catholic districts; he lost four districts that were heavily Protestant. Other things were involved, but the vote would be interpreted generally as a Protestant-Catholic split. The religious issue was very much alive.

In terms of practical politics, Humphrey had been eliminated. If he could not win next door to his home, Minnesota, in a state similar in voter make-up to his own, where could he win? Humphrey had worked as hard as Kennedy with a much smaller organization. He did not read the returns that way. He saw the close outcome as a moral victory. He would renew the contest in West Virginia.

West Virginia was a state of mountains and mines, poverty for many and politics for everybody. Most importantly, it was a state that took religion seriously—and it was the deep-dyed religion of the pioneers who carried Bibles with their squirrel rifles. Only five percent of the population was Catholic.

Lou Harris' first soundings of sentiment in December had found a 70–30 margin for Kennedy. Three weeks before the primary on May 10, he found a shift to 60–40 for Humphrey. What had happened, the pollsters asked. In December, they were told, nobody knew Kennedy was a Catholic.

O'Brien and Robert Kennedy flew from Wisconsin to take command of emergency

"Just as I went into politics when Joe died, if anything happened to me tomorrow my brother Bobby would run for my seat."

JOHN F. KENNEDY

*Three brothers: 1959*

measures: the conviction was strong that Kennedy's cause could not survive defeat in West Virginia. Eight main headquarters and an equal number of suboffices were opened. The workers rallied: O'Brien estimated the number on election day as 9,000. Tasks were assigned—mailings, telephone calls, door-to-door distributions of literature, speakers, social affairs. Kennedy television film portrayed him as a war hero, a scholar, a father, devoted to America's faiths and freedoms. Nowhere was the difference in the candidates' resources more apparent than in travel: Kennedy flitted around the state in his own plane, while Humphrey had to settle for a rented bus.

(Simultaneously with the West Virginia operation, other Kennedy teams of lesser proportions were at work in Maryland, Nebraska, Oregon and Indiana.)

Advisers divided on what to do about the religious issue. Kennedy decided to meet it head-on. A President swore on the Bible to uphold separation of church and state, he told listeners. If the President violated that oath, he would be guilty of a crime against the Constitution and a crime against God. Harris' pulse-takings began to show that Humphrey was slipping in favor.

Humphrey grew snappish under the pressure, an unwonted reaction for him. "Kennedy is the spoiled candidate," he said, "and he and that young, emotional, juvenile Bobby are spending with wild abandon . . . Anyone who gets in the way of . . . papa's pet is going to be destroyed." Then, mournfully, "I can't afford to run around this state with a little black bag and a checkbook."

Kennedy turned away the bludgeon with a rapier. "I got a wire from my father," he said in a speech. " 'Dear Jack: Don't buy one vote more than necessary. I'll be damned if I'll pay for a landslide.' "

(As a matter of fact, Kennedy's expenditures did not come close to matching the rumors. Many of his workers were unpaid volunteers. Their services could not have been purchased with anything but friendship. An exhaustive investigation did not turn up any evidence of wrongdoing.)

Election weather was a damp drizzle. The vote count was slow, with many local offices being decided, but there was little doubt of the outcome from the start. Kennedy swept forty-eight of fifty-five counties.

It was a heart-breaking loss for Humphrey. Bobby Kennedy walked through the wet streets of Charleston to Humphrey's hotel to thank him for the telegram conceding the election. Humphrey said he wanted to go back with Bobby to Kennedy headquarters to congratulate Jack who was flying in from Washington. Together, they walked in the rain. On the way, Humphrey stopped off at his own campaign center to salute the weary, desolate hangers-on. Folk singer Jimmy Wofford, who had toured the state with Humphrey singing old New Deal songs, strummed one last refrain: "Vote for Hubert Humphrey. He's your man and mine."

Humphrey, tears filling his eyes, stood before the television cameras and read a brief statement: "I am no longer a candidate for the Democratic Presidential nomination."

Wofford began to cry. Humphrey patted his shoulder. "Aw, Jimmy," he said. Bobby Kennedy, his own eyes wet, put his arm around Humphrey. They walked out into the rain together.

West Virginia gave the Kennedy wagon a momentum that seemed unstoppable, but there was no letup in the steady campaigning. No bloc of votes was too small for his attention. He was looking at multiples—a half-dozen blocs of three each was as good as one bloc of eighteen. Through May and June,

his assured total of convention votes mounted. By July 1, he could count 550 of the necessary 761 as certain; on convention eve, The Associated Press said he had the nomination "all but nailed down." The one mystery ingredient was Adlai Stevenson, the twice-defeated Democratic standard-bearer.

Stevenson was living in peaceful seclusion on his Illinois farm, determined to have no more to do with politics. The pressure of world events shattered his privacy.

Stevenson had never lost his magic for devoted followers. Early in 1960, at least four small but serious movements for a third Stevenson candidacy were under way. Efforts were redoubled when the world erupted into a series of chaotic events, most of them constituting a setback of one sort or another for the United States. There was the U-2 incident and the consequent collapse of the Eisenhower-Khrushchev Summit; Syngman Rhee's government in Korea was overthrown; Fidel Castro flung new insults from Cuba; a rampage of terror broke out in the Congo; riots in Japan were so violent that a visit by President Eisenhower was canceled. Stevenson heard the overtures politely and turned

them down. Friends were convinced that he still had a deep-down yearning for the Presidency, but he would not seek it; the party would have to come to him.

"Draft Stevenson" clubs began to appear. Metropolitan newspapers carried full-page advertisements appealing for Stevenson campaign funds, and drew enthusiastic response.

The Stevenson strategy was simple: stop Kennedy. If Kennedy could be held short of majority on the first ballot, his strength would start melting away.

But this time the Kennedy forces left nothing to chance. This was not 1956, not a makeshift grab.

They set up headquarters at the Biltmore (with an annex of sorts at the Beverly Hills mansion of film star Marion Davies where Joe Kennedy and Rose had taken up residence.) "Shepherds" were assigned to state delegations, armed with cards listing the name of each delegate, his family, his profession, hobby, religion, characteristics. They had their own system of communications from the convention floor to command post: walkie-talkies.

On Wednesday, July 13, leaders of the

Kennedy team assembled for stock-taking. Robert Kennedy told them, "I don't want generalities or guesses. There's no point in fooling ourselves. I want the cold facts. I want to hear only the votes we are guaranteed on the first ballot." The "cold facts" added up to 740 votes, 21 short of majority. Bobby had a farewell message: "We can't miss a trick in the next twelve hours. If we don't win tonight, we're dead."

As the roll call progressed, it became apparent that the Kennedys had been conservative. They picked up an unexpected vote here, another there. West Virginia carried the total to 725, Wisconsin to 748. Wyoming was next. And there, in the midst of the western delegates upon whom he had been bestowing affection for months was Edward Kennedy, the political ingenue.

"Wyoming," boomed the state's committee-man, "casts all fifteen votes for the next President of the United States!" That was it. The hall exploded with thousands of shrieking, thundering voices. The Kennedy banners pumped up and down. The band struck up "Happy Days Are Here Again." The final tally was Kennedy 806, Johnson 409, Symington 86, Stevenson 79½, all others 140½.

There were conflicting stories about the proffer of the vice-presidential nomination to Johnson. A publisher recalled that the suggestion had come in an offhand remark from Jack Kennedy. Another version insisted that the motivation came from Johnson. Whatever the truth, Johnson was an unlikely choice. There had been bitterness between his camp and the Kennedys' in preconvention maneuvers. There was more conflict in stories about Johnson's reaction; here again, the point was that he accepted. It was another point that the hard-headed Kennedys, before the final decision was made, calculated how many votes Johnson, representing the Old South, would bring to the ticket in November.

Nevertheless, the liberals were bitter at the choice, and this affected the candidate and his brother. As Arthur Schlesinger wrote, "All emotions did not subside. Jack and Bobby were sitting gloomily around the swimming pool when their father appeared at the doorway, resplendent in a fancy smoking jacket, and said, 'Don't worry, Jack. In two weeks everyone will be saying that this was the smartest thing you ever did.'"

One more convention ritual remained: the acceptance speech. On Friday, July 15, John F. Kennedy addressed 80,000 people in Los Angeles Coliseum:

*We stand today on the edge of a New Frontier— the frontier of the 1960s—a frontier of unknown opportunities and perils, a frontier of unfulfilled hopes and threats."*

*Woodrow Wilson's New Freedom promised our nation a new political and economic framework. Franklin Roosevelt's New Deal promised security and succor to those in need. But the New Frontier of which I speak is not a set of promises—it is a set of challenges. It sums up, not what I intend to offer the American people but what I intend to ask of them. It appeals to their pride, not their pocketbook—it holds out the promise of more sacrifice instead of more security.*

A fortnight later, the Republicans met in Chicago and nominated Vice-President Richard Nixon as their choice to succeed Dwight David Eisenhower. Nixon had virtually no opposition.

The Kennedys consistently looked at politics in terms of people. The people were divided into leaders and followers and the leaders were the most important, to be sure, but all should be cultivated. Cultivating meant not cursory acquaintance but warmth, intimacy even, to give a sense of participation. The Kennedys had their own values of leader-

ship and personality and they had an instinct for passing by the straw men to reach those who truly were in control. Instead of relying upon party machinery, they relied upon themselves.

Moreover, they recognized the vast changes afoot in the country—the great growth of suburbia at the expense of big cities and rural communities, the expansion in white-collar jobs with resulting changes in what people wanted from life, the growing importance of the Negro vote and—most of all —the rising tide of youth. The World War II generation was reaching maturity, bringing new demands, new sets of values to the political scene. The awareness of youth was again reflected in the men close to the Kennedys—virtually all of them veterans of long service in World War II, and those who were not youths still had a youthful outlook and could concede and adjust to the strength of youth. The "new leader" offered in 1946 by a "new generation" was older now but still close to a slightly newer generation.

Jack Kennedy, of course, was the perfect personification of the Kennedy philosophy. So, in another way, was Robert Kennedy who never was far from his brother's side on the long road to the White House. But, where Jack was warm, outgoing as ever on campaigns —or almost always—Robert was often abrasive, as he had been in 1952. Mennen Williams, then governor of Michigan, encountered the younger Kennedy in preconvention days and remembered: "He was rather brash and cutting. He didn't ingratiate himself and the candidate but rather created antagonisms . . . Whether we got used to him or whether he changed, we learned to cooperate on the basis of mutual understanding."

Another observer of the RFK personality commented on his relentless drive to win, with no quarter asked and no quarter given.

Robert told a meeting of Democrats in New York: "Gentlemen, I don't give a damn if the state and county organizations survive after November and I don't give a damn if you survive. I want to elect John F. Kennedy." The resemblance between Robert and his father was not lost on Jack. When the youth of his campaign manager was mentioned, he would say, "If I need somebody older, there's no need to go outside of the family. I can always get my father."

Really, though, where did Joe Kennedy fit into this picture of youth on the march? He was in the background, so deep in the back-

ground that a doggerel went the rounds: "Jack and Bob will run the show/While Ted's in charge of hiding Joe." The father did not attend the acceptance ceremonies in Los Angeles; he declined even to speak at the twenty-fifth anniversary dinner of the Securities and Exchange Commission, the agency he had helped found. The onetime ambassador and Washington power had his own definition of his role: "I just call people. You call people that you know and ask them to help in any way they can."

Still, there was no denying that Joseph P. Kennedy was very much in the picture as head of his family. In addition to calling people, he was on the phone often, cheering his boys, offering advice. "The great thing about Dad is his optimism and his enthusiasm and how he's always for you," Jack said. "He might not always agree with what I do, just as I don't always agree with him, but as soon as I do anything, there's Dad saying: 'Smartest move you ever made.'"

Thus, in the Kennedy camp, the campaign was conducted in an atmosphere of camaraderie, affection and understanding. In the Nixon camp, there was confusion, discontent, misunderstanding.

Richard Nixon had been a representative at thirty-three, a senator at thirty-seven, Vice-President at thirty-nine. In eight years in the Eisenhower administration, he had carried the vice-presidency to new heights of prestige and earned respect by his restrained conduct under stress. He also had a reputation for hard-hitting tactics and blunt conservatism that offended liberals.

The reputation influenced his campaign plans. He intended to devote the early weeks to erasing "the image of pugnacity," then gradually increase his pace to reach a climax on election eve. Nixon believed that a campaigner should not run too fast too early, but should conserve his strength for a final sprint. The Kennedys believed in running as fast as they could all the way.

Whatever the merits or demerits of the plan, it was Nixon's own. Insofar as it was possible, considering the scope of the effort and the great number of people inevitably involved, his was a one-man show. He did not spare himself; he insisted on keeping a pledge to visit every one of the fifty states even after an injury. He cracked his knee against an auto door and infection developed, putting him in the hospital for two weeks.

But physical troubles were only part of his woes. Communications between him and his staff, between him and the press, were faulty. He was criticized for not bringing President Eisenhower into the arena before the last week, for not making better and earlier use of television. There were disputes over policy; it was said that he did not pay enough attention to his advisers.

One national commentator complained about the "painful monotony" of the campaign speeches. Another saw the campaign as only "a great popularity contest." But then the drama picked up. The candidates agreed to a series of four face-to-face debates

before a possible television audience of 120 million Americans.

Jack Kennedy arrived in Chicago on Sunday, September 25. He was met by his brain trust of Sorensen, lawyer Dick Goodwin, and law scholar Mike Feldman, all of them laden with research on the problems that faced the United States. They worked around the clock condensing the critical questions and on Monday met with Jack Kennedy to begin a day-long brainstorming session. That night, although he rarely ate before speaking engagements, Jack Kennedy dined alone in his room.

Richard Nixon, arriving late Sunday, kept a full schedule of speaking engagements Monday, and showing his tiredness, made a dash for the television studio. Jack Kennedy dressed leisurely in his hotel room in what his aides called his television suit—a dark gray. As friend Dave Powers remembered: "He stood in front of the mirror, and he looked great. He said, 'I feel like a boxer going into Madison Square Garden.' And I said, 'No, no, Senator, it's more like the opening day pitcher for the World Series because you are going to have to win four.' And he chuckled, and out the door we went."

Most observers felt Jack Kennedy was the clear winner of the first debate, not so much for what he said, but because his temperament and demeanor put down the charge that he was too young, too inexperienced. Added to that was the effect of the lighting and camera angles on Nixon's televised image, an effect that produced deep shadows on his face and in his eyes.

In later debates, which went more evenly but drew smaller audiences than the first, Nixon avoided the ravages of the electronic tube with careful make-up, but the damage had been done. Jack Kennedy always looked at the debates as the turning point in his

run for the White House. And he always wondered why Nixon, with eight years of White House exposure to his favor, had ever agreed to put it on the line with a Senator hungry for the same kind of exposure. Before the debates, Jack told his father and Bobby, "I think I can beat him."

Then the religious issue rose to plague Kennedy again. His troops had hoped they had finished with it in West Virginia. But so had the Dearos so long ago when they marched on Boston City Hall. John Kennedy

had come far since then, but he was back with the issue that had frustrated his grandfathers.

There were murmurs in the South, in the farm belt. Echoes in 1960 of Boston, 1860. Traveling campaigners found the most hard-shelled Democrats disturbed by their candidate's Catholicism.

A group of prominent Protestant churchmen issued a pronouncement questioning whether a Catholic could or should be President.

Jack Kennedy met the new situation as he

*As the campaign lengthened, the polls looked good.*

had met the old one—head-on. He accepted an invitation from the Greater Houston Ministerial Association to discuss his religion. He and Ted Sorensen—a Unitarian—drafted a speech, and on September 12, he delivered it. Here are excerpts:

*I believe in an America where the separation of church and state is absolute—where no Catholic prelate would tell the President (should he be a Catholic) how to act and no Protestant minister would tell his parishioners for whom to vote— where no church or church school is granted any public funds or political preference—and where no man is denied public office merely because his religion differs from the President who might appoint him or the people who might elect him.*

*I believe in an America that is officially neither Catholic, Protestant nor Jewish—where no public official either requests or accepts instructions on public policy from the Pope, the National Council of Churches or any other ecclesiastical source— where no religious body seeks to impose its will directly or indirectly upon the general populace or the public acts of its officials—and where religious liberty is so indivisible that an act against one church is treated as an act against all.*

Kennedy would speak in similar vein on other occasions, notably to the American Society of Newspaper Editors. The filmed record of the Houston speech was shown on television and became a basic campaign document, exhibited to both Protestant and Catholic audiences. The election result was the best possible evidence on how the head-on tactic worked.

And then there was the much-publicized incident of the arrest of Dr. Martin Luther King Jr.

King was a respected spokesman for his race and an exponent of non-violence in the cause of civil rights. On October 12, he and fifty-two other Negroes were arrested when they tried to integrate a restaurant in an At-

lanta department store. Fifty-one defendants were freed. King was sentenced to four months of hard labor and taken to the Georgia state penitentiary.

The idea that Kennedy should respond came from Harris Wofford, a university law professor in the campaign's civil rights section. Kennedy was told, and he promptly telephoned Mrs. King, assured her of his sympathy and promised to do anything he could. Robert Kennedy followed up with a telephoned appeal for King's release to the judge who had sentenced him. King was freed on bail, pending appeal.

Publicly, the Republicans said and did nothing. A statement advocating King's release was drafted in the Department of Justice, and one copy was sent to the White House, another to Nixon. Neither saw the light of public print. The effect of the Kennedy intervention upon the Negro community was incalculable. But there were hints of its impact after the votes were counted. For instance, it was estimated that a quarter of a million Negroes voted for Kennedy in Illinois, a state he carried by only 9,000 votes, a state he would not forget.

The mood of the Kennedy forces had been increasingly optimistic in the climactic weeks. The polls were telling a bright story. Every one around the candidate was confident. Worries among party sachems in Washington were discounted. Warnings of a last-minute Republican surge were shrugged away.

And so, as it did in all campaigns, the tumult and the shouting stilled. It was time to vote.

A candidate on Election Day is a lonely man. All that can be done has been done. Nothing now will rectify mistakes. All that matters is the muted click of voting machine levers, the thin rustle of paper ballots.

*On November 25, 1960, the President-elect breaks the news to Caroline: a baby brother.*

John F. Kennedy voted early, in a one-time branch of the Boston Public Library. He journeyed by car and plane to Hyannis Port, accompanied by Jacqueline, now eight-months pregnant with their second child, and by reporters who had traveled with him up and down the country for three months. He had breakfast with members of the family, huddled for a while on a porch, wrapped in an overcoat against the chill. He posed for photographers, took his daughter Caroline, almost three, for a walk, and idly tossed a football with his younger brothers. He was tired, so tired.

He and Jacqueline lunched together. He wandered across the compound lawn to Bobby's home, the command post, which soon would be receiving and analyzing election returns. He tried to nap. Restless, he went back to the command post. He made some phone calls. He returned to his home. He went back to the command post.

When the first solid returns began to appear, there was cause for concern among the Kennedys. Kansas, where some communities permitted a progressive vote count, was giving Nixon bigger majorities than it gave Eisenhower in 1956. Kentucky, counted by poll-taker Harris as safe for Kennedy, would be a hairline state. Then came a real jolt: the computer of the Columbia Broadcasting System predicted 459 electoral votes for Nixon, seventy-eight for Kennedy. But then the tide began to turn. Connecticut produced a flood of Democratic ballots. The first returns from Philadelphia exceeded expectations. The candidate went to dinner, then settled down to watch television in his own living room.

Disappointing results in Detroit and Cleveland were only momentary setbacks. Texas fell into the Kennedy column; so did South Carolina after an early show for Nixon. The

*In family photos there was now a President.*

popular vote margin mounted to 1.5 million, 1.6 million, to 2 million by midnight. The CBS computer changed its mind, was now predicting 311 electoral votes for Kennedy, forty-two more than needed. First returns from California had a pronounced Democratic tinge. Kennedy sent his wife to bed. He crossed the compound again to the command post.

About 3 A.M., it was apparent that four states held the key to the Presidency—Michigan, Minnesota, California and Illinois. Kennedy needed any two. If he took only one, the election would be decided by the House of Representatives.

Tension supplanted the earlier elation. Nixon appeared on television to speak briefly and encouragingly to his followers. There was fleeting anger among the Kennedy people that he had not conceded. "Why should he concede?" asked Kennedy. "I wouldn't." There was nothing more John Kennedy could do. At 4 A.M. he went to bed. Exhausted, others turned in too. Only Robert Kennedy remained up through the night, phoning, checking all around the country, tabulating and retabulating. Sometime during the night, Michigan went into the Kennedy column to stay. Jack Kennedy was five votes short of the magic 269. Minnesota decided it. At 12:33 P.M. on November 9, The Associated Press bulletined that the state's eleven electoral votes were assured for Kennedy. Illinois fell to him later. California's decision was not known until November 16. It went for Nixon by 35,000.

At Hyannis Port, photographer and friend Jacques Lowe remembered the feelings:

"Jacqueline Kennedy described the period between the closing of the polls and the moment of victory as 'the longest night in history.' Now she seemed dazed as people rushed up to congratulate her. After a while,

she donned her raincoat and went for a solitary walk along the beach.

"Finally there was certainty, and the long struggle was over. A sigh of relief was almost audible, and all got up and walked into the sun room, where they stood with bright smiles, looking up at their brother. Then John Kennedy asked for his wife, and he went down to the beach to find her. While Jacqueline went in to dress for a picture . . . John F. Kennedy went for a long walk with Caroline."

In the final tabulation, Kennedy amassed 303 electoral votes from twenty-three states to 219 for Nixon from twenty-six states. (Mississippi's support went to a slate of independent electors who voted for Sen. Harry F. Byrd of Virginia.) The total number of ballots was 68,832,818—eleven percent more than in 1956 and the greatest number cast in any free election in history up till then.

Typically, Kennedy wanted to know the facts of what was really a narrow victory. He had taken 49.7 percent of the popular vote, and Nixon 49.5 percent. He set Dave Powers to analyzing the vote. "He wanted," Powers said, "to know what fifty electoral votes he had come closest to losing." Those key votes came from just five states: Illinois, where he had taken seven out of ten Negro votes, and barely carried the state; Missouri, New Mexico, Nevada and Hawaii. A shift of 11,874 votes to Nixon in those states, just two hundredths of one percent of the total vote, would have defeated Jack Kennedy.

Robert Kennedy gave the final word:

"We simply had to run and fight and scramble for ten weeks all the way, and then we would win. We got on top with the debates, we fought to stay on top, and we did win. And if we'd done one bit less of anything, then we might have lost."

# White House Years

It all lasted a little over one thousand days: one thousand and thirty-six to be precise.

Each day had its problem, or decision, or triumph, or national memory, or private moment. Some days went as fast as the clock and dropped from sight, as forgotten as yesterday's appointment list. Some became not days but dates. Students would read and write about them generations hence. Among them were:

JANUARY 20, 1961.

Inauguration Day. Twenty degrees above zero.

The City of Washington was clothed in a cover of snow and the whiteness returned the glare of a brilliant noonday sun in the Plaza of the Capitol. The crowd on the inaugural platform and the hundreds of spectators in the grandstand in front stamped their feet, slapped their arms, turned up their coat collars, blew into cupped hands and awaited in shivering anticipation the arrival of the man who would become the thirty-fifth President of the United States.

John Kennedy had awakened in his Georgetown home at eight o'clock in the morning after an evening of gaiety. First there was an Inaugural Concert at Constitution Hall, then an Inaugural Gala at the Armory. Jacqueline, at his side, was dazzling in a white gown and a necklace he himself had chosen for the occasion. On the way from the concert to the gala, driving through a snowstorm that had left motorists stranded along the route, the President-elect instructed his driver: "Turn on the lights so they can see Jackie." Driving through the snow-whitened streets, lights on, he thumbed through the concert program in which appeared a reprint of Thomas Jefferson's inaugural address. John Kennedy read it. "It's better than mine," he said. He was a student of graceful expression. Since his days in London he had collected rhetoric in a small black leather book. At the gala, Kennedy sat with his wife and his close friend William Walton, and, according to Walton, "saw the whole thing and adored it—sat in the front of the box, with a big cigar, and you knew this was one of his great moments, you could tell. Here was the reigning prince, and he was loving it."

To the delight of his mother, the President-elect began his administration by attending mass. Mrs. Rose Kennedy awoke early, dressed herself up against the cold, and walked to nearby Trinity Church in Georgetown. "When I got to the church," she recalled, "I saw policemen around and I thought, well, possibly Jack is coming to mass. I went into the church and subsequently he came in. I didn't sit with him because I was all bundled up with a lot of funny-looking scarves and things, but I was delighted to think that he had gone. He had gone on his own. Jackie hadn't been able to go because she wasn't, of course, very strong at that time. I hadn't urged him to go. I would have, except I thought he was so overwrought with work and with responsibilities. But the fact that he did go on his own, and did think it was important to start his new administration out with mass in the morning, gave me a wonderfully happy feeling."

After mass the President-elect returned home for Jacqueline, drove to the White House for coffee with President and Mrs. Eisenhower, accompanied them to the Capitol where the shivering crowd awaited. It was the President-elect's prerogative to choose the costume for the occasion. John Kennedy selected strictly formal attire, including high silk hat.

The inauguration ceremony began. The old priest and family friend, Richard Cardinal Cushing, gave the invocation, an excruci-

*Inauguration Day. January 20, 1961.*

atingly long one, and the nation became aware of his distinctive nasal twang and stentorian tones. Then arose the old poet, Robert Frost, whose aging eyes could not read in the sun's glare the poem of dedication he had written. So he recited from memory. Then, at 12:51 P.M., the Chief Justice arose to administer the oath of office. John Kennedy would be the first man in history to take that oath with his hand on a Douay Bible, as the Catholic version was called. It was the Fitzgerald family Bible, passed down to Honey Fitz, thence to Honey Fitz's son, Thomas. When John F. Kennedy sent to Boston for the Bible, his Uncle Tom retrieved it from his attic, put it in a shopping bag and dispatched it to Washington in the care of two Secret Service agents.

Now John Kennedy arose, stripped off his overcoat, placed his hand on his family Bible and swore the same oath that every President before him had sworn, while his mother, his father, his sisters and brothers, shipmates who had been aboard *PT 109*, old pals from the Eleventh Congressional District who had helped him in his first campaign, new friends who had helped him in his last, watched him assume the highest office in America.

Then President John F. Kennedy stepped to the podium and in the firm, crisp accents of his native New England delivered his Inaugural Address:

*We observe today not a victory of party but a celebration of freedom, symbolizing an end as well as a beginning, signifying renewal as well as change. For I have sworn before you and Almighty God the same solemn oath our forebears prescribed nearly a century and three-quarters ago. . . .*

*Let the word go forth from this time and place, to friend and foe alike, that the torch has been passed to a new generation of Americans, born in this century, tempered by war, disciplined by a hard and bitter peace, proud of our ancient heritage, and* unwilling to witness or permit the slow undoing of those human rights to which this nation has always been committed, and to which we are committed today at home and around the world.

Let every nation know, whether it wishes us well or ill, that we shall pay any price, bear any burden, meet any hardship, support any friend, oppose any foe to assure the survival and the success of liberty. . . .

To those peoples in the huts and villages of half the globe struggling to break the bonds of mass misery, we pledge our best efforts to help them help themselves. . . . If a free society cannot help the many who are poor, it cannot save the few who are rich. . . .

So let us begin anew, remembering on both sides that civility is not a sign of weakness, and sincerity is always subject to proof. Let us never negotiate out of fear, but let us never fear to negotiate.

Let both sides, for the first time, formulate serious and precise proposals for the inspection and control of arms . . .

Let both sides seek to invoke the wonders of science instead of its terrors. Together let us explore the stars, conquer the deserts, eradicate disease, tap the ocean depths and encourage the arts and commerce. . . .

All this will not be finished in the first one hundred days. Nor will it be finished in the first one thousand days, nor in the life of this Administration, nor even perhaps in our lifetime on this planet. But let us begin. . . .

Now the trumpet summons us again—not as a call to bear arms, though arms we need; not as a call to battle, though embattled we are; but a call to bear the burden of a long twilight struggle, year in and year out, "rejoicing in hope, patient in tribulation," a struggle against the common enemies of man: tyranny, poverty, disease and war itself. . . .

And so, my fellow Americans, ask not what your country can do for you; ask what you can do for your country.

My fellow citizens of the world, ask not what America will do for you, but what together we can do for the freedom of man.

Finally, whether you are citizens of America or citizens of the world, ask of us here the same high standards of strength and sacrifice which we ask of you. With a good conscience our only sure reward, with history the final judge of our deeds, let us go forth to lead the land we love, asking His blessing and His help, but knowing that here on earth God's work must truly be our own.

The America that John F. Kennedy took command of in 1961 was like an old ship, unsure of its course and strength, tired, apprehensive. The Russians had landed a rocket on the moon; Cuba had fallen to communism; American efforts to stem the spread of communism in Southeast Asia, especially in Laos, appeared to be faltering; American prestige had suffered from the U-2 incident. Was America perhaps no longer Number One in the world?

And so when the young, handsome, eloquent President stood before the Capitol, hatless and coatless on that raw January day, claiming personification of a new generation of Americans to whom he said the torch had been passed, the claim did not seem improbable. The eye of America, through the eye of a television camera, could not miss the striking contrast when the outgoing and incoming Presidents took their places on the podium that blustery inauguration day—the oldest man ever to serve in the nation's highest office; the youngest man ever elected to it. One could believe, or at least hope, the prophecy of Robert Frost would come to be, that Americans were to be legatees of "a Golden Age of poetry and power, of which this noonday's the beginning hour. . . ."

The men who would stand at the head of the New Frontier had been selected in the weeks after election in a nationwide screening process that paid more attention to quality

than to party. One of the big surprises was the naming of Robert S. McNamara, who had just become head of the Ford Motor Company and was a Republican, as Secretary of Defense. Dean Rusk was brought in from the Rockefeller Foundation as Secretary of State. Douglas Dillon, who had held high position under Eisenhower, became Secretary of the Treasury. Dillon, too, was a Republican.

McNamara had been a reluctant draftee. He said he didn't know enough about military affairs to head the Pentagon. "There's no school for Presidents, either," Kennedy replied.

One of the later Cabinet posts to be filled was that of Attorney General. Kennedy wanted brother Bob. Bob was hesitant. It would open Jack to the charge of nepotism. Joe Kennedy scoffed. Why would any one think that Bob had any need for a job just to keep him busy?

Joe Kennedy, himself, had to overcome Jack's initial resistance to naming Bob. But his father pointed out that as President he would need a man near him whom he could trust absolutely. Jack came around. "I want the best men and they don't come any better than Bobby," he told Dave Powers. But he

was ever aware of the implications of the appointment. Said the President-elect, wryly:

"I think I'll open the front door of the Georgetown house some morning about 2 A.M., look up and down the street, and if there's no one there, I'll whisper 'It's Bobby.' "

Bob finally surrendered at breakfast at Jack's house. At thirty-five, he was the second youngest Attorney General in American history. It was a risky selection for reasons other than nepotism. Union labor was not happy with Bob because of his role in the labor rackets investigation. Others believed there was more truth than humor in Jack's later comment that he "saw no reason for not giving Bobby a little experience before he goes out to practice law."

Bob, reportedly, didn't think it true or funny. And he joined the team.

So did Orville Freeman, the liberal midwesterner, as Secretary of Agriculture; Stewart Udall, young congressman and former basketball star, at Interior; Abe Ribicoff to become head of a new Department of Health, Education and Welfare. Ribicoff was a good choice from a political as well as personnel standpoint, but Kennedy's overall aim was embodied in a conversation one day with Schlesinger.

"All I want to know is: is he able and will he go along with the program?"

It seemed to be a Cabinet both willing and able, and over in the White House were such nimble minds as Sorensen and Fred Dutton and McGeorge Bundy—a Republican —and Schlesinger.

It was a sharp break, on the surface, with the faces of the Eisenhower years. But there are also private areas of the government of the American people, areas off limits to the public. One such was a holdover from the Eisenhower administration. It had to do with Cuba.

APRIL 17–19, 1961

Among the many crises raging around the head of the young President, none was so close to home as the Red tempest stirred in Cuba by the bearded rebel, Fidel Castro, who had managed to conceal the fact that he was a Communist until after his successful revolution which had the sympathy of most Americans.

President Eisenhower broke off relations with Castro January 3, 1961, but long before that he had agreed to a Central Intelligence Agency recommendation that Cuban exiles be given a chance to pull their sunny island back from the shadows of the Iron Curtain. The CIA began recruiting a brigade from the Cubans.

As President-elect, Kennedy was briefed by the CIA at Palm Beach. He reportedly expressed strong doubts. But six years earlier, CIA "guerrillas" had engineered the overthrow of the pro-Communist government of Jacobo Arbenz in Guatemala. Allen Dulles, the CIA chief, told Kennedy, "The prospects for this plan are even better than they were for that one."

Prompt action, Kennedy was assured, was imperative. Parts of the plan had been rumored by the news media. The brigade was fully trained and restless for action.

The clinching argument was that Russia soon would move to build up Castro's defenses. Already, Cubans were being trained as MIG pilots behind the Iron Curtain. Four Russian jet trainers had been sent Castro. But still Kennedy wavered.

Kennedy listened to the chorus but there was one loud and discordant note. It was the voice of Senator J. William Fulbright, chairman of the powerful Senate Foreign Relations Committee. "To give this activity even covert support," Fulbright said in a memorandum to the President, "is of a piece with the hypocrisy and cynicism for which the United States is constantly denouncing the Soviet Union. . . . This point will not be lost on the rest of the world— nor on our own consciences."

Kennedy invited Fulbright to Palm Beach and heard his plea for a policy of isolation and containment of Cuba. "The Castro regime," Fulbright said, "is a thorn in the flesh; but it is not a dagger in the heart." The President invited Fulbright to attend a final review scheduled April 4.

"What do you think of all this?" Kennedy asked Schlesinger, his adviser on Latin America. He replied: "I think it's a terrible idea." The world would sympathize, Schlesinger said, not with Goliath but with little David, and the operation "might recklessly expend one of the greatest national assets—John F. Kennedy himself."

"This would be your first drastic foreign policy initiative," he concluded. "At one stroke you would dissipate all the extraordinary good will which has been rising toward the new administration through the world. It would fix a malevolent image of the new administration in the minds of millions."

At a party celebrating Ethel's birthday, Robert Kennedy called Schlesinger aside. "I hear you don't think much about this business. You may be right, or you may be wrong, but the President has made his mind up. Don't push it any further. Now is the time for everyone to help all they can."

At the final review meeting April 4, the President polled the room. No one dissented. "Let 'er rip," said one man.

On April 12, the first question popped to Kennedy at his weekly news conference was about Cuba. He ruled out, "under any condition, an intervention in Cuba by United States armed forces."

"The basic issue in Cuba is not one between the United States and Cuba," the President said. "It is between the Cubans themselves, and I intend to see that we adhere to that principle. . . . This administration's attitude is so understood and shared by the anti-Castro exiles."

But it was not so understood. The Cubans, understandably emotionally fired with patriotism, could not be blamed for a natural assumption that the United States could not let them down. They thought the spoken denial of U.S. intervention was just for propaganda purposes.

The beachhead chosen was the Bay of Pigs in southern Cuba.

On April 10, the brigade moved to Puerto Cabezas in Nicaragua, the point of embarkation. At the wharf, the Cubans felt their first misgivings. Instead of well-equipped transports, they found old unpainted cargo vessels. The landing craft were open fourteen-foot boats powered by outboard engines. When he protested, one Cuban said he was assured that the landing parties would be protected by sea, by air, "and even from under the sea."

As the ships pushed off for Cuba, eight B-26s took off from Puerto Cabezas for the strike that was to knock out Castro's air force. It didn't. Castro's four jet trainers were unscathed.

President Kennedy, meanwhile, kept up appearances, going off with his family to Glen Ora, his rented estate in Virginia, for the weekend, the same weekend the brigade was at sea. He looked on from a rail fence at the first race of the Middleburg Hunt Race Association. "First time I've seen one of these steeplechases," he remarked. Then he left, saying he had to go back to the house "and do a little work." Later he hurried back to Washington. The next day was April 17: D-Day.

As the brigade neared the Bay of Pigs, radio stations in the United States began to pick up strange messages broadcast repeatedly by "Radio Swan." They said, "Chico is in the house. Visit him. The fish will not take much time to rise. The fish is red." This was the alert to the Cuban underground to rise. But as the invasion developed, Castro's police rounded up 200,000 rebel suspects in Havana. In one stroke, Castro erased all chance of an internal uprising.

The first frogmen to go ashore were startled when they encountered immediate fire from a militia patrol. Landing craft foundered on sharp coral reefs that had not been mentioned in the briefings. But the invaders managed to fight their way inland, and at dawn their paratroops landed successfully at interior positions.

But the rising sun exposed a rapidly developing disaster. Castro's air force, far from destroyed, was over the Bay of Pigs by 9 A.M. His fast T-33 jet trainers shot down four of the brigade's World War II B-26s in their first runs and sank two freighters carrying most of the arms, ammunition and communi-

*Presidents Kennedy and Eisenhower meet at Camp David during the first Cuban crisis.*

cations equipment. Commanders of the two remaining ships fled.

Soon nothing was left but the final escape valve to the Escambray Mountains. But between the remnants of the brigade and the sheltering hills lay eighty miles of swamp. Without food, water or ammunition, they were quickly rounded up by a 20,000-man Castro force complete with Soviet tanks. By April 19 it was over.

When the awful truth of the Bay of Pigs came home to Americans, Schlesinger wrote, "the nation was in a state of shock."

Kennedy was "aghast at his own stupidity," said Sorensen. But he took the disaster like a President. "There's an old saying," he told a post-invasion news conference, "that victory has a hundred fathers and defeat is an orphan . . . I am the responsible officer of the government and that is quite obvious."

Kennedy had also played into the hands of the critics of his youthfulness, giving them, Sorensen said, "a stick with which they would forever beat him."

But he also remained philosophical. "We can't win them all," he said. "I have been close enough to disaster to realize that these things which seem world-shaking at one moment you can barely remember the next. We got a big kick in the leg—and we deserved it. But maybe we'll learn something from it."

One lesson borne in on him was not to rely so unquestioningly on the military. He developed a healthy disrespect for the opinions of the so-called experts. He resolved to work much more closely in critical matters with those he felt he could trust. One such was his brother. Bob had not been in on the invasion discussions, but he was in the Monday morning quarterbacking. At a White House rehash he stepped outside for a breather with a key Kennedy aide. The aide told him to be patient. "When you're in a fight and

*Macaroni and friends on the White House lawn*

*Macaroni and friends on the White House lawn*

you're knocked off your feet, you don't come up swinging wildly because that's when you get hurt. I told him there would be plenty of time, plenty of opportunity in the future to prove to the world that we weren't a paper tiger. He thought for a moment and finally said, 'That's constructive. That's all he said.''

Not quite all. Bob later went up to assistant secretary of state Chester Bowles, who had written a memo opposing the operation, and said, "I hear you were against the invasion. From now on you were for it."

Jack Kennedy had found—again—the man he could trust above all others, the man who would do whatever the President bade above all others.

In retrospect, the President said: "Thank God the Bay of Pigs happened when it did."

There was still time to regroup, even though innocence had fled. Perhaps there would come a second chance. Perhaps even in Cuba.

## 1961—NOVEMBER 22, 1963

John Kennedy was elected by one of history's narrowest popular vote margins. Yet a Gallup Poll taken after he had been in office only thirty-nine days showed that seventy-two percent of Americans approved of the way he ran the office. Even the Bay of Pigs debacle apparently did not hurt the new President's popularity; by November, six months after the event, his Gallup Poll rating was up to seventy-seven percent. Why? Americans, one close associate of John Kennedy observed, "had confidence in him. They liked what he said and they liked his courage. But most of all they were young again."

There were swing sets in the White House Rose Garden; Caroline's pony, named Macaroni, grazed on the White House lawn. Laughter, gay and young, echoed in the White House nursery, music and song in the White House drawing rooms. Writers, artists, poets drew the interest and attention of the Kennedys, and thus of the nation. Pablo Casals, the cellist, played for the First Family and their friends. (The President's wife could become annoyed because his interest in opera and ballet did not match her own. Once she chided him that apparently the only music he liked was "Hail to the Chief.") A ballet troupe entertained White House guests. Authors, Nobelists, Pulitzer Prize winners came to White House dinners.

Part of the President's popularity resulted from his wit. His press conferences, televised live, had quick repartee. He rarely was without a comeback at any time. Just before the inauguration he spent a few days at the home of artist William Walton. During a hectic, appointment-filled afternoon, Marietta Tree, the diplomat, stuck her head in the door and said, "I'm terribly proud to have you for my President." John Kennedy looked up at her and said, "Well, Marietta, I'm terribly proud to have you for my citizen." On another occasion John Kenneth Galbraith complained that the New York Times had called Kennedy arrogant. "Why not?" shrugged the President, "Everybody else does." On a trip to France, during which his wife charmed the Parisians, he referred to himself in a speech as "the man who accompanied Jacqueline Kennedy to France."

While John Kennedy found it easy to turn his needle upon himself, he insisted that his office be accorded the utmost dignity. The rumpled, shirttail-out young congressman now would slip into a coat and tie whenever he was to be photographed at work and, according to Sorensen, "On more than one occasion he handed out coats and ties to his aides before our pictures were taken with him." The President was inclined toward lightweight, dark fabric, two-button suits, monogrammed shirts, PT-boat tie clasp. He

# "But most of all they were young again."

also believed that those outside the White House should have the same deference that he himself felt toward the office he held. While he was relaxing in the swimming pool of an exclusive Rhode Island club, a guest plunged into the water with him, greeted him as "Jack," rambled on about himself and at length said, "You can call me Chuck." "And you," the President replied crisply, "can call me Mister President."

If John Kennedy's thrusts could be sharp and well aimed when his dander was up, he also was quick to forget, and forgive. "He bore no man lasting grudge or envy and his readiness to love was instinctive," wrote Benjamin Bradlee, his close friend and long-time Georgetown neighbor. "John Kennedy reveled in love for the Irish patrimony that he had left so far behind. He laughed with love at the roguery of his grandfather, Honey Fitz, and his trip to Ireland [in 1963] was a pilgrimage to that love."

The full measure of John Kennedy's love was directed toward his children, Caroline and John Jr. He was a devoted father, but he really did not get to know his daughter until they moved into the White House. Indeed, one of Caroline's first words was "plane," for during her first three years her father was forever flying off somewhere. (And, conversely, his plane's name was *Caroline*.) They flew off many times during their White House years, too, but as a family—to Camp David, Hyannis Port, Palm Beach. At the White House, Caroline and young John became national personalities; members of the press corps took every opportunity to photograph and question them. One day Caroline wandered into the press lobby and said her father was "sitting upstairs with his shoes and socks off not doing anything." Such quotable tidbits were grist for a public hungry for information about the first children to

inhabit the White House in years. Like every devoted father, the President spent as much time with his children as possible. He called them in from play in the Rose Garden for a few moments of relaxation in his office during working hours, often while government dignitaries were present. While the First Family was visiting in Palm Beach, Caroline clomped into a Presidential press conference wearing a pair of her mother's shoes.

The American public's appetite for news about the Kennedys extended to in-laws, relatives, friends. The Kennedy manner of living, familiar to many, soon became known to all. One fascinated Kennedy guest, given perhaps to hyperbole, wrote in 1957 a set of "Rules for Visiting the Kennedys," which read in part:

"Prepare yourself by reading the *Congressional Record, US News & World Report, Time, Newsweek, Fortune, The Nation,* How to Play Sneaky Tennis and *The Democratic Digest.* Memorize at least three good jokes. Anticipate that each Kennedy will ask you what you think of another Kennedy's a) dress, b) hair-do, c) backhand, d) latest public achievement. Be sure to answer 'Terrific.' This should get you through dinner. Now for the football field. It's 'touch' but it's murder. If you don't want to play, don't come. If you do come, play, or you'll be fed in the kitchen and nobody will speak to you. Don't let the girls fool you. Even pregnant, they can make you look silly. If Harvard played Touch, they'd be on the varsity. Above all, don't suggest any plays, even if you played quarterback at school. The Kennedys have the signal-calling department sewed up, and all of them have A-plusses in leadership. If one of them makes a mistake, keep still . . . But don't stand still. Run madly on every play and make a lot of noise. Don't appear to be having too much fun though. They'll accuse you of not

*"He'd rather have walked the beach with Caroline at the Cape than have met Khrushchev in Vienna."*

TORBERT MacDONALD

taking the game seriously enough. Don't criticize the other team, either. It's bound to be full of Kennedys, too, and the Kennedys don't like that sort of thing. To become really popular you must show raw guts. To show raw guts, fall on your face now and then. Smash into the house once in a while, going after a pass. Laugh off a twisted ankle, or a big hole torn in your best suit. They like this. It shows you take the game as seriously as they do.

"But remember. Don't be too good. Let Jack run around you now and then. He's their boy . . ."

Their boy, and also the despair of Secret Service agents who moved in force to Hyannis Port whenever the President visited home. Early in the Kennedy administration three agents stationed themselves at intervals along the Yacht Club pier when the many Kennedy children went sailing. Faced with the dismaying sight of their charges scattered to the four winds all over the harbor and the fact that lifejacketed Kennedys float as well as the next person, the dockside staff shrugged and reduced its forces.

As the curious gathered, a fence was put up along the street by Jack's house inside the family compound. (Jacqueline Kennedy sometimes referred to it as the stockade). With scads of little Kennedys romping around the compound it could become difficult for the President to relax, which, after all, was his main purpose in visiting Hyannis Port. Very early on the morning President Kennedy was to take off for Vienna to meet with Soviet Premier Nikita Khrushchev June 3 and 4, 1961, a lawnful of Kennedy siblings massed on the compound for a pre-breakfast game. The game came to a frozen halt when a voice that had become unmistakable to a nation roared from an upstairs bedroom: "Godammit, knock it off!"

Wherever the President went, whether out on the family yacht, *Marlin,* or even to the home of his Hyannis Port neighbor across the street, the famous "black box," the box that contained the coded mechanism to set in motion the nation's nuclear striking force, was never more than a few footsteps away. Despite such Presidential encumbrances, despite the tight security, the endless parade of sightseers, the coming and going of helicopters and governmental limousines, there were occasions when it must have seemed almost like old times at Hyannis Port. On the Fourth of July in 1962, for example, the Barefoots and the Pansies decided to have their traditional softball game. The President was sidelined because of his back, but the originals who were still around were back at their old positions. The Barefoots, however, found themselves short of manpower—and the prerogatives of the Presidency were put to use. A call went out to nearby Otis Air Force Base asking the commandant if he had any hotshot softball players. He sent over three, one a former player with the crack Phillips 66 Oilers team, who smote baleful drives about the compound all afternoon. Despite the ringers, the Pansies were so confident of their customary victory they planned a postgame call to Richard M. Nixon to cheer him with news of their triumph. Nixon never got the call. The Barefoots won, fifteen to six.

If Hyannis Port could be hectic at times, the President's home in Middleburg, Virginia, was a place of almost total seclusion. The Kennedys rented Glen Ora while their own white stucco home was being constructed atop a nearby knoll called Rattlesnake Mountain. This was hunt country, and horsewoman Jacqueline Kennedy loved it.

A few of the Secret Service agents took riding lessons in case they drew the hunt detail, but in general they regarded Virginia duty as rather soft. The President, no horseman himself, rarely ventured out of Glen Ora except to attend Sunday mass or perhaps check on the progress of his house. He preferred to sit in his rocking chair on the flagstone patio looking off in the distance for long, silent periods. Often his children would snuggle in his lap and listen to the latest adventures of Charlie and Bruin. Bruin was an imaginary bear, invented by Caroline. Charlie was her pet Welsh terrier. The President weaved them both into an engaging bedtime story in which Bruin, who lived out in the woods of the hunt country, was always needling Charlie about the soft living at the White House. Charlie's defense was that he had awesome responsibilities—guarding a 134-room house and playing watchdog for the President of the United States and his family.

Jacqueline Kennedy, too, enjoyed the tendency of the Virginia residents to respect her privacy. She could, and regularly did, drive to town in a jeep, dressed in blue jeans and bulky knit sweater, to pick up the morning papers at the drugstore, scan new arrivals on the magazine rack, stroll down the street licking an ice cream cone, plop down on a packing case in the saddlery shop and go through the latest shipment of riding gloves, browse for French period pieces in the town's three antique shops. Often she brought Caroline with her for a bit of lunch. They took stools at the far end of the drugstore counter, ordered a pair of hamburgers well done, and engaged in the battle of the beverage:

"You'll have a nice glass of milk, won't you, Caroline?"

"No, Mommy, I want a Coke."

"Milk is better for you . . ."

"Please, Mommy, a Coke?"

A negotiated peace often resulted in a com-promise choice: chocolate milk. (Caroline's father, too, worried about her sweet tooth, apparently a Kennedy hallmark. Once, in the midst of a crisis with worldwide implications, he asked her: "Caroline, have you been eating candy?" No reply. Twice more he put the question, still no reply. Finally he said, "Caroline, have you been eating candy? Answer me—yes, no or maybe.")

President Kennedy was the picture of health but the fact was he suffered steady pain in his back. One close friend remarked that he never knew whether the President's wry smile was the result of hurt or amusement. He could joke about his pain (once remarking that its severity depended on the weather—"political and otherwise") and did his best to conceal it from the public. Before performing his annual spring chore of tossing out the first ball for the opening baseball game of the Washington Nationals, he would practice a few throws on the White House lawn. On a 1961 visit to Ottawa, Canada, he aggravated the back injury severely and used crutches around the White House. When appearing in public, however, he determinedly put them aside.

After the 1961 injury the President practiced a strenuous daily regimen of calisthenics, which not only strengthened his back but kept him muscular and held his weight to a steady 175 pounds. He also tried to get in a round of golf on weekend trips to Hyannis Port or Palm Beach. John Kennedy was a natural athlete and a good golfer. Playing a match with his friend "Red" Fay at Cypress Point, California, during the 1960 campaign, Kennedy hit a teeshot that headed straight for the hole. "Don't go in! Don't go in!" he pleaded, figuring a hole-in-one would in no way help a candidate trying to succeed a President whose addiction to golf had produced considerable comment. Ben Bradlee said the President had a Walter Mitty streak

sailing, for instance, they were more likely to discuss child-raising than NATO.

John Kennedy also had a personal as well as official relationship with his staff. One close aide observed, "The boss is never a hero to his staff. But John Kennedy was a hero to his staff on a personal basis, which is quite unusual because it was tough [work] and he was demanding; the return was far greater than anyone gave him." An enthusiastic Kennedy fan was his secretary, Evelyn Lincoln. Sorensen remarked that Kennedy had said, if he told Mrs. Lincoln, "I have cut off Jackie's head, would you please send over a box?" she would have replied, "That's wonderful, Mr. President. I'll send it right away." The President's feelings for a person extended to the rest of the Kennedy family. "If he liked you," said Dave Powers, "the rest of them would find a reason to."

According to Schlesinger, "Access to him was easy for his staff. In fact it was often easier to get him by the telephone than to get officials of the government or some of one's own colleagues at the White House." At the end of the morning and the end of the afternoon he ordinarily would leave a little time, and any member of his staff who chose could simply stick his head in the door for a Presidential audience.

This was not to say the President wasted time. Quite the opposite. He began his day by shaving in the bathtub and found similar ways throughout the day to cut corners. Some of his appointments lasted no longer than fifteen minutes. He kept his visitor on the subject, and when it was covered he might just stand up and say "good-bye." Apart from hours of work in his private quarters, he spent an average of fifty-five hours a week in his office. Still, he managed, unfailingly, breakfasts and lunches with his family and a daily dip in the pool with Powers.

in him "as wide as his smile" which showed most on the golf course. "When he was winning," Bradlee wrote, "he reminded himself most of Arnold Palmer in raw power, or Julius Boros in finesse. When he was losing he was 'the old warrior' at the end of a brilliant career, asking only that his faithful caddy point him in the right direction and let instinct take over."

John Kennedy adamantly refused to allow the press to observe him at golf. When relaxing he wanted nothing more than—to relax. He enjoyed the companionship of old friends, like Lem Billings and Fay and Chuck Spalding and Dave Powers and other amusing, easygoing pals from the old days. "The Presidency is not a very good place to make new friends," he once remarked. "I'm going to keep my old friends." One old friend, and frequent golfing companion, was Sir David Ormsby-Gore, the British ambassador. The President and the ambassador had no difficulty in dropping their official roles; out

"Jack works harder than any mortal man," his father once said, and then added: "Bobby goes a little further."

No question, Robert Kennedy set a torrid pace for his staff at Justice—and for the nation. He once took a fifty-mile hike to Camp David (during which he wore out even his big, black dog, Brumus, and the hikes quickly caught on as a national fad. Attorney General Kennedy's unaffected, shirt-sleeve style of work and life became the subject of newspaper feature stories and magazine articles. He often shunned his chauffeured limousine and drove to work in his red Ford convertible, Brumus on the front seat beside him, perhaps two or three of his many children with him. His wife would drop by the office—and stuff the suggestion box with notes, such as: "Why doesn't the Attorney General come home and have dinner with his children?" or "Fire J. Edgar Hoover." Once Bobby showed up at a White House reception for the judiciary with Mrs. Wright, an elevator operator at the Department of Justice who lacked a ride.

Apart from the predictable charge of nepotism that followed Robert Kennedy's appointment as Attorney General, there also were suggestions that he was unqualified for the post. Editorialized the New York Times: "If Robert Kennedy was one of the outstanding lawyers of the country . . . the situation would be different. But his experience as counsel to the McClellan [Labor Rackets] Committee, notably successful as he is, is surely insufficient to warrant his present appointment." Other critics agreed, and Bob himself said he had originally preferred a post "somewhere in the State Department or over in the Department of Defense." But, he said, his brother "felt that it would be very helpful if I went over to the Department of Justice as Attorney General. And that is what I ended up doing." Before his term was up the same New York

Times would find several occasions to commend the young appointee.

Bob selected as his deputy Byron "Whizzer" White, his brother's longtime friend who became John Kennedy's first appointment to the Supreme Court in the spring of 1962. Other men of eminent legal background and talent surrounded him in key Department jobs. And, as if to demonstrate to the nation that he could handle himself in a courtroom, Bob argued one case before the Supreme Court personally—the case which resulted in reapportioning legislatures on the principle of one man, one vote. Traditionally the Court does not question Attorneys General on the rare occasions when they present cases in person. Bob waived that privilege. He made his presentation without notes, then answered the justices' incisive questions without stammer. Legal onlookers were impressed.

Outside the courtroom, Attorney General Kennedy pushed through Congress a half-dozen anti-racketeering bills; saw his favorite project (some called it a vendetta), the prosecution of Jimmy Hoffa, end in Hoffa's eventual conviction; put the prestige of his office behind a new Juvenile Delinquency Control Act; brought to court Virginia operators of "whites only" private schools—the first time the government ever played the role of plaintiff in a case involving segregation.

It was in the field of civil rights that Robert Kennedy was most in the headlines as Attorney General. He sent federal marshals to Montgomery, Alabama, to protect groups of "Freedom Riders" who sought to integrate bus terminals; sent another force of marshals to the campus of the University of Mississippi (while his brother federalized the Mississippi National Guard) when riots broke out over the admission of Negro James Meredith; used the same tactics, with swifter and more peaceful results, a year later when two Negroes

registered at the University of Alabama; dispatched a top assistant, Burke Marshall, to Birmingham, Alabama, to negotiate a settlement between city officials and Martin Luther King; pressed without letup for a civil rights bill which eventually passed in Congress in 1964.

In his years at the Department of Justice, Robert Kennedy clearly established that he was not just his brother's brother. He was Attorney General of the United States.

There is an odd recurrence in the history of the Kennedy family. It wasn't until some time well after he had made his first million and his many movies that Joseph Kennedy Sr. was no longer known around his hometown as "Honey Fitz's son-in-law" and stood out in his own right. Similarly, it was a long time before Jack Kennedy stopped being an ambassador's son.

But as the White House days lengthened and Jack Kennedy became a household word —good or bad— as he and his kin popped up on TV tours of the White House, magazine covers and every other public showcase, one face was invariably missing. It was that of Joe Kennedy.

Those who used to claim Jack moved only when Joe pulled the strings now seemed to pay scant heed as to whether he was behind the scenes at all. He was and he wasn't.

"When Jack was President, he leaned very heavily on his father," said a high adviser in the administration. "He would call him at least once a day. I don't mean the old man had any influence on national policy, but Jack did seek his counsel."

And his father would give it. He said, for instance, that he thought the Bay of Pigs might have some silver lining. At least it had hardened his son and removed some Presidential baby fat.

But it was legitimate to wonder at times what influence the attitudes Joe had instilled in his son had over the actions of the grown President. For example, Joe was with Henry Luce, the publisher, the night of Jack's acceptance speech for the nomination and Luce conjectured that the candidate would have to have rather less than conservative views in economic affairs. Luce's purged comment of Joe's reply was: "How can you imagine that any son of mine would be any blank blank liberal?"

Schlesinger thought Joe's orthodox views on the economy in particular did have some force on the President's thinking, but was not sure of the degree.

The steel industry, at any rate, was left no room for doubt during the week of April 8, 1962. On Tuesday of that week, Kennedy's secretary, Mrs. Evelyn Lincoln, reminded the President that he had an appointment with Roger M. Blough, chairman of the board of the United States Steel Company, that afternoon at 5:45 P.M. This puzzled the President. Big Steel had reached a wage agreement with the steelworkers only a few days before, an agreement that Kennedy had happily announced was "noninflationary."

When Blough arrived (a few minutes late) he handed the President a press release that began: "Pittsburgh, Pa. April 10—For the first time in nearly four years, United States Steel today announced an increase in the general level of its steel prices."

Kennedy, believing himself double-crossed, barely kept his temper until Blough left, then rasped: "My father always told me that all businessmen were sons-of-bitches, but I never believed it till now." (The President later amended his quoted reaction, saying he had not meant *all* businessmen and should not have generalized).

What followed was a classic example of

government pressure on an industry which ultimately resulted in U.S. Steel and other companies that had followed its lead rescinding the increase. Kennedy then extended an olive branch, but his father's reaction to his son's humbling of an industry for which he once worked was not recorded.

DECEMBER 19, 1961

Whatever difference the two Kennedys may have had, their affection had remained a strong bond after Jack took office. Late in 1961 Jack flew down to visit his father at Palm Beach. On December 19 the President flew back to Washington, remarking he didn't think his father was looking well. But Joe always had taken care of himself, a friend once said. "He exercised, didn't smoke or drink. You have to admire the organized human material, not a bit of waste."

Later that December 19, Joe went out with Ann Gargan, the daughter of Rose's late sister, to play golf at the Palm Beach Country Club. "I don't really feel well today, but it must be the cold I've had," he said.

He wasn't using a cart to tour the course and on the sixteenth hole he said he felt ill and sat down. A caddy went for a cart. They took Joe home. He didn't want any doctors, but they were called, and he was rushed to St. Mary's Hospital where it was determined a stroke had paralyzed his right side. A priest came and administered last rites. The President was notified and rushed back to Palm Beach, hours after he had left it, aboard Air Force One. Once again the Kennedys were gathering at the bedside of a stricken member. There was a reminder of one not there. A plaque on the door next to Kennedy's room read: IN MEMORY OF JOSEPH P. KENNEDY JR. DONATED BY MR. AND MRS. JOSEPH P. KENNEDY.

Joe Kennedy once said of Jack: "I know nothing can happen to him. I've stood by his deathbed four times. Each time I said good-bye to him and he always came back." And this time it was Joseph P. Kennedy who came back. But he would never be the same again.

He wasn't able to walk for two and a half years following a long period of retraining at the Institute for Rehabilitation Medicine of New York University. It had taken heroic medical measures to preserve what was left of the body of Joseph Kennedy. For several weeks the President, said Dr. Howard A. Rusk, director of the Institute, wondered whether the treatment had been too heroic, that it might have been better if his father's stricken body had not survived.

But when Joe recovered enough to visit the White House and take obvious pleasure in his grandchildren, Rusk said he told John Kennedy: "See how much enjoyment he has in seeing you as President of the United States, his dream of a lifetime."

"Yes, that's true," the President replied.

Joe was able to travel only after a long rehabilitation at the Institute. "He was not a very cooperative patient," said Dr. Rusk. "He was a man with definite opinions. He would take a few minutes of drilling in speech therapy, then wave the therapist away." Someone suggested they teach him to write. Rusk shrugged. "He hasn't written anything in thirty years other than his signature. He dictates to secretaries. This is no time to try to teach him the alphabet."

The one word that remained to Kennedy was "no." When he said "no no no no" he meant yes, said Dr. Rusk. "NO NO NO NO" meant no.

Ann Gargan, who had had nurse training, became a constant attendant to him.

"Our days in Hyannis Port are pretty much the same," she said. "In the morning Uncle Joe goes into the pool—it's heated—after he's been through the morning newspapers and

"When Jack was President, he would call
him at least once a day."

the mail. After the lunch, he naps, then we go out for a ride in the car." Joe visited New York and Chicago as well as the White House, went out on his boat, watched pro football on TV and in time even dropped in at his office.

After December 19, 1961, Ann Gargan said she never played golf again.

OCTOBER 22, 1962

The U-2 spy plane whisked through the air high over Cuba, invisible in the early morning sky. Later, the film from its cameras was studied frame by frame, acre by Cuban acre. Then photo analysts found what they were looking for around San Cristobal.

At 8:45 A.M., October 16, the President in his dressing gown was still going through the morning newspapers and finishing breakfast in his bedroom at the White House when McGeorge Bundy brought him the bitter news the photographs revealed: Soviet technicians were building missile sites in Cuba, bringing half of the United States into the range of their nuclear warheads. Soviet assurances that they would not install offensive weapons in Cuba were blatantly false.

Since August, United States intelligence had been scanning Fidel Castro's island, looking for unusual military activity, tipped by increased shipments of technicians and equipment from the Soviet Union. President Kennedy personally doubled the number of U-2 overflights, and a special daily intelligence report on Cuba was started August 27.

When the Cuban arms build-up began with Soviet aid, it was billed as defensive. In September the President made the United States position clear. He said that should Cuba become "an offensive base of significant capacity for the Soviet Union, then this country will do whatever must be done to protect its own security and that of its allies." He backed

that up by asking Congress for standby powers to call up the reserves.

At 11:45 A.M. on the sixteenth, the President called in his top advisers to discuss the crisis. The group was later called the Executive Committee of the National Security Council, or ExCom. The meeting begun this day would continue for a week with recesses, would study and plan the answer to the Soviet move, would find Robert Kennedy closer than ever before to the power of the Presidency.

"In every crisis," Dave Powers said, "Bobby was the first man the President turned to, his best friend and his best adviser." In the Cuban missile crisis, Ted Sorensen said, "The Attorney General was the best performer, not because of any particular ideas he advanced, not because he presided (no one did), but because of his constant prodding, questioning, keeping the discussions concrete and moving ahead."

In the following days, every alternative was laid out for close examination and reexamination. Among them: 1. A limited surgical attack against the sites themselves. 2. A general surprise attack. 3. Learn to live with the missiles. The President squelched that one firmly. "We must bring the threat to an end," he said. "One way or another, the missiles must go."

Between sessions, his brother kept up his questioning, trying men of lesser rank who may have been reluctant to speak up in the sessions with the President and top leaders present. In long, private discussions with the President, Robert Kennedy said, "we discussed the possibility of war, a nuclear exchange and being killed. The latter at that time seemed so unimportant, almost frivolous."

President Kennedy himself said: "I guess this is the week I earn my salary."

As the debate continued, the greatest mili-

*Mrs. Khrushchev shares a happier moment in American-Soviet relations.*

tary build-up on U.S. soil since World War II began in Florida, under the cover of amphibious exercises. The Army moved in more than 100,000 troops. Tactical fighters flew in from all over the country. Asked how likely it would be that this force would be unleashed, the President calculated, "The odds on war are between one out of three and even."

When Defense Secretary McNamara proposed a naval blockade of Cuba, it met at first with little support—but ultimately it seemed like the best move. The President had already tentatively agreed. The Joint Chiefs preferred either an air strike or invasion. But work had already begun on the limited blockade against offensive arms. It was decided to call it a quarantine.

Partly to cloak the military activity, the President that weekend continued business as usual. He had political engagements planned in Ohio and Illinois. In Springfield, he laid flowers on Lincoln's tomb.

In his brother's absence, Robert Kennedy held the line.

"Bobby was at his greatest at this time," Powers said. "While we were campaigning, Bobby was there in the White House, and having Bobby there was like having your right arm. He kept the President informed of everything that was happening, and he fought for President Kennedy's position, which was the blockade, and which in the end was to prove to be the most successful."

The President was addressing a group of

precinct workers for Mayor Daley in Chicago when his brother telephoned Friday. "Bobby suggested," Powers related, "that things were reaching a peak and it was time to come home."

Feigning a cold, Kennedy headed back. But before leaving Chicago, he called Jacqueline and suggested that she and the children return to the White House from Glen Ora where they had been vacationing. In this time of great danger, he wanted his family with him. Later, Sorensen said, Kennedy asked his wife if she wanted to move to a place near the underground shelter to which the First Family would be evacuated. The answer was no. "If the attack came," Sorensen said, "she would go to his office and share with him whatever happened."

Kennedy, after a final meeting Saturday, went for a swim in the White House pool with Powers.

"You know," he said, "if it were not for the children, it would be easier to say that you would 'push the button' or something like that."

"I looked at him strangely," Powers said, "and he went on, 'Not just Caroline and John, and not just children in America, but children all over the world who have never lived, who will suffer and die, like you and I who have lived.' Then he left the pool and walked over to the mansion."

Powers did not follow him immediately, "because there are times to talk to him and times to keep still, and this was one of the times for keeping still."

A bit later, in the living quarters, Powers heard the President's voice: "He was reading Caroline a bedtime story, and I had the oddest feeling—standing there in the wings, not wanting to interrupt—that perhaps he thought this might be the last story he would ever tell her."

*John Kennedy had already met Premier Khrushchev in Vienna.*

The speech announcing the blockade was set for Monday, October 22, at 7 P.M. All day Sunday the President was in "a calm and reflective mood," Schlesinger remembered. On Monday, he conducted White House business as usual. At seven that night, in even tones, the President read:

"Within the past week unmistakable evidence has established the fact that a series of offensive missile sites is now in preparation on that imprisoned island . . . To halt this offensive buildup, a strict quarantine of all offensive military equipment under shipment to Cuba is being initiated."

The United States, he went on in a voice hard but calm, now called for "prompt dismantling and withdrawal" of the missiles from Cuba. Then he drew the line more clearly: "It shall be the policy of this nation to regard any nuclear missile launched from Cuba against any nation in the Western Hemisphere as an attack by the Soviet Union on the United States, requiring a full retaliatory response on the Soviet Union."

The speech over, the waiting began. That night he whiled away the time before dinner playing with Caroline. He and his wife dined by themselves. The next day, the Russian technicians in Cuba continued their work at a feverish pace. Photographs showed they had already unpacked forty-two missiles, and a number of jet attack aircraft capable of carrying nuclear bombs. Even more important, at least twenty-five Soviet ships, some of them carrying new missiles, dotted the Atlantic on steady course toward the Caribbean.

The Navy had discovered that each of the ships was being tailed by a Soviet submarine as they approached the waiting American fleet on blockade duty. The Navy put a destroyer on each of the subs. One of the destroyers was a World War II ship, the U.S.S. *Joseph P. Kennedy Jr.*

On Thursday and on Friday, the break came. Sixteen of eighteen Soviet ships had either stopped or turned for home. Only one entered the quarantine zone, and was allowed to pass. It was a tanker, no nuclear weapons aboard. In the situation room, one of Kennedy's advisers watched the plotted ships put about and said wryly, "That's nice. The Soviets are reacting to us for a change."

On Friday, October 26, Khrushchev sent a rambling, vaguely worded letter to the President. Yet in tone and on balance, it seemed to be conciliatory. Kennedy set his aides to drafting a reply. But on Saturday came another message from Khrushchev, this one making new demands. Weighing one against the other, the question was clear, which reply was the real Khrushchev? Robert Kennedy suggested the second letter be ignored. Reply instead to the first. If it worked, fine. If not, the way was still open for harsher action. The President concurred. Done.

The next morning Khrushchev replied. The Soviet Premier said the missiles would be removed. He added:

"We should like to continue the exchange of views on the prohibition of atomic and thermonuclear weapons, general disarmament, and other problems relating to the relaxation of international tension."

Kennedy read the letter on the way to mass. "He took the news with tremendous satisfaction," Sorensen said. "It was a beautiful Sunday morning in Washington in every way."

JUNE 26, 1963

To Ireland, the gentle green land, back, as President of the land his forebears had come to. It was a returning, an act of state, but, too, a pilgrimage of family, one Patrick Kennedy could never have imagined on the dock, in New Ross, in 1848.

Said Powers: "I was with the President in Ireland when he said, 'It is that quality of the Irish, that remarkable combination of hope, confidence and imagination that is needed more than ever today.'

"When we flew into Dublin from West Berlin that day, he said: 'Those who suffer beyond that wall of shame I saw in Berlin must not despair of the future. Let them remember, as I did, the boys of Wexford who fought with heart and hand to burst in twain the galling chain, and free their native land.' "

Dave Powers, so often with John Kennedy, returned to Dublin in 1968 to represent the family at a celebration of the President's fifty-first birthday.

*America's first Catholic President visits Pope Paul VI.*

JULY 26, 1963

At 7 P.M. the announcer said, "Ladies and gentlemen, the President of the United States." The image of John F. Kennedy, sitting at his desk in his oval office, appeared on television screens throughout the country. He spoke:

*Good evening, my fellow citizens:*

*I speak to you tonight in a spirit of hope. Eighteen years ago the advent of nuclear weapons changed the course of the world as well as the war. Since that time, all mankind has been struggling to escape from the darkening prospect of mass destruction on earth. In an age when both sides have come to possess enough nuclear power to destroy the human race several times over, the world of communism and the world of free choice have been caught up in a vicious circle of conflicting ideology and interest. Each increase of arms has produced an increase of tension.*

*In these years, the United States and the Soviet Union have frequently communicated suspicion and warnings to each other, but very rarely hope. Our representatives have met at the summit and at the brink. . . . But too often these meetings have produced only darkness, discord or disillusion.*

*Yesterday a shaft of light cut into the darkness. Negotiations were concluded in Moscow on a treaty to ban all nuclear tests in the atmosphere, in outer space and under water. For the first time, an agreement has been reached on bringing the forces of nuclear destruction under international control. . . .*

*The treaty initialed yesterday . . . is a limited treaty. . . .*

*Nevertheless, this limited treaty will radically reduce the nuclear testing which would otherwise be conducted on both sides . . . and it offers to all the world a welcome sign of hope. For . . . the achievement of this goal is not a victory for one side —it is a victory for mankind.*

*A war today or tomorrow, if it led to nuclear war, would not be like any war in history . . . as Chairman Khrushchev warned the Communist Chinese, "the survivors would envy the dead."*

*. . . So let us try to turn the world away from war. Let us make the most of this opportunity, and every opportunity, to reduce tension, to slow down the perilous nuclear arms race, and to check the world's slide toward final annihilation. . . .*

*Now, for the first time in many years, the path of peace may be open. No one can be certain what the future will bring. No one can say whether the time has come for an easing of the struggle. But history and our own conscience will judge us harsher if we do not now make every effort to test our hopes by action, and this is the place to begin. According to the ancient Chinese proverb, "A journey of a thousand miles must begin with a single step."*

*My fellow Americans, let us take that first step. Let us, if we can, step back from the shadows of war and seek out the way of peace. And if that journey is a thousand miles, or even more, let history record that we, in this land, at this time, took the first step.*

*Thank you—and good night.*

The President had said in his Inaugural Address that America should never fear to negotiate, and he had pleaded—challenged—both sides, "for the first time, [to] formulate serious and precise proposals for the inspection and control of arms." On September 24 the Senate ratified the Nuclear Test Ban Treaty, to match Russia's assent. President Kennedy counted it the greatest accomplishment of his administration.

AUGUST 7, 1963

"It is against the law of nature for parents to bury their children," the President once said. Children were his delight, his concern.

On this date, Jacqueline Kennedy gave birth to her third child, nearly six weeks premature, baptized hours later Patrick Bouvier Kennedy. Doctors noted almost immediately the baby's difficulty in breathing. It was a grim reminder of other troubles, a miscarriage in 1953, stillbirth in 1956.

*A bouquet for her mother in the hospital*

The baby was transferred immediately to the famed Children's Medical Center, Boston, the mother remaining at Otis Air Force Base Hospital on Cape Cod. The President rushed to Boston, as did Robert and Ted. Jean Smith went to Jacqueline's bedside.

Doctors placed five-pound Patrick in a large chamber to force more oxygen to the lungs. For a while, it seemed to work.

His head bowed, face heavy with worry, Kennedy haunted the hospital corridors, the courtyard where other worried parents, too, waited. His arrival brought crowds of nurses and pajamaed children to the front hall and windows. His entourage of Secret Service agents, aides, newsman seemed out of place in this house of hope and sadness.

But now, for the first time in the two days and one night of his vigil, he was seen to smile. On this second night, he decided to stay in special quarters in the hospital. Then, at 2:10 A.M., while most of the hospital slept, he was awakened and told his new son's condition had worsened. Two minutes later, he was joined by Robert.

At 4:04 A.M., August 9, Patrick Bouvier Kennedy died, after 39 hours and 12 minutes of life. Said a doctor sadly, "We fired all the guns there were to fire."

The next morning, Cardinal Cushing, who bound them together in marriage, who then spoke of the hidden future of joys and sorrows, pleasures, pains, now read the Mass of the Angels in the private chapel of his home. Wearing white, rather than the black vestments of requiem, the Cardinal spoke the saving words: "Because of my innocence You have received me and given me a place in Your sight forever."

Cardinal Cushing remembered of the President: "He wouldn't take his hands off of that little coffin. I was afraid he'd carry it right out with him."

*The glitter of the New Frontier: Pearl Buck, Robert Frost, Nobelists*

# Another America

The lights glittering through the windows of the old mansion, the limousines lining up at the portico were evidence for any to see that the Kennedys were hosting yet another ball.

In the East Room of the White House the Marine Band in scarlet tunics limited its repertoire to selections from *My Fair Lady* and *Camelot*, particular favorites of the President of the United States and his lady. In the lobby the Strolling Strings of the Air Force serenaded the swirling dancers. It was a timeless frieze, that ball of November 20, 1963 as old as the noble old house, as modern as the Broadway lyrics:

> *Don't let it be forgot*
> *That once there was a spot*
> *For one brief, shining moment*
> *That was known as Camelot. . . .\**

It was to be a gala season for the dwellers of the White House. Thanksgiving was coming and birthdays and Christmas. The President was going to be out of town for a few days but would be back in time for John Jr.'s third birthday the next Monday. He was going to Texas on a political trip.

He was going out to a different America, too, from the genteel and elegant world of that White House reception and the dignitaries of the Supreme Court and Justice Department who were there. Not that that different America was Texan. It wasn't any more Texan than it was of any other one place.

It was a world foreign to people raised, as the Kennedys were, with wealth and love. It was a world of hate, private or public hate, hate born of envy or frustration or despair or sickness of mind or sickness of spirit. It was a world where hate could explode in a knife thrust because of an accidental brush by a stranger in a tavern. It was a hate that

could nourish itself into a jealous rage at some one who had what the hater did not, did not have it because of impersonal fate or personal lack. Such a world could hate a Kennedy because a Kennedy had everything it had not. It was a deep irony—and it became a deep tragedy—that a father who had done what every father would hope to do for his children by achieving the American dream would see his children taken from him by those of this world of hate, this other America where lived the ones for whom the American dream was only nightmare.

The world is not always Camelot once one passes beyond its gates.

Those who had come to the White House, however, found Camelot all it had been advertised. The President passed smilingly among the quests. A young bride of a Justice staffer couldn't contain herself. "He's *beautiful.*"

Later John Fitzgerald Kennedy left the gaiety of the party. There was the work that never ends. He sat in his office, giving an hour to reading over foreign cables. Jackie, regal in a mulberry-colored velvet gown, had gone to the family quarters. This was her first public emergence since the death of Patrick. Her physician had expected that she might not begin public activities until the beginning of the New Year. But a recuperative trip abroad had worked magic. Only three weeks before, Jacqueline Kennedy had announced to her husband that she would accompany him on his Texas tour. That was to be tomorrow, November 21.

To Robert Kennedy, the reception had gone well. He had a moment of doubt, earlier in the evening, that somehow the minor members of the judiciary would not receive their due in greeting the President. Protocol required that certain homage be paid rank, and

*When he arrived—and when he left—little John was there to see him.*

the justices of the Supreme Court had received that at a small and private reception earlier. But lesser judges, some of them still out-of-joint because they had been herded among Justice Department minions at the annual receptions in 1961 and 1962, needed to be singled out for special attention this time and greeted before the others. The Attorney General had specified this be done, but he wasn't sure it would be. It had. And now he could look forward to Hickory Hill, and a private party celebrating his thirty-eighth birthday. In the afternoon, his staff had surprised him with a birthday gift: a Monopoly set.

For John the last moments of this day were spent free from the formalities and restraints that attend being President. Here, in his quarters, with Jacqueline, and with Bob and Ethel Kennedy, "Mr. President" became "Jack."

John Kennedy could use some buoying. No one in this intimate circle needed telling that he didn't relish this Texas trip. There were others, too, to whom he expressed his undisguised disenchantment with the whole idea.

At the reception, in greeting Secretary of the Treasury Douglas Dillon, the secretary had said, "This is hello and goodbye. We're leaving for Japan."

"I know," said the President. *"You're* off to Japan—and I've got to go to Texas. God, how I wish we could change places."

Pierre Salinger was also going to Japan with the hidden mission of paving the way for a Presidential tour in 1964. John F. Kennedy wanted to polish America's tarnished image in a land where President Eisenhower canceled a visit because of leftist riots.

To his press secretary, the President had said: "I wish I weren't going to Texas." But Salinger put this down to a weariness of travel. They had returned early the morning of November 19 from a trip to Miami Beach, and

though the brief sojourn left the President with the veneer of a light tan, in Salinger's view there was a tired man beneath it. But it was a time for reassuring: "Don't worry about it," said Salinger. "It's going to be a great trip, and you're going to draw the biggest crowds ever."

To Jacqueline Kennedy the trip would be her first to America's Southwest.

There was a note from her mother, wishing her daughter well on her journey. Enjoy yourself, she wrote. Jackie's mother-in-law did the same.

The awesome machinery of a Presidential move had been put into motion weeks earlier with advance men tending to the constellation of details.

In the time of McKinley, or Garfield, or Lincoln, when America was a young nation, an American President could go to a theater, attend a ribbon-cutting ceremony or board a train without some high-level logistics involved. But now, even to a Jack Kennedy who resisted red tape, it was clear that there were few moments for spontaneous trips or improvised diversions.

The morning began to slip away. It was 9:15 and Caroline was off for school. John Jr. went along to Andrews Air Force Base. John took his place in Helicopter One. The President waited for his wife. Even a President does that. Maj. Gen. Chester Clifton and Secret Service Agent Clint Hill were sent searching for her and found Jacqueline Kennedy near the Rose Garden, dressed in a white wool dress, selected in anticipation that it would be cool in Texas. However, it was going to be hot, quite hot, and the President fretted because he thought this would ruin the trip for Jackie and perhaps sour her on campaigning when the time came for that.

At Andrews, boarding Air Force One—the Presidential jet—John F. Kennedy bid his boy

good-bye. At 11:05 the plane was airborne, hurtling toward Houston at 550 mph.

Lost in the distance were the stone spike of Washington Monument, the broad mall beyond to the domed Capitol, the House on 1600 Pennsylvania.

> . . . once there was a spot
> For one brief, shining moment
> That was known as Camelot. . . .

In the weeks of October and November 1963, had there been urgings that John Fitzgerald Kennedy keep a cautious distance from Texas. These warnings came not from those who hated him, but those who loved him.

Byron Skelton, Democratic National Committeeman, couldn't hold back. Even if he were put down as an alarmist, it didn't matter. This trip—particularly Kennedy's scheduled visit to Dallas—worried him. There was a hatred for John F. Kennedy. He had tried to persuade Kennedy's aides to steer clear of Dallas, but failed. Senator William Fulbright of Arkansas, who had endured violent newspaper attacks during the 1962 campaign, personally urged the President to bypass Dallas, saying it was very dangerous.

But there was no avoiding it. Texas required special attention for a successful reelection campaign in 1964. Much mending had to be done there to escape serious losses as the result of an acrimonious struggle between Gov. John B. Connally, whose conservatism pleased the powerful, and his fellow Democratic Senator Ralph Yarborough, whose liberalism did not. Texas had twenty-five electoral votes, and if a Kennedy ticket in 1964, were to win them, much patching had to be done to seal the rent. Vice-President Johnson, with all the power he had commanded in his home state, still could not do it alone. It needed both of them—President Kennedy and Vice-President Johnson.

The political necessity, finally, muted the warnings of danger. But deeper still ran the conviction that America as a nation would cease to have meaning the day an American President felt he could not enter any city because to do so would be placing his life on the line. To be fearful of American streets, for the President to feel such jeopardy, is unconscionable. And so, forearmed and forewarned, or not, John F. Kennedy went. The President must.

He went to a land whose flat horizons occasionally were marked with billboards saying "Impeach Earl Warren."

If John F. Kennedy's name was not always cherished in the Deep South or in the unyielding conservative compounds of Southern California or the Protestant territory of the wheat-growing plains of the Midwest, at least it could be said that the association of his name with the Presidency was sufficient to bring it a measure of due respect. But were there children in classrooms of Kansas or Vermont or California who booed at the mention of the President's name? Quite possibly. And in Texas there were, too.

A child does not boo just because he is a child. He has to be taught. A killer, most students of the mind agree, is not born. He has to be made.

Above the roar in the darkened tunnel, a subway motorman hears a banging on his cab door. He opens it and is stabbed to death by a man he's never seen before.

A young girl is found strangled in a clump of bushes in a park. Police hold her young boyfriend. His suburban neighborhood is stunned. He was such a model boy.

A teen-age youth with a troubled past slashes his mother's underwear with a pair of shears. He is taken to a psychiatrist. The mother later stops the visits although the

Two First Families

doctor protests. Still later the boy rapes and kills a schoolmate.

A young war veteran, fond of Bible reading, strolls along the streets of Camden, New Jersey, dropping in here, dropping in there. He has a gun and in twelve minutes he kills thirteen people who were strangers to him.

Guns. Murder. Violence. Bonnie Parker and Clyde Barrow. John Dillinger. Machine Gun Kelly. It would seem there is an American way of death. Perhaps there is.

"Violence by gun is an American trait," said Dr. David Abrahamsen, a New York psychiatrist. "We are still living under the shadow of the Wild West where action was the easiest solution."

The gun, of course, did do much to make America: maybe more than it has done to wound America. The Spaniard, Pizzaro, and his countryman, Cortez, toppled vast empires with only a few hundred men not just because they were brave as well as predatory but because they had the gun and their foes did not.

The American Indian was edged back from the sea in part because the first arrivals from the Old World had guns and he did not, in part because there was a vast continent behind him to retreat into. But the white man followed and eventually conquered—with the gun. And as the white man pushed his way West, he left further and further behind the refinements of law that were one of his greatest cultural contributions. Law, rather, was made of steel, and its judge was too often the quickest hand and surest eye.

The imprint such a heritage can make on a people is most difficult of definition. Surely, however, it is there. The TV shows of violence may or may not have caused violence in contemporary America. They reflected it, however.

The infant turned child drops its rattle for—a toy gun. There was in the nation what psychiatrists call a gun fetish. Man, being an animal, is a descendant of predators. But man, unlike his fellow animals, can kill wantonly. That he is restrained from doing so is the result of the civilization he has developed over the ages of his evolution. And yet there are men who kill. Why?

When a child wants something, it seeks gratification instantly. If hungry, it cries till fed. If it wants to wet, it wets. Gradually, said Dr. Abrahamsen, the child learns that if it is to get, it must give. If it does not learn this, its self-control will be shallow, easy prey to its whims, be they conscious or subconscious.

"In criminal behavior we find an exceedingly great amount of family tension as well as emotional deprivation," said Abrahamsen. The twig, bent, twists as it lengthens. It twists privately but against a public background, one that may or may not be preceived with reality.

So the stimulation of the potentially homicidal mind may have social and political overtones. John Wilkes Booth believed he was murdering a tyrant who had oppressed the people of the South. But if he thought of himself as a public patriot, was he also a private psychopath? Booth did not live in an era that recognized such distinctions. A madman was a madman, period.

Later, in a psychologically oriented age, interpreters of behavior have given much study to the murderer and to the public murderer, the assassin. One psychiatrist, Frederic Wertham, called the assassin's crime magnicide: the killing of someone who is of stature.

"Public figures are symbols of what America stands for," said a criminal psychiatrist. "They become authority figures and as such have to be killed by those who feel frustrated by authority."

The assassin, said another analyst, "has the infinite ability to transfer hate from the individual who deprived him to the fountainhead, particularly to public figures who raise emotions."

John F. Kennedy was, in 1963, a public figure of stature who had raised emotions.

He was also a man of wealth, inhabitant of a hilltop world that most Americans see, if at all, through the gates, as it were. And how did Americans look upon their countrymen who had made fortunes when they had not?

In their great days, the Robber Barons regarded the accumulation of wealth as theirs by right. And, by right or wrong, they accumulated. This did not endear names such as Rockefeller, Morgan or Carnegie to the American lower-class ear. The names of some of the bloody labor battles of the late nineteenth century bore the names of some of America's newly rich families—the Pullman Strike—or of the factories and companies that made them rich—the Homestead Strike—or, later, the sanguinary Ford Strike of 1937. The bank founded by J. P. Morgan was bombed in 1920, and thirty were killed.

No one could avoid hearing about, if not seeing, the wealth that was growing in America. But any father could hope his son would grow some day to share it if he, himself, did not. Immigrant families could dream that their offspring would erase the hyphen that made them Irish-Americans or Italian-Americans and stand as simply Americans.

But there are those who see America's melting-pot society as not that at all but rather a pressure cooker. A child taught he is being raised in a land of free opportunity can also learn frustration when, as an adult, he finds it denied him. And denied the fruit of the tree, he may resolve to cut it down. The assassin is such a person. Doctors at Massachusetts General Hospital in Boston said the public killer has better control of his impulses than a "normal" psychotic. He wants his act to *mean* something.

At the Medical Center for Federal Prisoners in Springfield, Missouri, Dr. David Johnson studied twenty-seven men imprisoned for threatening the life of a President. There were things they had in common: unhappy homes, dominant mothers, absent or ineffectual fathers, a resentment transferred to their mother and later to male authorities and, finally, to the government and its leader.

There were, in mid-century America, groups as well as individuals that disliked what they saw and what they felt or imagined had frustrated them. There was fear—and hate—of Negroes, of Communists, of Catholics, of Jews, of those who would fluoridate the water or collect pennies at Hallowe'en for the United Nations to distribute food to the hungry children of the world. There were 100,000 names stored in the memory banks of Secret Service computers, people whose hate was so great they were considered potential assassins of a President.

There was political hate. Lyndon Johnson and his wife, Lady Bird, had been spat at in Dallas, and Adlai Stevenson had been spat at in Dallas, and now John Kennedy was making his way to Dallas.

Dallas had known for some weeks that President Kennedy was coming to town and for several days knew the route he would follow.

Pupils at the W. E. Greiner Junior High School were told they could be let out of school to see the motorcade pass nearby provided their parents came for them. The school was across the Trinity River from the Texas School Book Depository, about the last downtown building along the route. One teacher at the school, however, was not so permissive as the school's policy. She said:

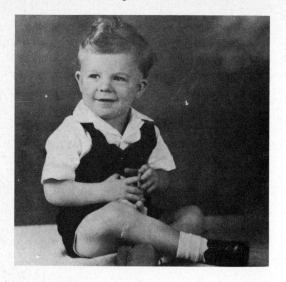
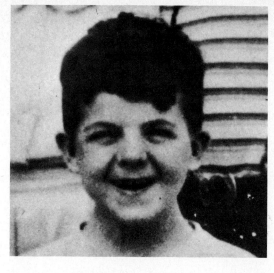

"Nobody here will be let out for that parade. I don't care if your whole family shows up. You still have to be in this class. He's not a good President, and I don't say that because I'm a Republican. It doesn't matter whether it's him or his brother Bobby. One's as bad as the other. You're not going. I'm not going. Period. If I did see him, I'd just spit in his face."

At this time in Dallas there lived, at 1026 North Beckley, a roomer known as O. H. Lee. He was born Lee Harvey Oswald. He was twenty-four years old.

And hundreds of miles away, in Pasadena, California, at 696 East Howard Street, there lived a young man of nineteen. His name was Sirhan Sirhan. He was an Arab, born in Jordan, and displaced in the Israeli-Arab war of 1948.

Oswald worked at the Texas School Book Depository, near the intersection of Elm and Houston streets. It was a modest job, but then he'd never had any job of any consequence. But he was known in a way other obscure workers are not: he had been a defector to Russia.

He had had his fill of it, as a factory worker in Minsk, and returned to America—with a Russian wife and infant daughter. But the marriage had its problems, and the wife, Marina, and daughter, June, lived at the home of Michael and Ruth Paine, in Irving, a community about fifteen miles from Dallas.

Before Russia, there was the United States Marine Corps, in which Oswald enlisted

October 24, 1956. There was little to distinguish his service career. He had pretensions of knowledge on world affairs and politics but was a high school dropout. He was court-martialed twice.

Oswald had left high school in Texas to enter the Marines. It was one of nine schools he attended in as many years of schooling.

As a child, he spent four weeks in New York's Youth House for Boys, undergoing psychiatric care. And as a young man, already in Russia, he tried to commit suicide when the Russians told him they wouldn't let him become a citizen.

Lee Harvey Oswald was alienated, isolated, malcontented.

And there was the other, much like him, growing up in Pasadena. There were many parallels.

Both came from troubled families. Oswald's father, Robert E. Lee Oswald, died two months before Lee Harvey was born on October 18, 1939, in New Orleans. His mother, Mrs. Marguerite Claverie Pic Oswald (once divorced, once widowed), married again in May 1945. For a time, she was to remember, her boy found in Edwin A. Ekdahl, her third husband, the father he never had. But that marriage collapsed at the beginning of 1948.

Sirhan Sirhan was the fourth of five boys born to Bishara and Mary Sirhan in the Musrara Quarter of Jerusalem, March 19,1944. The father was an employee of the city water-supply department, a post which placed him

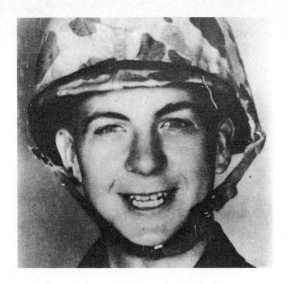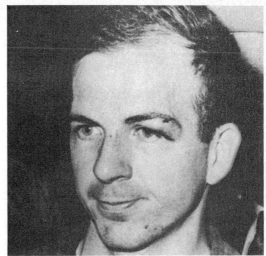

a cut above most Jordanian workers. It was 1947. In the next year, there was war. The father went to Amman to seek work. The mother ruled the family. And they remembered that when the father was there he punished his children with sticks and his fists. Once, it was said, he held a hot iron to one of Sirhan's heels.

While Lee Harvey Oswald and his wife and child were befriended by the Paines, who gave them great help, so were the Sirhans to benefit from compassionate Americans. The Sirhan family was brought to Pasadena, California, at the beginning of 1957, under the sponsorship of Dr. and Mrs. Haldor Lillenas, members of the First Nazarene Church of Pasadena. But Bishara Sirhan longed for his old land. He abandoned his family. Sirhan was then thirteen.

In Longfellow Elementary School in Pasadena, according to the recollection of a classmate, he was made the butt of jokes. He could not speak the language well and boys taught him dirty words, which he did not understand.

It was the sort of slight that also afflicted Oswald. When he was in the Marines some of the men in his unit nicknamed him "Ozzie Rabbit."

As a grade-school pupil, Oswald was a loner. It seemed that nowhere was he able to make meaningful, abiding connections with others.

And Sirhan? Before coming to America, at the Jerusalem Evangelical Lutheran School in Jerusalem, he was fifth in his class of twenty-six. A classmate remembered him, and said: "He had no really close friends."

Sirhan, said one boy who knew him in Eliot Junior High and John Muir High School, was a sort of non-person.

"Sirhan was just there. He didn't seem to be part of anything, so if he wasn't around, he would not especially be missed, and if he was, he would not especially be noticed."

There were those who could testify to a different side of Oswald, or Sirhan. Polite, courteous, quiet. If there was rage beneath this, it was a controlled impulse that seldom went beyond threats.

When frustrated, Sirhan was apt to withdraw or quit. He wouldn't play softball in high school because he couldn't understand the rules, according to Frank Matuzak, who was the athletic director.

"It is true that he did not perform well in American sports. He seemed to be a very good soccer player, but we did not have soccer at that time." said Matuzak. "When it would come to a game like softball, he seemed uneasy and would ask me to explain the rules and say, 'Mr. Matuzak, why is there this rule?' Maybe it was the rule about not leaving the base on a fly ball, or something like that. Perhaps he was caught off base. But that made him feel very inadequate. He wouldn't play. He said he could not play until he understood all the rules."

Lee Harvey Oswald, in the summer of 1952, boiled over. He and his mother moved in with his half-brother, John Pic, in New York City. This was the brother he had once chased with a knife, an incident Mrs. Oswald dismissed as "a little scuffle." Now, when it appeared that Lee and his mother might try to settle in for more than a visit, there was a quarrel, and Lee, defending his mother's side, threatened young Mrs. Pic with a pocketknife.

Oswald and Sirhan both saw the world from the aspect of men who could do something about it. Oswald seemed to vacillate between being a champion and critic of communism. He had his reservations about capitalism. Before defecting to Russia, and before leaving the Marine Corps, he applied for entrance to the Albert Schweitzer College in Switzerland, stating his reasons with his usual bad spelling.

*In order to acquire a fuller understanding of that subject which interest me most, Philosophy. To meet with Europeans who can broaden my scope of understanding. To receive formal Education by Instructers of high standing and character. To broaden my knowledge of German and to live in a healthy climate and Good moral atmosphere.*

Sirhan, so far as was known, did not keep as extensive a diary as Oswald but he was known to have jotted down a few matters that interested him.

He had become a member of the Rosicrucians, a philosophic group which essayed to develop "psychic powers."

He also, like Oswald, seemed to have had an interest in Russian. One report said he studied it while in John Muir High School. And Mrs. Totsey Boyko, who worked in a food store with Sirhan, said she had talked with him often and the thing she remembered most was his admiration for Russia. "He thought Russia was the best," she said, and she thought that he spoke a little of that language.

These were two youths of America; one who had left it for a time to live in another country, the other who had been brought from his homeland to live in the United States. But they both dwelled in the same world, a world where there was more have-not than have.

It was somewhat ironic that in the undistinguished, one-story boarding house in Dallas where O. H. Lee was staying—where rooms for the transients who came and went rented for seven dollars a week—there was a battered tin wastebasket. It was stained with old coffee and tobacco juice over its original decoration, the pennants of the leading universities of the nation. There was Notre Dame's, California's, Michigan's. And there was the crimson and white of Harvard.

One day of the Texas trip had passed and had gone well, and now, on the morning of Friday, November 22, President Kennedy was in a parking lot outside the Texas Hotel in Fort Worth, talking to an audience out in the open; seeing and being seen. Jacqueline Kennedy was in the hotel, readying for the flight to Dallas.

That morning, Lee Harvey Oswald hitched a ride with Buel Wesley Frazier, who also worked at the Texas School Book Depository. He hadn't expected to see Lee. Lee usually came to the Paine home in Irving only on weekends. For some reason he decided to come Thursday night instead. He wanted to get some curtain rods, he explained to Frazier. And when he got into the car Friday Oswald had a large brown package. Frazier was curious. "Curtain rods," said Oswald. They drove to Dallas.

In the Texas Hotel, President Kennedy, Jacqueline, and Ken O'Donnell had a few moments together before starting on the next leg of the trip. The crowd at Rice Stadium the day before, and the brief moments with people in the parking lot, led to talk

about the risks of public appearances. There were risks, no question about it. But the President told O'Donnell that "If anybody really wanted to shoot the President of the United States, it was not a very difficult job—all one had to do was get on a high building someday with a telescopic rifle, and there was nothing anybody could do to defend against such an attempt."

That this prophecy was realized scarcely two hours later does not need much repeating in a nation whose memory froze for a time on November 22, 1963. Was there any one of age who did not recall where he was when he heard? Recall as those somewhat older would remember the day of Pearl Harbor or the death of Franklin D. Roosevelt?

The events did not die with the years . . . the Presidential limousine . . . the President seated in the right-hand corner so that he would be closest to the people who wanted to see him . . . Governor John Connally of Texas and Mrs. Connally in the seat in front of Mrs. Kennedy . . . the President stopping en route downtown to shake hands . . . the enthusiasm along Main Street . . . Mrs. Connally turning to the President and saying, "Mr. President, you can't say Dallas doesn't love you". . . . the President answering, "That is very obvious. . . ."

The electric clock atop the Depository read 12:30. For John Fitzgerald Kennedy, descendant of immigrants, son of Joseph, son of Boston, son of Massachusetts, son of hope, son of ambition, son of politics, time stopped.

At Hyannis Port, Joseph Kennedy arose from his customary midday nap and, as was his custom, signaled to Ann Gargan to turn on television. It seemed curious that she was there. She was supposed to have left for a trip on this Friday. "There's been an accident," she said, intending to tell her uncle

as gently as possible that his son John was dead in Dallas. But nurse Rita Dallas caught her, and let her know that Mrs. Rose Kennedy wanted one of her sons, Bob or Ted, to break the news. Ann Gargan finished her sentence by saying the accident involved an automobile.

They told Joe Kennedy the TV set wasn't functioning. He was in no mood to read, so Ann played his favorite records to occupy him, and Rita Dallas set up a movie in the basement theater and gave him a milkshake with a sedative. The drug took little effect.

Ted Kennedy arrived. He was due for a speech in Boston, he explained, and stopped by to say hello. Eunice had come from Washington, too. Their mother was fearful that the dreadful news would kill her stricken husband. They sat with Joe as he had his supper. Eunice and Ted engaged in some artificial argument, just to keep the talk going.

Joe Kennedy, irritated, gestured for them to turn on the TV. Ted said it didn't work, and secretly pulled the plug from the wall socket. But the old man saw the dangling cord, gestured for them to connect the set. Ted, on his knees, did so. As the set warmed he reached into the back and tore out some wires. It was still no good, he said. It would be fixed in the morning.

More milk, more sedative, and Joe Kennedy went to sleep.

The next morning Mrs. Rose Kennedy went to seven o'clock mass, and decided to remain for a second mass. Ted attended the eight o'clock mass while Ann Gargan returned to the house to breakfast with her uncle.

Ted and Eunice came to the bedroom. They sat by Joe's bed. Ted said they'd all been to mass. And then he said:

"There's been a bad accident. The President has been hurt very badly." Then he told him.

*ask what you can do for your country."* JOHN F. KENNEDY

# The Third Son

During his recovery from his back operations, John Kennedy said:

"Just as I went into politics when Joe died, if anything happened to me tomorrow my brother Bobby would run for my seat. And if anything happened to him, my brother Teddy would run for us."

That was the way in the Kennedy family. In sailing in the young days Joe Jr. taught Jack who taught Bob who taught Ted. Now, in a time of grief in the nation and in the family, the torch had passed down to Robert.

Robert Francis Kennedy was not given pause, even in the convulsive trauma of John's death, to sob long for the brother with whom he had shared so much. There were things to do. The Kennedy family turned to Bob for support as a matter of rote. He functioned well, shunting aside his own anguish to comfort and steady the others, to annex the role of substitute father to Caroline and John, and particularly to devote his attention to Jack's widow, Jacqueline.

But the public Robert Kennedy, Attorney General of the United States, Cabinet member in the administration of the incoming thirty-sixth President, legatee of the Kennedy political mantle, had no appetite for those roles at first. They joked in Washington that Bob was not the number-two man in his brother's administration but number one-and-a-half.

Behind that joke lay a bigger truth. No brothers could have been closer, more single-minded in purpose, more united in their efforts. In times of Jack's greatest crises, he had turned to his brother. It was that way when their father suffered his stroke. It was that way when Jack and Jacqueline's son, Patrick, died in a Boston hospital; and it was that way during the Bay of Pigs. He was his brother's total partner; their bond was complete and mutual. "There was nothing he would not do for him," Pierre Salinger said. "His advice to JFK was sound and his judgment good. And the President knew that when he turned to Bob for advice he was going to get it straight, whether he liked the advice or not."

Their sister, Eunice, said it was an exaggeration to call them blood brothers. "First there was a big difference in years," she said. "They had different tastes in men, different tastes in women. They didn't become really close until 1952, and it was politics that brought them together. That's a business full of knives. Jack needed someone he could trust, someone who had loyalty to him."

None of this was a consideration for Robert Kennedy in those early dark days of 1963 although "What Will Bobby Do Next?" was a question pondered by columnists and the country almost as soon as his image as one of the principals in the unforgettable drama of John's funeral had faded from the television screens.

The private Bob Kennedy became and remained the family's fount of strength, its underpinning. The public Robert Kennedy, regarded by many as the best Attorney General the country had had since Francis Biddle twenty years earlier, became diffident and withdrawn. "I don't know, I don't have the heart now," he told a colleague who asked solicitiously when he would return to his office. He took long, lonely walks, sometimes for hours.

"After the assassination, I got the feeling—he never said so but I feel it—that he wondered about the existence of God," said one friend. His thin, boyish face took on new lines, the carefree manner left him. "Bob grew up then, fast," another friend said.

He performed his duties but was abstracted. By chance he walked into President Johnson's first Cabinet meeting—held while his brother's coffin rested on a catafalque in another part of the White House—and sat moodily while

# "Their associations had been distant and barely polite."

the President pleaded for support. Two days later, when the President stood before Congress and eloquently asked "Let us continue" the work begun by John Kennedy, Robert sat stony-faced, staring straight ahead.

There was speculation that he would resign from the Cabinet, that he would not resign, that he would run for governor of Massachusetts, that he would accept any number of posts out of government.

The relationship between Lyndon Johnson, the anomaly in the New Frontier, and Bob Kennedy—a symbol of the frontiersmen—aroused public curiosity and private concern. As Vice-President and Attorney General their associations had been distant and barely polite. Johnson had admired John F. Kennedy but he was convinced that Robert had attempted to sabotage his nomination for the vice-presidency in 1960. Many tried to dissuade Johnson from the notion without much effect. Other biographers have said that most of the early problems between the two men stemmed from misunderstandings—including the issue over the nomination—that usually could be traced to one aide or another. The misunderstandings later grew into an almost open feud.

As William Manchester put it in *Death of a President:* "To the new Chief Executive Bob Kennedy represented a problem which was unique in the history of Presidential succession.

Here was a Cabinet member who looked like, sounded like and thought like the slain leader; who had been his second self; who was one of his two chief mourners . . . clearly he regarded the late President's brother as a formidable obstacle."

But Kennedy did not resign. Nor did the President ask him to. In fact, it was Johnson who helped rekindle Robert's interest in the public arena.

In those first months after Dallas Ethel Kennedy did her best to bring her husband out of his depression, without notable success. Swim, she said. Ski. Do the things he loved best. He reluctantly followed through with a few days at the Florida home of Cabinet mem-

ber Douglas Dillon, and a few more on lonely slopes in Colorado. "Without Ethel," an intimate said, "Bobby might well have gone off the deep end." Thanksgiving—six days after the assassination—and Christmas, ordinarily gay, contented days at Hickory Hill for the family-centered Kennedys, were times of despondency. In fact, one friend observed, it was not until March, 1965, when Bob scaled Mount Kennedy—the 13,900-foot Yukon peak named for his brother—that he was able to shake the gloom. "Bob had to climb that mountain," the friend said. "It was the final catharsis for him."

In mid-January 1964, the President asked Kennedy to undertake a diplomatic mission in Tokyo, consulting with President Sukarno of Indonesia whose troops had been threatening the Federation of Malaysia. It was the beginning of an election year and perhaps concern for Robert would woo Kennedy factions to Johnson. Bob had been sent by President Kennedy to talk with Sukarno in 1962, and their meeting had been pleasant and productive. The Asian trip, whatever else it did, served to bring Bob back.

In his brother's Presidency, Bob had stopped in Japan on the first leg of a four-week world tour as good-will ambassador. One afternoon he went to Waseda University. Trying to make their way into the university's memorial hall to deliver a speech, Bob and Ethel were mobbed by enthusiastically friendly students. But inside, members of an ultraleftist student organization drowned out his remarks with hoots and catcalls. "It was the first time anyone had heard the cry 'Kennedy Go Home,'" said staff aide John Seigenthaler who was there with him. The Kennedy people borrowed a police bullhorn and Bob, with icy calm, tried to speak.

Finally a student cheerleader climbed the platform and closed the meeting with the school song. That was 1962.

There was need for a bullhorn on the 1964 trip, too. But only so that Robert could talk over the *banzais* he received. On his return to Waseda University 1,000 cheered themselves hoarse, particularly when he said Jack "was not only President of one nation. He was President of young people around the world. If President Kennedy's life and death are to mean anything, we young people must work harder for a better life for all the people of the world." They hurrahed in Manila, Indonesia, and Malaysia. The journey was not merely a trip. It was a voyage of discovery.

As the journey progressed, Kennedy began to feel that the youth of the world was look-

ing to him to carry on his brother's work. His personal secretary, Angie Novello, said then: "This trip has helped him get away from himself." And to find himself.

Nicholas Katzenbach, his deputy attorney general, thought he saw a change in Bob. "I don't think Bob had any great sense of dynasty, but when Jack died Bob felt he had a responsibility to carry on what Jack had started."

Bobby, himself, had said: "I think you have one time around and I don't know what's going to be in existence in six months or a year. I think that there are all kinds of these problems [to] which you are here on earth to make some contribution of some kind. I think if one feels involved one should try to do something."

But, for a still grieving Robert Kennedy, to do what?

Robert Kennedy was still in his deepest sorrow when James Hoffa was convicted in March 1964. The staff presented Robert with a wallet embossed: "We, the jury, find the defendant guilty as charged." But nothing could cheer the Attorney General then. He said only "nice work," to Walter Sheridan, the aide who had carried the biggest load.

He felt he had done all he could as Attorney General. The able staff he had gathered could carry on. He had won the biggest fight of his legal career, finally convicting teamster boss Hoffa. The civil rights bill he had espoused at last was heading for passage. Months before, with Jack Kennedy in the White House and Ted Kennedy newly in a Senate seat, someone mentioned to Ethel that Bob had won no elective office. "Of course he will run for office," his wife said, "he'll have to to prove he can win."

In Ethel ran the same competitive strain that was in Robert. Their eldest daughter, Kathleen, named for an aunt she had never

seen, once asked Ethel whether it was better in touch football to play offense or defense. "Well, both are good," she said, "but Mummy likes offense best. That way you can make touchdowns."

They both had the combative instinct, to be sure, the kind that makes touchdowns. And admirers. And enemies.

Everyone had his opinion of the Kennedys. Those who knew them. Those who pretended to. Those who didn't. Enter the arena, walk into the light, prepare to be judged. The Kennedys understood this. Set a pace. Some will admire you. Others will knock you for grandstanding. Have ambition. It's the American dream to get ahead. But there will be some who say you are buying your way. Have drive. There will be those who applaud your

energy. There will be those who call you ruthless.

Fill in the blanks. The Kennedys are_____.

. . . arrogant . . .? compassionate . . .? ambitious . . .? opportunist . . .? Americans . . .? Catholics . . . ? honest . . .? blunt . . .? warm . . .? cold . . .? competitive . . .?

Find an adjective. It's been used already.

Of the three elder brothers, Bob Kennedy earned the most expletives.

Ruthless. The word came easily to his enemies. He laughed about it. One morning, before leaving for the office, he took a copy of the *New York Times* upstairs to Ethel. "That's my good deed for the day," he said. "Now I can go back to being ruthless." And on the campaign trail, in the way he always had of turning humor onto himself, he took note of a baby crying in the audience. "I'm not ruthless, but if you don't stop crying, I'll come over there and. . . ."

Ruthless? "I think he is the most compassionate person I know but probably only the closest people around—family, friends and those who work for him—would see that." Jacqueline Kennedy said that. "People of private nature are often misunderstood because they are too shy and too proud to explain themselves." She said that, too.

But the people who sat in judgment of the Kennedys—it seemed to be a national pastime—were polarized. You liked them or you didn't. They drew unreasoning love—and unreasoning hate.

Ted missed this searching analysis, partly because he was a latecomer on the national scene and partly because there was so much to talk about his elder brothers.

People noted that Jack walked erect. Bob slouched. He was often photographed with his tie loosened, his sleeves rolled up. Jack was urbane, polished and slid easily into his many-sided role as President, politician, diplomat. Bob, more a doer than a thinker, plainly felt unease in the backslapping world of the politician. He was blunt to the point of rudeness: introspective, given to moods of silence and solitude, was aloof. His inborn shyness was a major personal obstacle to competition in the political world. In conversation he was a counter-puncher. When he first met Burke Marshall, who was under consideration for head of the civil rights division at Justice, he opened the conversation by saying hello. Marshall, no man to use two words if one would do, said hello. Silence. More silence. Then Alphonse and Gaston got down to business. If they didn't waste words, they didn't waste time, either.

If nothing else, Bob Kennedy was a realist. Of his ability to draw crowds he said: "In the politics of the country at this moment, this is a fad."

And the man who had lost two brothers and a sister said: "Existence is so fickle. Fate is so fickle. Not only can this feeling pass, but also your existence can pass. Robert Frost once said that you go on the tennis court to play tennis, not to see if the lines are straight. So you do what you can while you're here and the future will take care of itself. I'm not going to guide my life by what may or may not come to pass."

All the Kennedy brothers, with the partial exception of John, exemplified the underlying theory of progressive education: learn by doing. Only when they encountered a problem in practical terms did its intellectual significance become interesting to them. This was true of Bob Kennedy probably more than the others. At one point he felt he should know more about Red China and started what became the so-called Hickory Hill seminars. Each week he would invite an expert in a particular field over for the evening—with only the proviso that he not be from within government—and hold open house in the big rambling mansion for friends and acquaintances. Ethel Kennedy asked the most questions.

A member of the Kennedy administration characterized Bob as considerably more primitive toward ideas, people and institutions than his brother. "He doesn't have the literary background or interests the President does," he said at that time. "Bobby has a limited, but growing, acquaintance with intellectualism. The more he is exposed, the more he is impressed." Said Seigenthaler who was Kennedy's confidential assistant at Justice, "He personally came to appreciate the arts. There was a period in which he really concerned himself with deeper reading, like Camus. In the mornings he often played Shakespeare

readings (while showering) and there was usually music in the house: Broadway plays, semi-classical."

Some professorial types doubted the intellectual depth of a man who force-fed himself culture in the bathroom. Others pointed out it was better than listening to the hiss of a shower. In any event, it was learned—and retained.

Bob once spent an evening with Richard Burton and Elizabeth Taylor in Rome. When the Welsh actor, noted for his Shakespearean virtuosity, recited the St. Crispin's Day speech from *Henry V* ("We few, we happy few . . ."), Kennedy caught him in a slight misquotation. Burton insisted he was right. So did Bob. He was.

Ted Kennedy had been written off as intellectually the least able of the three. But his record in the Senate, where he was better liked than either of his brothers had been, did much to render such judgment hazardous. John said Ted was "the best politician in the family." George McGovern, Democratic senator from South Dakota, said of Ted: "He is more conservative and orthodox politically than Bob. In the broad sense, Ted has the greatest personal appeal of all the Kennedys."

A close family friend, echoing the prevailing Washington sentiment, said, "In affability, I'd say Ted was first, Jack second and Bob third. The social amenities came hard to Bob and he despised stuffed shirts. He couldn't ignore one. When he found one he usually cut him apart. He would bear down so hard on an issue he thought was wrong, he'd leave no stone unturned in trying to correct it."

As Attorney General, Bob Kennedy felt there were no more stones he wanted to turn. "I'm tired of chasing people," he said. "I want to go on to something else."

At Hickory Hill, so full of memories, he set his thoughts down in an introduction to the memorial edition of Jack's *Profiles in Courage:* "If there is a lesson from his life and from his death, it is that in this world of ours none of us can afford to be lookers-on, the critics standing on the sidelines."

In South Vietnam in the summer of 1964 the struggle against the communist Viet Cong was intensifying. American troop strength doubled and redoubled from the 16,000 men who were there when Jack Kennedy died. One June afternoon at Hickory Hill, Bob sat in his study and wrote a letter to President Johnson in longhand (he couldn't type) and underlined *Personal* on the envelope. He volunteered to replace Ambassador Henry Cabot Lodge in South Vietnam, should Lodge resign to return to politics. The President was grateful and told Robert so in a warm telephone conversation, but urged him to continue as Attorney General to handle increasing civil rights problems. Privately the President commented the assignment was too dangerous. "The last thing I'd want is another Kennedy killed." But to Bob he was appreciative.

"In that one exchange, both men hurdled the barrier of pride and a few of the tripwires of suspicion that separated them," one reporter wrote. But it wasn't really so. Lyndon Johnson still had what he referred to as "the Kennedy problem." He was trying to mold an administration of his own, proceed with programs of his own, preparing for a campaign to be elected President in his own right. But he met with strong antagonisms from the young idealists Jack Kennedy had attracted to Washington who thought, as one cruelly put it, Camelot had become Dogpatch.

If this was unfair to a man trying to establish his own government and image, it nonetheless was understandable in the resentment of those who mourned their dead leader. The nation itself seemed to be thinking more of the Kennedy past than the Johnson future. The very landscape of the country changed. Cape Canaveral, named by Spanish conquistadores in the days of discovery, became Cape Kennedy. Idlewild Airport in New York became Kennedy Airport. Countless streets and parks across America took the family name. Kennedy books crowded the shelves. As can happen in a world inhabited by humans, the mourning could become more crass than dignified.

There was no end to Kennedy books, Kennedy dolls, Kennedy phonograph records, Kennedy buttons, Kennedy photographs, Kennedy dinner plates, Kennedy everything. The movie fan magazines shelved their gushy peeping at the heroes of the screen and ground out meaningless, often defamatory, accounts of the Kennedys, Jacqueline, Bobby, Ted, their parents, their children, their lives. Pierre Salinger called it an insidious invasion of the Kennedys' privacy and spoke of "the revolting exploitation of Mrs. Kennedy, primarily by the movie fan magazines. Issue after issue, these magazines ran pictures of Mrs. Kennedy on the cover with suggestive titles. When you read the articles, they said nothing. But the titles said just enough to sell the magazines."

No matter what their content, this reiterance of Kennedy, Kennedy, Kennedy, pounded into the national consciousness—and Lyndon Johnson. The Kennedy problem. It grew.

Democratic politicians, sensitive to sympathy that enveloped the whole Kennedy family, began talking of Bob as a running mate with Johnson. Without any overt moves on his part, Kennedy got 25,861 write-in votes for Vice-President in the March 10, 1964 New Hampshire primary, while LBJ got 29,861 for President. There were impressive write-ins for the Attorney General in the Presidential primaries in Illinois, Pennsylvania, New Jersey, Massachusetts and Nebraska.

Lacking word from Johnson, vice-presidential aspirations were out for Bob Kennedy. What else then? Return to Massachusetts and run for office? In the Senate he would be junior to his own younger brother even if Massachusetts voters could be sold on a tandem Kennedy team. Wait in limbo two years for that election? What in between? There was another possibility. Democratic leaders in New York had been searching for a candidate with the strength to oppose Kenneth Keating in the fall. Bob Kennedy? What of his residence? There was nothing in the consitution to bar it—the only requirement was that a candidate be inhabitant of the state at the time of election. Kennedy was not unreceptive.

June 19, 1964, tragedy struck another Kennedy. Once more the clan had to gather in affliction, once more word had to be relayed to the Hyannis Port compound, to long-suffering Rose and her paralyzed husband that a son, their youngest, was critically hurt.

As it was with Joe, the oldest son, and Jack, the second son, Ted Kennedy was hurt in the line of duty—in his case, political duty. The 32-year-old senator voted at 7:49 P.M. in Washington for the civil rights bill that Bob Kennedy had worked so hard for. Then he took off from Washington National Airport to attend the Massachusetts Democratic State Convention at West Springfield. He was to accept its nomination as candidate for a full-term Senate seat once held by Jack, the unexpired part of which he had filled the past two years.

The private plane, piloted by Edwin Thomas Zimny of Lawrence, Massachusetts, bore Senator Birch Bayh, the young Indiana Democrat who was to be the convention's keynote speaker, Mrs. Bayh, and Edward Moss, Senator Kennedy's administrative assistant. Zimny

*At Palm Beach, Ted walks again with his wife, Ted Jr., three, and Kara, four.*

filed an instrument flight plan to Barnes Airport in Westfield. As he neared the field, the pilot asked for a weather report. Foggy, visibility poor. He was cleared for a radio beacon approach to Runway 20. At 10:49 P.M. Zimny reported he was over the radio beacon.

Out the left window, Bayh saw black objects. He thought they were storm clouds. They were the tops of 65-foot trees.

"Are we in trouble?" said Mrs. Bayh.

"No, everything's fine," her husband replied.

Kennedy, the only one who didn't have his seat belt fastened, turned in his seat, half standing. The plane ripped into the trees and plunged into an apple orchard. Zimny died in the crushed cockpit. Kennedy and Moss sprawled unconscious in the aisle. The Bayhs squirmed through an eighteen-inch window and pulled Ted after them. A farmer who lived nearby, Robert E. Schauer, arrived soon and raced for help. Moss died in the hospital at nearby Northampton seven hours later.

"It's amazing he is alive," one of the doctors said of Ted Kennedy. He had suffered fractures of the spine in six places. He had two broken ribs. He had many cuts and bruises on his hands and legs. Condition: critical.

A woman behind the counter of the coffee shop at the hospital spoke for the nation. "How much," she asked, "do these people have to give?"

Not the life of another son, it seemed, as Ted's condition slowly improved. But for months he lay strapped in a special frame, immobilized. He spent the time reading, learning. Once free of the frame, there were long periods of retraining muscles, building up his once sturdy body. He vowed, however, that he would walk into the Senate and take his back row seat, third from the left, when the second session of the Eighty-eighth Congress convened in January 1965.

Robert's family responsibilities were all the heavier with Teddy disabled. "The relationship between Teddy and Bob has become far deeper in the last six months," said one of the Kennedys of the time before the accident. "Teddy has become to him now what Bob was to Jack. They talk every morning and every night, wherever they are. They're like crossed fingers."

Bob spent the weekend after the accident with his family. The following Tuesday, the day before he was to leave on a European trip to West Germany and Poland for Johnson, Bob issued a brief statement. He said he appreciated the loyalty and friendship of the New Yorkers who had urged him to run. "However," he said, "in fairness to them and to end speculation, I wish to state that I will not be a candidate for United States senator from New York."

Lyndon Johnson, still publicly sitting out his decision on his running mate, plainly didn't want Bob on his ticket. Then the Republican National Convention, in San Francisco's cavernous Cow Palace, picked Senator Barry Goldwater as its standard-bearer. That cinched the President's decision. Goldwater was a man he could beat, could beat easily, could beat without the help of a Bob Kennedy.

The President pulled the switch in typical Johnson style. He invited the Attorney General to the White House, greeted him cordially, and so there would not be any misunderstanding, read Bob his prepared verdict: "Ever since San Francisco I have been thinking about the Vice-Presidency. You have a bright future, a great name and courage, but you have not been in government very long. I have given you serious consideration but find it inadvisable to pick you."

Then he asked that Bob announce publicly that he was not interested in the vice-presidency. Kennedy refused and murmured as he left "I could have helped you, Mr. President." The President said the parting shot was wistful. Bob's friends said it was sarcastic.

On July 30, the President assembled the press. It would be inadvisable, he said, to select "any member of my cabinet or any of those who meet regularly with the cabinet." Exit Attorney General Kennedy.

In a speech to Democratic Congressional candidates the following month Robert said: "I must confess I stand in awe of you. You are not members of the cabinet and you don't meet regularly with the cabinet and therefore you are eligible to be Vice-President." He waited for the laughter to subside and added: "I decided to send a little note to the cabinet members saying "I'm sorry I took so many nice fellows over the side with me."

In New York state, brother-in-law Steve Smith—Jean's husband—tested political waters for Bob. Smith, a reticent man with the look of a sophisticated schoolboy, found the temperature warm.

The day following Johnson's ruling on Bob there gathered at Hyannis Port a group of close friends: David Hackett, a Justice Department aide; W. Averell Harriman, Undersecretary of State for Political Affairs, and Schlesinger. Two principal topics were discussed as the men sunned themselves: would there be a place for the Attorney General in the Johnson administration? If not, what were his alternatives? Kennedy made it clear he had no reluctance to get out of politics for a year or so. After all, he had seen twelve years of furious activity. But he also said he saw no indication there would be an opening for him in 1965 or 1966. A friend said Bob "was looking down the well," and he felt strongly inclined to try for the Senate if the nomination could be had without a protracted fight. Appearances, all agreed, were

most important. "We had to be sure," said a key Kennedy man, "that this thing didn't look like a coup by the Irish Mafia."

In a way, Kennedy's design on the New York Senate seat was as audacious an undertaking as Joe's buying the Merchandise Mart years earlier. It opened the 39-year-old Attorney General to new and bitter charges of ruthlessness, opportunism and carpetbagging. The dictionary says a carpetbagger is "any person, especially a politician or promoter, who takes up residence in a place to seek special advantage for himself." Kennedy commented: "Don't they know any other word?"

But Kennedy's inclination to run had hardened into determination to do so. The reason for confidence, as one Kennedy aide said, was "the oldest reason in politics—you can't beat somebody with nobody and the anti-Kennedy people had nobody."

"If this was a steamroller," someone put it aptly, "it was a steamroller sitting on a steep hill. All they had to do was release the brake. There was almost nothing standing in their way."

Almost nothing. But there was the matter, first of all, of Bob's residence. He had the home in Virginia. He also had a home in Hyannis Port. But he was not an inhabitant of New York.

The ubiquitous Stephen E. Smith took care of that nagging matter. At Glen Cove on Long Island stood a house, much like Bob Kennedy's at McLean: roomy, surrounded by trees, with a swimming pool, five bedrooms on the second floor, several on the third. A far cry from the Boston apartment where Jack established residency years before. Smith leased the house and Bob's residence problem was solved.

On August 21, Mayor Robert Wagner of New York publicly endorsed Bob Kennedy, citing his "personal eminence," his "heroic" advocacy of civil rights and "the dazzling magic of his name." Four days later, at Gracie Mansion, the mayor stood by Robert's side as Kennedy announced his candidacy.

That same month in Atlantic City, the salt-water taffy New Jersey resort, the Democratic National Convention met. The party's theme song, "Happy Days Are Here Again," boomed through the world's largest auditorium. To a degree they were. But over it hung a long shadow of sorrow. Each mention of John Kennedy's name brought thundering applause. It was also a convention staged, produced and staffed by a master director, Lyndon Baines Johnson. To eliminate any possibility of a stampede for Bob Kennedy, Johnson instructed Democratic National Chairman John Bailey to schedule an emotional film on John Kennedy's life and achievement on the fourth, rather than on the second, night of the convention—after the vice-presidential nominee had been safely chosen. The president milked the last bit of suspense from the convention by waiting until his final words to announce his choice. He took great delight in discussing the various prospects with Hubert Humphrey, as though he were a disinterested observer. "It's like a guy calling the girl next door—who he knows is madly in love with him—to ask the phone number of the newest broad in town," complained the senator. He learned he had been chosen only a few hours before the delegates did.

Not until August 27, the final day of the convention and Lyndon Johnson's fifty-sixth birthday, did a Kennedy go before the delegates for the first time. Robert stood there in the bright lights, as flashbulbs stabbed the scene like harsh fireflies, his eyes moist and distant. The delegates, whose rendering of "Happy Days Are Here Again" had been tempered by the realization that Lyndon Baines Johnson was their choice chiefly because of that day in Dallas, for thirteen minutes poured out their emotions in applause as if it could penetrate the flame and the concrete and the cool earth of that grave in Arlington.

His introduction to a twenty-minute filmed eulogy to President Kennedy began:

"When I think of President Kennedy I think of what Shakespeare said in *Romeo and Juliet:*

*When he shall die*
*Take him and cut him out in little stars*
*And he will make the face of heav'n so fine*
*That all the world will be in love with night*
*And pay no worship to the garish sun.*

The delegates wept.

That fall began for Robert Kennedy a replay of 1960, but now he was the candidate. He showed up at fish markets and bakeries before dawn, plant gates when the evening shift left. Between the convention in early September and the election in November, he went to every corner of the state. It was estimated up to one million people saw him personally in the first few weeks.

Was it the allure of his name? Was it curiosity about this man about whom so much had been said? Was it sympathy? Whatever the answer, Kennedy was a political hurricane.

Women smeared his face with lipstick, ran beside his car to grab and kiss his hand. In Plattsburg, a man gripped him around the neck and pounded his back, yelling "Bobby! Bobby!" He was showered with flowers, confetti and rice as his open convertible passed. Often, while standing in the car to shake hands, he was almost pulled over backwards. An aide then grabbed his belt and another a leg to keep him upright.

Much of the time he traveled in the *Caroline,* the 1960 campaign plane. Relman Morin of The Associated Press traveled extensively with Bob Kennedy as he had with John.

*Adulation on the sidewalks of New York*

"When I first came aboard," said Morin, "he was at a window seat toward the rear of the plane, looking out. His eyes were more deep-sunken than usual, it seemed to me. Almost a year had passed since the assassination, but the grief and shock were still there in his expression. He did not appear to be looking at anything specifically, just staring through the window. From time to time, if a member of his staff asked him about something you could see that he pulled himself together. The expression of sadness changed and he was the alert, hard-driving guy who had worked so hard for his brother.

"It was a rather eerie moment . . . the same plane, the same pilot and co-pilot as in 1960 . . . the same table where we had written so much about his brother . . . Neither of us said a word during the forty-five minutes or so to his first stop. On the stump, he changed. His expressions ranged from grim conviction to thoughtfulness to a kind of gaiety. It occured to me that a hard, exhausting campaign was exactly what he needed. But back on the plane again, he sank into that deep moodiness, with the far-away expression in his eyes, staring out the window. At nothing, I suspect."

On the way to another stop, Morin asked Bob how he explained the size of the turnouts. "He thought for a moment," Morin said, "then said, 'I think they are looking at me and seeing my brother. I think they feel somehow that if I am elected, things will somehow be as they were before ' . . ."

The dizzying pace took its toll on tempers. Bob Kennedy, always less tactful than his brothers, once exploded at a minor miscue. "What I need is an s.o.b. like me to run my campaign."

Writer Gore Vidal, an acid critic of Bob's whose stepfather is also Jacqueline Kennedy's stepfather, wrote about Robert: "His obvious characteristics are energy, vindictiveness and a simple-mindedness about human motives which may yet bring him down. To Bobby the world is black or white. Them and Us. He has none of his brother's human ease; or charity."

As always, his wife Ethel matched her husband's punishing schedule, even though she was in the latter stages of pregnancy. She spent two to four days a week doing everything from pounding the pavement in Harlem to making two-minute speeches by telephone to meetings of women Democrats. Jack Kennedy used to say, "With Jackie by my side, I can do anything." Bob said "With Ethel by my side, nothing is impossible."

Of the wives of the Kennedy brothers, Ethel threw herself into campaigning with the most zest. Once Joan Kennedy, Ted's wife, had accepted an invitation to christen a ship in Massachusetts. But when the time came, she was six months pregnant and begged off. Ethel took her place. At a reception afterward, she acknowledged applause by saying, "My sister-in-law was supposed to be here, but she couldn't come. She's pregnant." Ethel herself at that time was only a few weeks away from delivering her eighth.

Hostile signs met Bob's eyes at every stop. One said "New York doesn't want LBJ's leftovers." Some commuters wore buttons: "Connecticut Carpetbaggers for Keating." Bob would snap: "Who grew up in Westchester County? I did, that's who. Keating didn't."

Keating, a one-time Latin teacher, graduate of Harvard Law School, was a formidable opponent for Bob. Keating had been in Washington eighteen years. He ran on his record, and one woman's comment was typical: "Keating has done a good job and I don't like seeing a young whippersnapper come along and try to take it away from him."

The President came in to help Keating,

telling crowds to "vote for Bob Kennedy for Senator and don't forget Hubert Humphrey and Lyndon Johnson either." Kennedy, in turn, plugged the Johnson-Humphrey ticket as if there had been nothing in their past to separate them.

The *New York Times* supported Keating, saying, "New York may soon have only one senator and Massachusetts three, two of them Kennedys."

For weeks a television debate had been discussed, and finally a date was set. Keating's aides contended that an afternoon deadline passed with no word from Bob that he would show up. But at 7:30 Kennedy knocked on the studio door. Keating, having bought a half-hour spot, was inside "debating" an empty chair. Kennedy said: "I was invited to appear and I am here to debate him." He was barred from the studio. So Robert also bought a half-hour and went on immediately after Keating. He had the last word.

Bob was spending money on a grand scale but, as was a common Kennedy trait, never seemed to have any fraction of his wealth in his pockets. (Joe Sr. once took a mammoth check to Cardinal Cushing as a donation to a hospital fund and didn't have enough for cab fare.)

Early in the 1964 campaign, Bob went to buy a plane ticket. He didn't have any money, and offered the girl at the counter a check.

"I'm not allowed to take a check without identification," she said. Kennedy didn't have any.

Seigenthaler, who was with Kennedy and told the story, said: "Did you ever hear of Robert Kennedy? He's Attorney General."

The girl shook her head.

Finally a man behind them said "I'll write a check for Mr. Kennedy," and did.

It was only a temporary setback in the massive Kennedy campaign.

On November 3, when New Yorkers at last spoke their will, Robert Kennedy was elected a United States senator with 3,823,749 votes to Keating's 3,104,056. "We didn't have as much money as he had," said Keating. "I wish the situation hadn't arisen that made me run for the Senate in New York," said Robert, "but I'm looking forward to serving— to serving the people of New York." Kennedy ran far behind Johnson's margin over Goldwater in the state, but he had made it to Washington a second time—on his own.

And in Massachusetts, Ted Kennedy was reelected by an even bigger margin than he had been two years earlier to fill John's seat, getting 1,716,907 votes to his opponent's 587,663, far more even than his brother's '58 landslide. The opponent? Leverett Saltonstall, one of the Brahmins from the family old Joe Kennedy had jockeyed to meet years before. Never before in the history of the United States had one family produced three senators.

The inkwells were full and there was the traditional sand for blotting on each desk as the United States Senate convened for the first session of the Eighty-ninth Congress on January 4, 1965. Every one of the 584 seats in the galleries above the great chamber was taken—first choice to families and friends of senators, the rest to the public.

In the galleries were the Kennedy women —all except Jacqueline, who had just returned to New York from a skiing vacation, and Rose, who was at her ailing husband's side in Palm Beach. Joan Kennedy, Ted's wife, was in a front row at an opposite side of the Senate galleries.

Ted Kennedy had arrived in Washington the day before after spending Christmas at Palm Beach. His hospitalization had lasted exactly 180 days and he was ready, as he had vowed, to walk into the Senate chamber unaided. But first he went with his wife and daughter Kara to Arlington and stood with bowed head by his brother's grave. When he stepped, stiff but steady, into the Senate chamber, he appeared thinner than usual. He was fifteen pounds underweight.

Sixteen days later, in sub-freezing temperatures, Bob Kennedy also paid a visit to Arlington, head bowed by the grave. He picked up a chunk of snow and crushed it. Then he left for Johnson's inaugural. At the 1961 inauguration, Bob and Ted had been in upholstered seats in the front row of the inaugural platform. This time their seats were unpadded benches in the seventh row of the section reserved for senators.

Seldom had so many Capitol Hill eyes been focused so intently on a single Congressional newcomer as were on Bob Kennedy. Was this office, as many believed, just his way of staying in the game for the big Presidential stakes in 1968 or 1972?

As Ed Guthman, Bob's friend and press secretary, put it: "Here was a completely unique figure in American history. No one had ever played the role in government that Robert had played. There was a sharing of power, not in the literal sense but in spirit and in a spiritual way." Was this a man geared to being at the bottom of the heap among ninety-nine others?

Kennedy noted his Senate desk position: "I had better seats to *Hello Dolly,* he quipped to fellow backbencher Joseph Tydings of Maryland. And he showed his impatience with the niceties of lawmaking at one meeting of the Senate Labor and Welfare Committee when Senator Jacob Javits of New York and Wayne Morse of Oregon were flyspecking about the wording of one sentence in a resolution. "Oh, hell," Bob exploded finally. "Why don't you just flip a coin." And then he stalked out.

On the floor, too, he acted unsenatorially. Normally when a senator wants to butt into another's speech, he can expect the sugary response: "Yes, I yield to my good friend, the distinguished senator from. . . ." Bob Kennedy, on a request to yield, would simply nod or wave his hand.

But as his colleagues soon found out, he did put himself to the task of representing his state, concentrating in his freshman year on legislation for minority groups and the poor. He joined with Republican Javits in co-sponsoring an amendment that would allow 100,000 non-English-speaking Puerto Ricans to exercise their franchise. And later he poured his efforts to improving the Bedford-Stuyvesant slum area of Brooklyn. The *New York Times* commented that in contrast to many of his colleagues whose interests were linked with money and power forces, Kennedy made the ghetto areas his special constituencies and that they in turn "considered him their special senator."

Fred Dutton, once again a Washington lawyer, described the differences between John Kennedy and Robert Kennedy as senators: "Jack was more interested in international relations, education, economic matters. Bob's priorities were the poor and discrimination. Bob could talk other things, but where he really warmed up was when talking about the poor. I think Bob got involved out of the civil-rights fights of the '60s and got to feel strongly about the lower part of society. That turned off the middle class and Bob knew it. A Robert Kennedy administration would have been far more concerned with social and domestic policies than Jack's was—social rather than economic, domestic rather than international. Bob's emphasis was fairly pronounced. He hurt more—identified more deeply with the poor."

Robert Kennedy's impatience did not endear him to fellow senators.

"Basically, he was very unpopular generally with congressmen because he stirred things up and congressmen don't like to be stirred," said Nicholas Katzenbach. "I don't think he played senatorial politics and they didn't like him for that. Still people who opposed him strongly had genuine respect for him. Bob

was not a patient negotiator. He wasn't a half-a-loaf man."

As he settled into the job, Kennedy's staff was relatively small—a personal secretary, one administrative assistant, two legislative assistants and a pressman. But in a three-month period of 1967 there were eighty-three names on Bob Kennedy's Senate payroll, more than half of them full-time staff members. This was far above the funds provided by the government and Bob paid the rest out of his own pocket. "No senator had a staff and the number of volunteers he had," said Abraham Ribicoff, then senator from Connecticut. "He had a staff like the President has; he had position papers prepared, he gave careful work and attention to the things he was interested in. The research they produced was almost unmatchable."

He invited them to Hickory Hill on weekends—to work, not play. Richard Reeves, writing in the *New York Times* Magazine in 1967, said: "The only complaint—whispered of course—they ever make about Bobby is his habit of departing for a weekend with Ethel and the children and leaving the staff with

enough work to make sure they won't have time to play with their own kids. 'Give me a memo Monday morning on that poverty bill' is not a young father's idea of an ideal Friday afternoon farewell. 'You have to be willing to take a hell of a licking if you want to work for Bob Kennedy,' Ed Guthman said. 'But it's worth it,' he added."

Adam Walinsky, one of the brilliant young staffers Kennedy attracted, said "of course it's worth it. I wish I could find the words. Have you ever read about Lee's lieutenants during the Civil War? The feeling they had for him? I mean it's just that. It swings. We're part of an adventure."

John Kennedy's men had said the same thing about him.

Because of his impatience with the ofttimes boring business of the Senate, Bob Kennedy darted into the chamber only to vote or partake in a debate that particularly interested him, like a bird that touches down only when there is a fat worm. His every speech on the floor was heralded with a snowstorm of news releases in the press galleries on the third floor of the Capitol. When Bob walked into the chamber, there invariably was a rustle in the galleries as visitors leaned over the railing, pointing and saying, "It's him, it's Bobby." More than once there were girlish squeals, when the loosely kempt mop of hair bobbed into view among the bald and graying senators, bringing a frown to the presiding officer. In his walks through the Senate Office Building, or en route to his car, Bob Kennedy received the adulation of a movie star, obliging with autographs, pausing for pictures.

The public, with its habit of visiting the Senate where fireworks come seldom, often missed Kennedy when he was at his best— at committee hearings—where he put to full use his talents as a prosecutor. There was such a drama, for instance, during the cities hearings of August 1966.

Mayor Samuel Yorty of Los Angeles was a witness. He had testified that his jurisdiction, in solving his city's problems, was limited and he did not have all the facts at hand. Robert Kennedy became enraged.

"I do not need a lecture from you on how to run my city," Yorty retorted, flushing. "I think you should confine your questions to things that are possible for me to answer without bringing a computer."

Kennedy: "The mayor of Los Angeles I would like to have stay here through all of these hearings, and I think he could safely do so, because as I understand from your testimony you have nothing to get back to."

Yorty: "That is sort of a ridiculous statement. . . ."

Relations would remain soured between Robert Kennedy and the mayor of Los Angeles.

The exchange with Yorty, clashes with others, and Bob's constant exhortations that the government ought to do more, got him headlines. So did his extracurricular activities.

In 1965 he went to South Africa, then wrote a magazine article entitled "Suppose God is Black." It set off shock waves.

Cynics said Bob's associations with Negroes, such as Olympic decathlon winner Rafer Johnson were calculated to gain political image and advance his ambitions to become President. But Robert had met Johnson in Kansas City in 1962 and admired him as a man and a successful athlete. Johnson became a frequent visitor at Hickory Hill and was roped into the athletic contests that were as regular a feature as breakfast and dinner. On one occasion he teamed with columnist Rowland Evans in a tennis doubles with Bob and David Hackett. It was the first time Johnson had ever played tennis. Kennedy and Hackett were leading 5–1 in the second set and Bob teased Evans, "How do you like getting beat with the greatest athlete in the world as your partner." But as the joking went on, Johnson got better and his side wound up winning 7–5. "It sure killed Bob to lose that game," Ed Guthman said later.

In his early months as senator, Bob performed the ritualistic act of climbing Mt. Kennedy. With him went climbers Jim Whittaker, a conqueror of Everest, and Barry Prather and five others.

"I began the climb," Bob wrote later in a magazine article, "I remembered my mother's last words to me: 'Don't slip dear.' . . . Then I began to think 'What am I doing here?' I stopped and held onto the mountain with both my hands and remained there. Again I thought 'What am I doing here? What can I do now?' I had three choices: to go down, to fall off, or to go ahead. Then I heard Jim Whittaker say, 'Come on, it's not much farther.' I really had only one choice. . . .

"When I returned to Washington I opened a letter from a young girl who had written, 'I understand you are going to climb a moun-

For Robert, Mt. Kennedy was a catharsis.

tain. I don't know why. I asked my daddy why. He doesn't know why either.' "

Why does any man climb a mountain? Said Robert:

"I think Jim Whittaker summarized the answer when we reached the summit. He turned to me and said 'I am glad there was the last difficult part—this climb and mountain have some meaning now for President Kennedy.' "

Liberals found Bob Kennedy's Senate record impeccable. He gave his support to Medicare and the Voting Rights Act of 1965, he criticized cigarette manufacturers for not stressing the hazards of smoking, and he spoke out strongly on problems of minority groups, the Negroes and Indians.

But the crisis was not only in the cities. There was Watts in 1965, the first of the recurring seasons of long hot summers that left smoking scars in the major cities of America. (Many people began buying guns for protection after Watts including one man near Los Angeles who picked up a cheap $30 pistol, an Iver Johnson.) There was the widening gap between generations—or so it seemed. For if there was no more of a chasm than there ever is between the young and their parents, the differences were more vocal. At the Berkeley campus of the University of California student dissent tore the campus.

The voices of the young were protesting the growing war in Vietnam, protesting what they regarded as the hypocrisy of their elders in preaching a democracy that they did not practice. Bobby Kennedy appealed to many of these young. He became increasingly vocal against the Vietnam war, a fosuc for many of the so-called doves.

Once, in the dark times after his brother's death, the nation had wondered what words applied to Robert Kennedy. One was being heard more and more often: President?

*Should he run?*

# *Again*

The voices were many and strident. The young said Run. The experienced said Wait. The disbelievers said Act. The professionals said Don't. The cynics said, "Hell, he's been running since the day he was born."

Everywhere the pressures were on Bob Kennedy. Events were hastening the timetable for the Presidential accession his supporters assumed for him. When Lyndon Johnson was elected in 1964, it was assumed that there would be no White House vacancy until at least 1972; no party had ever denied an incumbent President renomination. But in election year 1968 the country was riven by one of the deep and emotional issues of its history. Mainly as a result of that division, Johnson's popularity was at the lowest point since he was elected. So low, in fact, it made it ironic that he had been elected in the greatest landslide any President ever recorded.

That issue was the war in Vietnam, a troublesome, diffused conflict. Robert Kennedy stood among the critics, aligned in opposition to the President. No issue stirred him like the war. Not civil rights. Not James Hoffa. Not the urban crisis. Not the poor. Not anything.

"Although the world's imperfections may call forth the acts of war, righteousness cannot obscure the agony and pain those acts bring to a single child," he wrote. And he did not mute his own participation in the events that led to the war. "I was involved in many of the early decisions on Vietnam," he said, "decisions which helped set us on our present path. It may be that the effort was doomed from the start, that it was never really possible to bring all the people of South Vietnam under the rule of the successive governments we supported. . . . If that is the case, as it well may be, then I am willing to bear my share of the responsibility, before history and before my fellow citizens."

He regarded with concern the course the United States pursued in Vietnam, what he felt were its missed chances for peace. In a speech he said: "There are three possible routes before us. The pursuit of military victory, a negotiated settlement, or withdrawal." Kennedy plainly favored negotiations, pointing out that the result would have to be "less than a victory for either side."

But in the Senate, he was only one voice in a hundred. His assignments as a freshman senator gave him a poor base from which to influence policy. Fellow Vietnam critics, like Senators William Fulbright, Eugene McCarthy and Wayne Morse, sat on the powerful Foreign Relations Committee. Senator Kennedy had no such platform. He served only on the District of Columbia Committee, the Government Operations and Labor Committee and the Public Welfare Committee. When he spoke on the Senate floor, it was often to empty desks and vacant galleries. So Robert Kennedy went more and more before the public to voice his dissent.

Was it enough simply to speak out?

For a long time, apparently, Robert Kennedy thought so. He was not only aware of the party tradition that said, "Don't challenge an incumbent President" but felt that such a challenge would splinter the Democratic Party. So he rejected suggestions that he become a candidate for President. In March 1967 he was prepared to give an affidavit to that effect to keep his name out of the Oregon primary. All that year, he said he would support Lyndon Johnson for reelection.

There came a time when the boyhood nickname "Bobby" didn't quite fit Robert Kennedy anymore. It stuck, of course, among close friends from the old days and, for quite different reasons, among people who disliked him. There were plenty of both.

*Eventually Joseph Kennedy was able to go to a ball game.*

John Kennedy once said, "I'll take all his enemies—if I can have all his friends too." Bob protested to John once that it was undignified for the President to call his Attorney General "Bobby," at least in public, but John took no heed. It was a privilege an older brother could exercise. The friends of later years all called him Bob.

The years since the assassination had matured Bob Kennedy. Lines removed some of the boyishness from his face; he laughed less often and less easily. No one who came close to him could fail to notice the hurt in his eyes and in his bearing. Robert Kennedy relived Dallas perhaps as much as anyone. On the third anniversary of the assassination, his wife Ethel telephoned some friends and asked them to come over to play tennis with Bob to rouse him from depression.

It wasn't just the assassination that changed Bob. A Harvard professor, who knew the Kennedys well, observed, "You have to remember all these Kennedys are late bloomers—much more impressive at thirty than at twenty and much more so at forty than at thirty."

(A classmate of John Kennedy observed the same thing at their twentieth reunion. "He hadn't been the brightest student, but I was amazed at how far he had come since graduation. He had kept on learning. A lot of us just stopped.")

His brother's death tied Robert even more to his own family. He would come home for lunch to spend time with the younger ones. Their pursuits were his pursuits. With ten active youngsters there was competition for their father's attention. There was a frog to describe, a new tree house, a swimming achievement. He listened intently, always asking, always encouraging. On Sundays, after mass, Bob was careful to single out each child, to spend a private moment alone

with each. A normal father doing what came normally.

Nicholas Katzenbach, the deputy attorney general, once mentioned he had to leave work early to visit his young daughter in the hospital. Within hours the child received a get-well note from the Attorney General. "He loved kids, all kids," said a close friend, "and they adored him. All you had to do was go out to Hickory Hill on a weekend to see that. There were always kids. His kids. Neighbors' kids. Friends' kids. And when he traveled to a foreign country or was trying to learn more about a foreign country, the first thing he would always ask was about that nation's youth. He had an emotional attraction for young people around the world and they flocked to him, sometimes almost frenzied." Keeping in style with youth, Robert Kennedy allowed his hair to grow long—prompting his mother to suggest he ought to get it cut.

In the Kennedy household, there were four refrigerators, two for food, one for drinks, one for ice cream. With a staff to take care of the feeding of the large brood, Ethel Kennedy could spend more time on her children's development. She admitted she was no cook. When she won the title of Homemaker of the Year, in 1958, she was amazed. "I don't even know where they keep the butter," she said. Ethel amazed other homemakers in other ways. Not infrequently her husband would phone to say he was bringing five, ten, twenty, even sixty people to lunch—in an hour. When they arrived, the table was ready. "They must have had a fantastic catering bill," said Katzenbach, a frequent visitor.

Ethel, always on the go, seemed "more a Kennedy than the Kennedys," said one friend. Ethel was unaffected and utterly devoted to Bob—as he was to her. When Senator Kennedy toured Europe in January 1967, he

*Two senators, 1967*

sent her a telegram every day, the same message, in the language of the country where he happened to be. Ethel said afterward she was grateful the first telegram came from London.

Robert Kennedy's close friends remarked frequently about his great capacity for compassion. If the trait was true of him, it was perhaps even truer of Ethel. Once her soft-heartedness—and her penchant for taking direct action—landed her in trouble. In 1963 she noticed an emaciated, neglected horse penned near Hickory Hill. She took him home and cared for him. The owner formally charged her, in effect, with horse stealing. The jury acquitted her, accepting her reason for taking the horse: "It was the saddest sight I ever saw." Still, they wondered why she hadn't returned him after he recovered. "Would you give it back to someone who was mistreating it?" she asked.

Ethel was a superb horsewoman. In fact no activity, however rough or risky, seemed to dismay her. She did, however, have an understandable fear of flying. Both her parents and a brother were killed in plane crashes. Landings especially frightened her, and she liked Robert in the seat next to her. "Would you mind getting my husband back here," she said during a 1968 trip with him

when he had left the seat. "He always holds my hand."

Bob Kennedy seemed always ready to lend a hand. Back in 1951 he shared a small office in the Justice Department with another young lawyer just starting out, John Davitt. The pay was low, and the time to buy clothes for the Davitt children was when there was a sale. "I remember one day after lunch," Davitt recalled, "I said to Bob, 'Hey, if you have time, why don't you come over to Hecht's basement with me. They've got a sale on kids' clothes.'" Hecht's was a large Washington department store, in the middle-to-low price class. "He went with me. All the sizes were just heaped together on one huge table and it was a mess. I told Bob I was looking for size two and size three. He got on one side of the table and I got on the other and we started going through the clothes. I remember him yelling—this millionaire— 'Hey, I found a two,' putting it under his arm so he wouldn't lose it. And then he dived in for more."

In those days—and in later days—Bob ate in the inexpensive lunchrooms government workers frequent in the Federal Triangle. "I never had a feeling that because I was with Bob Kennedy we should go somewhere more swank," Davitt said. Robert had the same habit as his brother Jack of carrying little or no money in his pocket. It got so, that Angie Novello, his longtime secretary, covertly kept track of the money he borrowed from the staff and repaid them. Reporters sometimes had to lend him money to put into the collection plate at mass.

As a senator, he received a $30,000-a-year salary. He always turned it over to charity. The huge staff in his office, which included young people who wanted a chance to get Washington experience, was largely paid from Kennedy's own pocket. The payroll far exceeded the allowance granted to a senator from New York.

A close friend said:

"Literally, money means nothing to them. Hickory Hill is a handsome estate, [it was the headquarters of General George B. McClellan during the Civil War] but if you were picking the one-hundred top suburban homes around Washington, you'd hardly include it. And have you ever seen the compound at Hyannis Port? I'd hardly classify it as impressive. Bob didn't seem to spend much on clothes either. I thought Jack always looked elegant, but Bob didn't seem to care much. I remember at one Cabinet meeting at the White House he walked in from the Rose Garden wearing an old beat-up pair of slacks and a crimson Harvard shirt with a big "H" on the front. That raised a few eyebrows but it was the way Bob was about appearance. In fact, I think all the Kennedys consciously underdressed. When you're invited out to dinner at someone's home, you'd expect that at least you'd wear a suit, wouldn't you? Well, I went out there once and everybody was in sports clothes with no jackets. They were very natural people."

As it often is with "natural" people, the bill of fare at the Robert Kennedys was plain—chicken, steak or chops on most days,

clam chowder on Fridays. Wine was not served often. Once a party of thirty guests gathered at Hickory Hill to honor the Duchess of Devonshire. There wasn't much elbow room. Ethel said grace (a mealtime practice never ignored) and ended the short prayer with " . . . and please, dear God, make Bobby buy me a bigger dining-room table."

Ethel Kennedy, the mother, wasn't much different from Ethel Skakel, the student, described in the 1949 yearbook of Manhattanville College of the Sacred Heart: "One moment a picture of mischief and, next, alive with mischief." Around her, even the most highly placed people shed rank and whatever stuffiness they might have elsewhere. Her home vibrated. Cabinet officers mingled with the Kennedy children, senators and teen-agers thumped guitars. And there always was Brumus, the lumbering Newfoundland that Kennedy intimates describe as "a most miserable specimen," mingling among the high-ranking guests. At one Christmas party there were so many dignitaries at Hickory Hill one newsman commented, "I think we've been invited out to cover the government in exile."

The Kennedy pool, a watering place by day for the young, also was a spot for some of Washington's wetter citizens who were known to have dropped in at times without first dressing accordingly.

Ruthless?

Margaret Laing, in *The Next Kennedy*, writes of Robert Kennedy: "He needs love because he is deeply vulnerable in himself, in spite of the almost impenetrable shield of protectors surrounding him. Except when he is in action . . . he seldom appears happy. Like the late President, he gets rid of anxiety and irritation in physical action . . . he is not complex. Each of his impulses is simple, extreme, intense and undivided in itself."

If physical action rid Robert Kennedy of

anxiety, it also won for him a long list of athletically inclined friends. Roosevelt Grier, for example, the tackle on the Los Angeles Rams professional football team, met Bob and Ethel during a charity telethon and became an immediate friend. "We just seemed to hit it off," Grier said. He became a frequent visitor at Hickory Hill, and he fit well into the roughhouse touch football games. "I just loved the Kennedys. I've never been overwhelmed by any people before, but they were so real. They liked you for you and you knew it. It was the easiest love in the world. None ever seemed to be talking about the 'Big I.' It was always about things done together. It was 'we.' And everyone was invited to participate. No one was dropped out."

In truth, some visitors to Hickory Hill were not totally enchanted. A Washington newsman commented after a game, "I'd like to hit him [Kennedy] right in the mouth. Every time I went up for a pass he gave me elbows and knees. The works. When our team got within one touchdown of his team, by God, he picked up the ball and said the game was over."

There also was the story of the Movable Goal Post. It began as a joke about Bob, that whenever the other team got close he pushed the goal line farther away. Ed Guthman said the joke "turned into something that was seriously reported as evidence that Bob was so intent to win he'd actually move a goal line."

"It isn't that I'm a saint," Kennedy once told a reporter. "It's just that I've never found it necessary to be a sinner." Some members of the business community, according to one friend of Robert Kennedy, regarded him as "a shallow, dangerously ambitious boy." Dick Schaap, in *R.F.K.*, describes Kennedy:

"His arrogance is not vicious, not premeditated; it is the milder arrogance of wealth and position. . . . Generally he does not open doors; others open doors for him. He does not carry his own attaché case. He does not wait for people. . . . Kennedy is not embarrassed by this excessive attention, not demanding, just accepting, which is irritating."

At no time in his career was Bob Kennedy cast in a any more critical light than in the imbroglio over publication of William Manchester's book *The Death of a President*. It was, in the language of show business and politics, a bad press. And a word was added to the lexicon about Robert Kennedy: censor. After John Kennedy's assassination the family realized that authors would want to write about the tragic day and settled on Manchester as the "authorized" chronicler, the one with whom they would cooperate. In return they sought to check the manuscript. Friends read the raw text and recommended major deletions, principally unflattering references to Lyndon Johnson. As far as anyone knew, none of the Kennedys read the book, but Jacqueline Kennedy eventually filed suit against Manchester. She later dropped the matter, none too gracefully. A writer noted the Kennedys erred in demanding the right to review a writer's work. "If they trusted him enough to choose him, they should have trusted his intelligence and art." If that was so, Manchester also erred in agreeing to the review. Bob Kennedy came out of the affair looking like a manipulator, a man capable of exerting cruel pressure. It was a time when he went to bat for Johnson.

There was another. In a 1967 St. Patrick's Day speech, Kennedy called Johnson an outstanding President and said he looked forward to campaigning for him. "I think we agree on most major issues," Robert said. "It is one of the prices of democracy that there is sometimes a difference of viewpoint. But sometimes we benefit by these differences." Just a few weeks before, Kennedy had returned from a European trip and urged a halt in the bombing of North Vietnam and had a stormy confrontation with the President in the White House.

It was said the two men called each other names and not family newspaper-type names. It was doubtful that many new ones were found to attach to Bob Kennedy. Because as a boomlet began building for him as a Presidential candidate, all the old adjectives were hauled out.

Again everyone had a word for Kennedy. But an old favorite also cropped up: opportunist.

As 1967 drew to a close the popularity polls showed Robert Kennedy consistently favored over President Johnson. He led 42-41 in September, 48-39 in October, 52-32 in November. Lou Harris, the veteran pollster for the Kennedys, summed up the situation.

"The basic fact about Democratic politics these days is reflected in these latest survey results: whenever Lyndon Johnson's political fortunes wane, Robert Kennedy rises as a possible alternative. To a degree, Senator Kennedy is also the beneficiary of his brother. Many Americans still wonder how President Kennedy would have handled these troubled times—and Mr. Johnson tends to suffer in the comparison." The poll showed the number of people who believed Robert had "many of the same outstanding qualities of JFK" had risen from 49 to 54 percent since June. His following jumped mostly among young people and women.

While Bob continued to reaffirm his support of the President as a candidate, another Democrat stepped up his challenge of United States policies in Vietnam. Senator Eugene J. McCarthy of Minnesota, ten years in the House of Representatives and in his second term in the Senate, had spoken of the war as a "highly questionable course."

Toward the end of November, McCarthy, pressing his demand for a negotiated settlement of the war, announced he would enter Presidential primaries in 1968. If his effort did not bring about a policy change, he said, "I think this challenge would have to go all the way to a challenge for the nomination for the Presidency."

Kennedy made no move. He called the McCarthy challenge "a healthy influence on the Democratic Party [that would] allow Americans to take out their frustration over the war in talk instead of violence." Both men laughed off suggestions that McCarthy, a former economics professor who was little known nationally, but whose liberal views remarkably paralleled Kennedy's, was a stalking horse for a future Kennedy entrance into the race.

Early in 1968 Senator Kennedy consulted his close friends, men like Seigenthaler, Fred Dutton, Schlesinger.

"We were unanimous that he shouldn't go in, that 1968 wasn't his year," said Dutton. But Kennedy was undecided. He waited until just before the New Hampshire primary to make up his mind, but kept his decision quiet.

Eugene McCarthy got 42 percent of the vote in New Hampshire. It surprised his supporters, his opponents, Kennedy, the country and Lyndon Johnson. Kennedy said McCarthy's showing reflected "a strong feeling against the war in Vietnam," but told friends three days after the primary: "To break with the party that made my brother President isn't an easy thing for me to do. My brother Ted still thinks I'm a little nutty for doing this, but he's an entirely different kind of person. You just have to march to the beat of your own drummer." Doing what? To a reporter, he said only, "I'm reassessing my position."

*Two senators, back among the Dearos, 1968*

*Senator Edward M. Kennedy*

The scene was familiar. There, in the same Senate Caucus Room where John Kennedy launched his drive eight years earlier, stood Robert Francis Kennedy. The opening words were the same: "I am announcing today my candidacy for the Presidency of the United States." Kennedy voice. Kennedy face.

"I do not run for the Presidency merely to oppose any man, but to propose new policy. I run because I am convinced that this country is on a perilous course. . . ." Again, a forefinger stabbing the air.

Now he was an "opportunist." Said McCarthy: "A lot of other politicians were afraid to come down into the playing field. They were willing to stay up on the mountain and light signal fires and bonfires and dance in the light of the moon, but none of them came down. And I tell you it was a little lonely in New Hampshire. I walked alone."

Then, the chief architect to those policies Kennedy criticized—Lyndon Baines Johnson—went on television to announce a curtailment of the bombing of North Vietnam and called on North Vietnam's president, Ho Chi Minh, "to respond positively and favorably to this new step toward peace."

Near the end of the speech, the President put a hand to his ear, a signal to Mrs. Johnson that he had finally decided a move he'd been considering for some time: ". . . I shall not seek, and I will not accept, the nomination of my party for another term as your President."

Soon after Johnson's announcement, Vice-President Humphrey entered the lists and made it a three-way race. But Robert Kennedy had something the other two did not—the Kennedy organization, back together again.

Lawrence O'Brien, Ted Sorensen, Dutton, Schlesinger, Kenny O'Donnell—the Irish Mafia and those adopted into it—came back to help John Kennedy's brother.

Politicking—the kind you do in the open—never came easy to Robert Kennedy. Some audiences felt coolness from him. He was not the speaker John was. Said Dutton: "Bob had almost a litany about the poor. He would get it in at least two speeches out of every five. His prepared speech was incidental, merely an introduction to the audience. What he really felt—that was in the question and answer session that followed every speech. At Fresno State College in California, he started comparing the affluent young white child with Indian kids. He kept weaving back and forth. Afterward he was totally drained emotionally, also exhausted. This was an area in which he really cared."

Vietnam and the Poor. "We Can Do Better." Again and again. He quoted Camus: "Perhaps we cannot prevent this world from being a world in which children suffer. But we can reduce the number of suffering children. And if you don't help us, who else in the world can help us do this?" In Welch, West Virginia, he was greeted by an editorial on the front page of the local daily newspaper describing him as uninvited, unwanted, undesirable, unethical, un-American, unfit, unprepared, unshorn, unpopular, unloved and overrated.

His campaign speech at the University of San Francisco was drowned out by hippies.

"We should let each one of us speak," he shouted. "I let you and now I get a chance."

Hippies: Go Home, Kennedy.

"Isn't there somebody friendly who will ask me how my family is or something?"

Hippies: What makes you think you can solve the problems of the country?

"I think the only person who can find the answers for the United States is probably God. And unfortunately he isn't running."

Kennedy could laugh at himself, sometimes from prepared matter, sometimes from the cuff. What advantage is the name Kennedy to you?, he was asked. "I think it's a tremendous advantage, and I like it very much."

At Sioux Falls, South Dakota: Senator, if you are elected President, what priority will you give the Sioux Falls economy? "Top priority. Just this morning at breakfast I said to Ethel, 'We've got to do something about the Sioux Falls economy.'"

In Omaha, in the rain, in a car with the top down: "You know, I'm not sure I'd vote for a man who didn't have sense enough to come in out of the rain."

In Elkhart, Indiana, Bob spoke to a large friendly crowd. "Are you going to go out and vote for me Tuesday?"

"Yeah, Yeah."

"And are you all going to go out and ring doorbells and tell your neighbors to vote for me?"

"Yeah, Yeah."

"Have you all read my book, To Seek a Newer World?"

"Yeah, Yeah."

"You lie in Elkhart, Indiana!"

At LeGrande, Oregon, there was no ramp to take the passengers off the plane. A forklift was used. The candidate was the last off the plane. He shouted: "We can do better."

In the midst of the campaigning came a sudden and violent occurrence, one that set off riots across the nation. Dr. Martin Luther King, the Nobel Peace Prize winner, was shot to death in Memphis, Tennessee, where he had gone to lead a march supporting striking garbage workers. King had been a friend, and the Senator chartered a plane to bring the body back to Atlanta for burial. Kennedy, as well as the other candidates, attended the funeral.

On the campaign trail again, having won Indiana, Kennedy ran into trouble in Oregon, the penultimate primary. He drew small crowds

and commented, "I can't account for it. If I don't win in Oregon, I'll have a tough time getting the nomination. California is going very well but Oregon is vitally important to me." Oregon wasn't a state much impressed with speeches about the plight of Negroes. There were few Negroes in the state.

He lost the primary, receiving 39 percent of the vote to McCarthy's 45 percent. "It's a setback which I could ill afford," he said. And he still could laugh at a sign in San Bernardino, California, that said SORRY ABOUT THAT—OREGON. "And so am I," commented Kennedy as he campaigned for the primary on the most crucial day of his life, June 4, 1968.

In the war that led to the birth of a new nation, Robert F. Kennedy was a frontline spectator as a correspondent for the Boston Post. He covered the Israelis' front line. And he cabled the Post: "They fight with unparalleled courage. This is their greatest and last chance; there will be no turning back."

Two decades had not diminished his admiration. Campaigning in Oregon, before the swing to California, he told worshippers in a synagogue:

"It is clear that in Israel—like in so many other places in the world—our commitment is clear and compelling. We are committed to Israel's survival. We are committed to defying any attempt to destroy Israel's survival. We are committed to defying any attempt to destroy Israel, whatever the source . . ."

He took a similar stance June 1 in a nationally televised debate with Senator McCarthy.

There were places where such words brought no joy, perhaps one a middle-class neighborhood of Pasadena, California, home of Sirhan Sirhan, the Jordanian Arab who had been uprooted by the Arab-Israeli war in 1948 as a

*Candidates Kennedy and McCarthy mourn Martin Luther King.*

child. Hatred of Israel was heightened in 1967 when the Jews humiliated the Arab nations in a six-day war. "It was all we talked about." said an acquaintance. Later some twenty pages of a journal were found. When the journal came to light, Mayor Sam Yorty of Los Angeles said one page mentioned the "necessity to assassinate Senator Kennedy before June 5." That marked the first anniversary of the Israeli-Arab war.

In Sirhan's neighborhood of small homes and small, neat lawns, he was seen as a quiet, polite, courteous young man. He had been around the $15,000 house often since March. That was when he left his job at John Weidner's Pasadena Organic Health Food Store, where he had worked as a $2-an-hour clerk. Weidner had been in the Dutch underground in World War II. "Sirhan argued a lot about the Jews. He hated them. He was consumed with himself."

The five-foot-five, swarthy Sirhan left Weidner's employ after the owner questioned him about his work, and Sirhan yelled, "So I'm a liar. I never lie."

To a former high school classmate, Jeff Kahn, anti-Jewish sentiments from Sirhan were no surprise. Kahn and Sirhan had the chance to talk every school morning as they walked around the school's track. The others ran, but Kahn and Sirhan chose not to, and walked and talked. Kahn, who is Jewish, recalled:

"Sirhan was very anti-Israel. He hated the Israeli nation and Ben-Gurion and Abba Eban. And he seemed to make a distinction between Israelis and Jews."

If Sirhan harbored hatred for Jews, apparently it didn't show itself when he was relaxing with some neighbors in games of Chinese Checkers. The players described him as polite and courteous. One of the players was a Jewish woman.

He also, like Oswald, seemed to have had an interest in Russian. One report said he studied it while in John Muir High School. And Mrs. Totsey Boyko, who worked in a food store with Sirhan, said she had talked with him often and the thing she remembered most was his admiration for Russia. "He thought Russia was the best," she said, and she thought that he spoke a little of that language.

Sirhan had an ambition. It was to be a jockey. It seemed an unusual one for the young man regarded as well-read and articulate, who had only a trace of accent in his speech. He had haunted tracks in the Los Angeles area, and at Santa Anita there was a general notion among track hands that Sirhan was a rider who was "buying real estate"—race track jargon for a rider with a penchant for falls.

One such fall, at the Granja Vista Del Rio Ranch at Corona, California, put him in the hospital September 25, 1966. He was a "hot walker"—a track worker who helps cool down horses after they've run. The doctor who examined him said X-rays showed no damage to the skull, but that he ordered him admitted as a precaution in case of internal injury. There was a small cut on the nose, near the right eye, and minor bruises.

Sirhan claimed the fall disabled him. A succession of doctors thought otherwise. One, Dr. Milton Miller, a Corona ophthalmologist, said that in December Sirhan became very agitated because Dr. Miller had said he could find no evidence of permanent injury.

"He became abusive, so I just left him in the office," said Dr. Miller. "I returned about ten minutes later, and he was gone." Dr. Miller prepared to put Sirhan's medical record away, hesitated and added a word: malingerer.

Ten minutes later Sirhan was on the telephone. " 'You better do what I want or I'll get you,' he said. I asked him, 'What do you mean by that?' and he hung up. That shook me up for a few days. When I'd leave my office, I'd look around."

Despite the conclusions of the doctors, Sirhan eventually received a $2,000 settlement. It came to him about the time he stopped working for John Weidner.

On the day that Californians went to the polls, June 4, to vote in the Presidential primary, Sirhan Sirhan was at the San Gabriel Valley Gun Club. He drew attention by the mound of expended shells at his firing position. "There were three hundred to four hundred," Henry Adrian Carreon, a college student and playground director, told a Grand Jury. He said Sirhan was firing very rapidly and "on the range you are supposed to shoot and pause." Carreon asked what sort of weapon it was and said he was told, "an Iver Johnson."

There was no campaigning this day and Robert Kennedy washed away the strain of travel and speechmaking by a swim off Malibu Beach and relaxation at the house of film director John Frankenheimer. Then the Kennedy entourage headed for Los Angeles and the Ambassador Hotel where they were to keep watch of election results.

Wherever he went, Bob Kennedy seemed quickly surrounded by people. And that worried his entourage. Bill Barry, the former FBI agent who acted as his unarmed guard, worried about it. And so did Roosevelt Grier, the Los Angeles Rams lineman, and Rafer Johnson, the decathlon champion.

Robert was as realistic as his brother had been. French novelist Romain Gary said Kennedy told him: "I know there will be an attempt on my life sooner or later. Not so much for political reasons but through contagion, through emulation." Ed Guthman, Kennedy's former press aide, said it was a private agreement among the Kennedy people that they would somehow form a human fence around him whenever possible. Bob Kennedy did not care for the idea of uniformed police or guards.

And some California police didn't care much for his idea. A ranking officer in the Los Angeles Police Department said there were reports from area commanders that the Kennedy people refused to cooperate. The Kennedy people could make the same charge. One motorcade going through Los Angeles was ordered to stop for red lights. A police sergeant waved the motorcade through a light—and then the motorcade was stopped and the lead driver given a traffic citation. The department had more than sixty citations issued, including one charging Fred Dutton with disturbing the peace. These were later dropped.

The absence of uniformed police in California—whether it was because Bob Kennedy rejected their help, or because they didn't offer it or give it when asked—certainly made it easier for crowds to get near Kennedy. Once, in San Francisco's Chinatown, firecrackers went off. Bobby Kennedy's face seemed to freeze in a half-smile. He shuddered.

There was no escort as he came rolling up to the Ambassador Hotel in singer Andy Williams' Rolls-Royce. It was about four in the afternoon. Jerry Costigan, the sound man recording the Kennedy campaign, said that as the Senator headed toward the hotel elevator, a slight man with something rolled up in his hand tried to get close to Kennedy but was shut out by Barry and himself. Costigan was sure this man was one whose picture he later saw.

In Suite 512, Kennedy had the usual run of telephone calls. And others not so usual. After the news came that he had won 50 percent of South Dakota's delegates, to 30 percent for President Johnson and 20 percent for Gene McCarthy, Robert Kennedy said:

"I think my campaign is at last reaching the people."

There was a feeling in Suite 512 that the Kennedy bandwagon was now rolling.

At about 9:15 in the evening, one party already was underway. It was for California's Max Rafferty, a conservative who challenged Sen. Thomas A. Kuchel for the GOP nomination. Rafferty's people were counting on victory even before the polls closed. They were having a fine time in the Venetian Room.

There was one uninvited guest, according to a 35-year-old unemployed mechanic who also was in the lobby outside.

Enrique Rabago said he and a friend ran into a slight, dark young man who complained he had been insulted at Rafferty's party. He was full of rage, cursing "the rich Rafferty people who step all over the poor." Rabago said he and his friend, trying to mollify the young man in white pants and white tieless shirt, suggested that he turn to Senator Kennedy, in the Embassy Room on the other side of the lobby. Rabago said the young man yelled:

"Kennedy! Kennedy! He should never be President. You think he really wants to help the poor? Kennedy just helps himself. He's just using the poor. Can't you see that?"

Later, in a kitchen passageway near the Embassy Room, a kitchen porter, Jesus Perez, said a young man asked him three or four times when the Senator would be coming. It was about a quarter hour before midnight.

Upstairs, Jesse Unruh, speaker of the California Assembly and a major voice among State Democrats, told the Senator they could start down. "There's no doubt about a victory," he said. Bob Kennedy's lead over Gene McCarthy had kept at a four percentage point margin, shifting slightly now and then, but it looked as if it would wind up as a 46–42 victory.

*dream things that never were and say why not."*

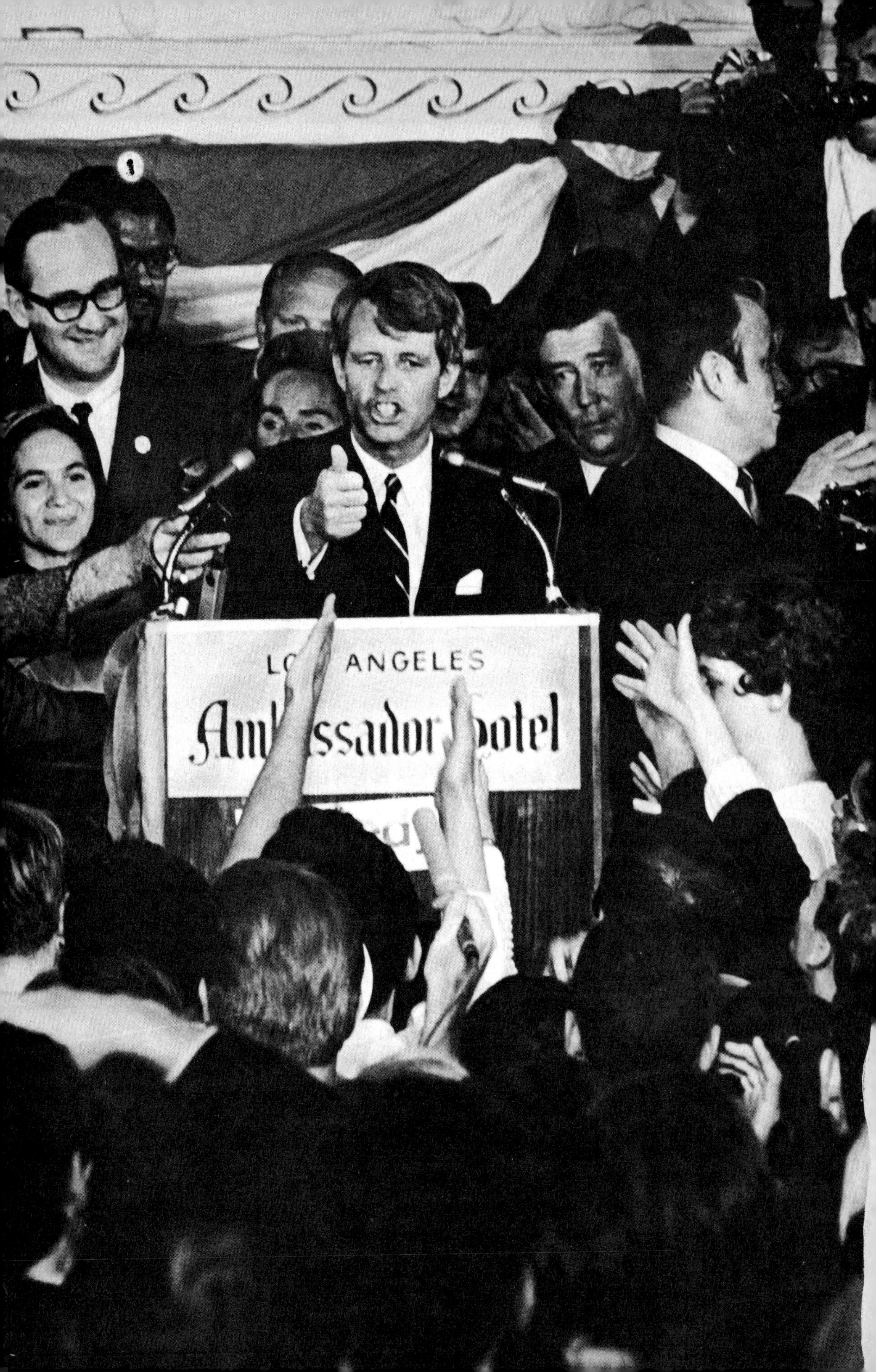
LOS ANGELES
Ambassador Hotel

At one minute after midnight, June 5, 1968 Robert Kennedy left his suite. He started downstairs, planning to use the regular elevators to the Embassy Room, but then decided to avoid some of the crowd by using the freight elevators. A hotel employee led the way, and they came off the elevator, went along a kitchen passageway into the Embassy Room. Here, Kennedy tried to quiet the mob of some 2,000 campaign workers.

"I want," he said, "to express my gratitude to my dog, Freckles, who's been maligned and I don't care what they say—as Franklin Roosevelt said—I don't care what they say about me but when they start to attack my dog. . . ." The crowd laughed. "Rosie Grier said he'd take care of anybody who didn't vote for me."

Then:

"I think we can end the divisions in the United States. What I think is quite clear, that we can work together in the last analysis.

"And this is what has been going on within the United States over a period of the last three years—the division, the violence, the disenchantment with our society, the division, whether it's between blacks and whites, between the poor and the more affluent, between age groups, or in the war on Vietnam— that we can start to work together.

"We are a great country, an unselfish country and a compassionate country. And I intend to make that my basis for running . . ."

The applause flooded the room.

"So my thanks to all of you and it's on to Chicago and let's win there."

The plan was to go to the Ambassador Ballroom where an overflow of campaign workers awaited him. The Senator had already appeared in interviews for each television network and writing reporters were anxious for a press conference. They were in the Colonial Room.

Jerry Costigan, self-advertised as "The Ambassador of Sound," was concerned about the people trying to get close to the Senator as he made his victory address. "If I saw anyone without a yellow badge, I'd chase them off." The badge was a press identification. "There was one guy I chased off twice before the Senator spoke." Later Costigan, too, said he could recognize him again.

The speech finished, Robert Kennedy started for the Colonial Room, from there to go to a party at The Factory, a popular and fashionable discotheque.

Instead of walking through the main door of the ballroom, Kennedy went out the back, toward the kitchen.

"We didn't know he'd take that route until just a couple of minutes before," said Fred Dutton. "I cleared the way with Bill Barry while Bob was giving the victory statement. Some people waited one floor down where the overflow crowd had gone. I made the decision that the place was overly congested and that he should go out through the kitchen. Bill and I were clearing the way down the steps, but Bob for some reason got off the back of the stage and that meant we were a few people behind him."

It was 12:16 A.M. Rosie Grier was with Senator Kennedy. And Rafer Johnson and Bill Barry and Milt Gwirtzman of the "issues staff" and Ethel Kennedy, pregnant for the eleventh time but looking bright and chirpy.

Bob Kennedy moved along, smiling, accepting congratulations, shaking hands, and one outstretched hand held a gun.

There were eight shots and then a violent inrushing of people. Karl Uecker, assistant maitre d'hotel of the Ambassador, and an assistant, had been leading the Senator. They clutched at a man holding a gun. Grier, whose playing weight was 287 pounds, crashed through the mob, ramming Uecker and the

*Senator Robert F. Kennedy, 1966*

Ethel Kennedy knelt low over her husband who was wide-eyed on the floor, his hands thrust upwards as if in surrender. "Give him air! Air!" she cried. But there were as many people trying to get in as out in the milling, horrifying confusion.

In the ballroom young girls shrieked. What were squeals of victory changed to shrieks of grief. "Oh, God! It can't be! Not again!"

Three doctors appeared, and one of them, a Negro, said Kennedy was still conscious. Then, after long minutes, police arrived. They wedged the young man who had been held by Grier and the others downstairs amid cries of: "Kill him!," "Lynch the bastard!"

Unruh bulled his way into the patrol car with the captive.

"I did it for my country," the youth told him.

An ambulance came for Robert Kennedy to rush him to Central Receiving Hospital, an emergency facility two miles away. Some remembered the senator said, "No, no don't," as he was lifted on the stretcher. No one remembered him saying anything more.

As the ambulance wheeled off, Kennedy aides and friends crammed into anything they could find to follow in pursuit. Pierre Salinger and his wife jumped on a motorcycle and clutched the rider as they roared off. Some had made a similar dash before, in Dallas.

Back in the ballroom Steve Smith, the brother-in-law, always a calm hand among the Kennedys, pleaded for the near-hysterical mob to leave.

Up in the candidate's suite, several aides had watched his speech on television and when he said "On to Chicago" and started walking out, they switched off the set with a kidding, "On to The Factory!"

In the kitchen, Grier dropped to a stool, face in his hands, and sobbed.

And at the hospital the receiving doctor

other two men against a serving table. George Plimpton, the jet-set author and dilettante athlete, and Johnson and Barry battled their way in. A gun, an Iver Johnson pistol, spun free and Johnson grabbed it.

Unruh screamed from on top of a table: "Keep him alive! Don't kill him! We want him alive!"

The short, swarthy man was alive, although battered.

But on the floor, on his back, lay Robert Kennedy, blood flowing copiously from a wound in his head. Five others had also been wounded. The Senator had been struck behind his right ear (near the spot where his brother's lethal wound occurred) and in his right armpit.

A radio newsman cried into his tape recorder: "Senator Kennedy has been shot! Is that possible? Is that possible?"

*Sirhan Sirhan: June, 1968*

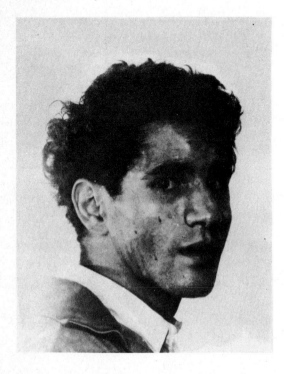

thought Robert Kennedy, at first sight all but dead, had steadied slightly but was showing indications of brain damage. The doctor let Ethel Kennedy hear her husband's heartbeat, and it seemed to calm her. Then Robert Kennedy was taken to Good Samaritan Hospital where doctors began brain surgery. It took three hours and forty-five minutes to complete.

Ted Kennedy had been the family's representative at an election night party in San Francisco. When it looked as if Robert had won, he left with aide David Burke for the Fairmont Hotel. In his room, Ted turned on the television set to get the latest returns. He learned, instead, his brother had been shot.

He said nothing. Then: "How bad is it?" Then: "What's the fastest way we can get the hell out of here?"

It was 8:30 in the morning in London. Princess Lee Radziwill heard the news and placed a transatlantic phone call to her sister. Jacqueline Kennedy was asleep in her apartment in New York. Had she heard the news and "how was he?"

Yes. She had heard. Wasn't it wonderful about California?

No, not that.

And then she was told.

In Hyannis Port, Ann Gargan was also awakened in the middle of the night. She was told. She talked to her aunt. Rose Kennedy decided not to tell her husband. Let him sleep. She went to six o'clock mass and returned to the compound. The phone rang. It was Ted Kennedy. The Ambassador was awake by then. And he was told, by Ted, for the second time in his long life.

Cardinal Cushing, who had shared so much of the grief and pleasure of this family, drove down to the Cape that afternoon to comfort Joseph Kennedy and his wife. "She has more confidence in Almighty God," said the Cardinal, "than any priest I have ever met."

It would be needed. For twenty-five hours the stricken son lay on the very edge of death. Even if he survived, doctors conjectured how much of his body and mind would remain as before.

But at least he was alive. It was not like Dallas when the President was beyond life after the shots. Then early Thursday morning the senator's press secretary walked out onto the front steps of Good Samaritan Hospital, into the white blaze of the television lights. Frank Mankiewicz was pale and haggard, but poised. In a soft voice he spoke into the microphones:

"Senator Robert Francis Kennedy died at 1:44 A.M. today."

And the world was told.

# Arlington

It was as much as the imagination—and the heart—could bear. One need not have been a partisan for or against to share the sorrow for family and shame for the nation. Once, if for nothing else, had been horrible simply because it could happen in the United States of America. But twice . . .?

"It's like watching a rerun of a movie you've seen years before," said Bill Moyers, who had left his job as President Johnson's press secretary to become a newspaper publisher. "But the difference is that when you turn off your set, the movie keeps running in your mind."

It *had* happened twice, so identically twice. A transcontinental flight bearing a body high above America towards home. A common forklift, sputtering up towards the great body of a jet, lifting its humble steel hands upwards almost as if in prayer to receive a coffin and bear it, and those great and small who carried it, back to the earth. The mourners filing out. Some new. Some not. Some who had made this awful passage home before. Eventide again and the lights prying the dark to glare on personal tragedy that was, however, also the people's.

But what had the people not learned from the first that they must look on a second? What, in God's name, was to become of this people whose leadership this murdered man had sought? Robert Kennedy had not made unity in a divided country in life, although he had tried by his own lights. In death, however, he had brought a unity of shock.

In Washington, Robert McNamara was at a ceremonial and broke into tears. A television station gave up two and a half hours of scheduled time and simply ran the word SHAME on its cameras. An American soldier in Vietnam said: "Good God, what's going on back home?"

A long autopsy had been performed in Los Angeles, unlike Dallas. Colonel Pierre Finck was one of the doctors, as he had been at Bethesda, November 22, 1963.

The body was then taken to the airport to be lifted in its mahogany coffin aboard a Presidential jet sent by Lyndon Johnson. Jacqueline Kennedy, who had flown to her brother-in-law's bedside, refused to board until reassured that the plane was not the one that flew that day from Dallas.

Those who came aboard were as varied a group as one could conceive. Fernando Para, a Mexican architect. Rafer Johnson. George Plimpton. James Whittaker and his wife. Mrs. Martin Luther King Jr., herself only recently widowed. Old friends such as Lem Billings who had traveled with Jack Kennedy so long ago; Ted Kennedy, the last son; Charles Evers, head of the Mississippi NAACP as his brother had been until he was murdered; Ed Guthman and his wife, and Burke Marshall, old colleagues from Justice; Andy Williams and his wife; Jesse Unruh; Jerry Bruno, once a forklift operator who had become a crack advance man for both John and Robert and looked out at the farewell throng at Los Angeles Airport and said: "He would have liked this crowd."

An oddly assorted group, one that those who did not care for the Kennedys would have said showed that either the family courted celebrities or welcomed celebrities courting them. That would be forgetting, however, that Joseph Kennedy had known queens of Hollywood and kings of England, that Honey Fitz had been friends with Babe Ruth, the Sultan of Swat, and William McKinley, the President of the United States.

In flight, Ted Kennedy rode up front with the coffin, drowsing, talking and heatedly discussing the "faceless men," ominous night riders from another America who had brought terror to the nation's public life. He talked, too, of his family, a family that suddenly

# "Love is not an easy feeling to put into words."

numbered fourteen children: his, Robert's and John's.

Back in the cabin the two so different women who had been joined by their marriages and now were bonded by death talked, the new widow showing the same stoicism her sister-in-law had before. Jacqueline Kennedy, in her last official night in the White House, had said she would cry later, after the public had turned its eyes from her trial. Ethel Ken-

nedy was to use almost identical words: "We'll all have a good cry later." She went forward and lay down beside her husband's coffin and fell asleep. Someone put a pillow beneath her head and a rosary into her hand.

The jet landed at La Guardia Airport in New York where another crowd awaited: notables, old friends, the curious. Jacqueline saw Mc-Namara, and they embraced. Ethel got into the front seat of the hearse with Ted Kennedy beside her to lead a procession to St. Patrick's Cathedral. Thousands stood in the steaming hot night to watch as the black cars slid by.

There was a short service for the family. Jacqueline wept as she had not before. Rose Kennedy comforted her. Later a hastily improvised honor guard stood brief vigil by the bier through the night. Its members bespoke much of the Kennedy family. There was Walter Reuther of the United Automobile Workers and Thomas Watson Jr., of IBM. The Rev. Ralph Abernathy, Martin Luther King's successor, and the poet, Robert Lowell. William Styron, the novelist, and Arthur Goldberg, lawyer, Supreme Court Justice and United Nations ambassador in turn.

Outside the church others waited. Nancy McGee, nineteen, had driven down from her home in West Roxbury, Massachusetts to New York for the first time.

"I had to get involved, and this was a start," she said.

In Los Angeles the arrested man was under a different sort of vigil. A guard remained in his cell at all times. Another watched through a peephole. There would be no repetition of the Dallas basement where Lee Harvey Oswald was shot down by Jack Ruby. He repeated over and over; "I wish to remain incommunicado." The Los Angeles law officers sought to keep official discussion of the case to a minimum, although Mayor Samuel Yorty was criticized for later mentioning that the prisoner had kept a diary and that his car had been seen outside leftist meetings.

The gun that had been taken from the man was quickly traced. Its serial number had been registered with the state by one Albert Hertz of Alhambra, California who bought it for self-protection at the time of the Watts riots in 1965. He later gave it to his sister, who did

not want it around the house with small children present. She gave it to a neighbor who recalled selling it in December 1967 to someone named Joe—"a bushy-haired guy who worked in a department store." This led to Munir "Joe" Sirhan, an employee in Nash's Department Store. Sirhan was asked to identify the prisoner, He did. He said he was his brother, Sirhan Sirhan. Police charged Sirhan Sirhan with murder.

The rumors had begun more quickly than they had the first time. Within days there was a hunt for a woman in a polka-dot dress seen at the hotel the night of the assassination. There was talk of plot, a conspiracy that somehow linked the deaths of the Kennedy brothers with that of Martin Luther King. There had been critics of the commission headed by Chief Justice Earl Warren, critics who refused to believe the commission's findings that Lee Oswald killed John Kennedy unaided. With Robert's death, they took renewed voice. The parasite, suspicion, fed on itself and flowered.

On Saturday, June 8, 1968, Robert, third son of Joseph and Rose Kennedy, was buried. The Requiem Mass at St. Patrick's was attended by 2,300 guests, a list quickly but carefully drawn up by Senator Kennedy's staff and close friends, a last, sad exhibition of their thoroughness. There was Kenneth Keating, the foe of 1964; Richard Nixon, flanked by Secret Service agents, as were all candidates, on orders of President Johnson, who was also at the cathedral; Earl Warren, whispering to Mrs. King; Barry Goldwater; Nelson Rockefeller; Eugene McCarthy; Billy Graham; names known to the nation, names known by the family. Thousands had passed the bier the day before, many the poor and the black who had seen in Robert Kennedy a hope they now had lost. The senator's older sons, Joseph

*"O, days of woe; O, days of wrath . . ."*

III, fifteen, and Robert Jr., fourteen, had stood vigil for a while. Ted Kennedy, for a time, slumped in a back pew, his thoughts his own.

But on this day of burial he moved to the altar to deliver a eulogy. It was an unusual departure from tradition. And it was an appearance of eloquence that some had thought would have been beyond the last son of Joseph.

*He was always by our side. Love is not an easy feeling to put into words. Nor is loyalty, or trust, or joy. But he was all of these. He loved life completely. . . . My brother need not be idealized or enlarged in death beyond what he was in life, to be remembered simply as a good and decent man who saw wrong and tried to right it, saw suffering and tried to heal it, saw war and tried to stop it. . . . As he said many times, in many parts of this nation, to those he touched and who sought to touch him: Some men see things as they are and say why. I dream things that never were and say why not.'*"

Cardinal Cushing, in a deep purple robe and white mitre over his scarlet cap, spoke a prayer: "May the angels take you into paradise. . . ."

Leonard Bernstein conducted thirty members of the New York Philharmonic in the slow movement from Gustav Mahler's Fifth Symphony, and Andy Williams sang the "Battle Hymn of the Republic."

The audience filed out of the shadows of the nave of the cathedral into the bright midday sun. The only sound was the hum of film cameras. Limousines took 1,200 of those invited to Pennsylvania Station where a twenty-one-car train drawn by a black engine waited for the final journey to Washington.

It seemed a return to earlier times. There had been Lincoln's crepe-draped train slowly moving across the country towards his home in the heartland, in Illinois. On this day in 1968 crowds gathered along the tracks, as they had done in 1865. There was tragedy

hardly after the train moved out of the tunnel beneath the Hudson River and across the marshland of the New Jersey Meadows.

A northbound train killed two people who had crowded onto the tracks in Elizabeth, New Jersey. Some aboard the Kennedy train witnessed the accident and were all but incoherent the rest of the trip.

Slowly the train moved southward, preceded by an advance engine as a precaution against a hidden bomb on the tracks. New Brunswick . . . Trenton . . . Philadelphia . . . Wilmington . . . Baltimore. . . .

Here and there a band gathered on station platforms and played "America the Beautiful" or the "Battle Hymn" as the train passed. Aged Negroes doffed their hats. Little children squirmed and fretted and wondered why they had to stand so long on such a nice day to see something they didn't understand. Down the tracks from Baltimore there was no band but the crowd broke spontaneously into the "Battle Hymn" when the train passed.

On board the train, drinks were served in the tradition of the Irish wake, and friends from the New Frontier, from Justice, from Hyannis Port, from Harvard, from '64, from '68, from New York, from Washington, from wherever this man had been known, talked, even laughed at times.

One passenger said, "There's enough talent here for two or three administrations." Joseph Kennedy III walked the length of the train shaking every hand: "I'm Joe Kennedy. Thank you for coming. Thank you for your sympathy. Thank you." Ethel Kennedy also came out from the rear car to talk to her husband's friends and colleagues.

The train reached Washington after dark, four and a half hours late. "I wish it had never ended," said one of those aboard. The cortege formed from Union Station and headed for Arlington, past the Capitol where he had

served, past the Justice Department where he had served, past the White House where he had served and so over the Potomac to Arlington. Just before the bridge, the cavalcade passed Resurrection City, the campsite where thousands of the nation's poor had gathered to demand Congressional help. Some of them raised both hands over their heads in farewell.

The cortege wound up the road into the National Cemetery. In the darkness, children held lighted candles. At graveside the pallbearers, including Robert McNamara and John Glenn, the first American to orbit the earth, jerkily folded the American flag that covered the coffin. Glenn presented it to the oldest son, who gave it to the widow. Slowly the mourners walked down the slope to their cars. The candles flickered out. The television lights were packed and trucked away.

All had gone, and a quarter moon shone down on the hill where Robert Francis Kennedy lay, a few feet away from his brother, John.

As with John, so with Robert. There was one mourner missing. Their father. He had considered coming to St. Patrick's, but the family said he was too distraught.

He was seventy-nine and, Dr. Rusk said, very feeble. He had outlived four of his children—something one of his three sons to fall in service to his country called a crime against nature.

He had sought a name for his family and had achieved it, a name that in two short generations had achieved a place in American history not many others had.

It was said this only happened because of money. The fame was bought, not earned. But America in mid-century was not an Irish ward of yesterday. Money helped, but no one bought sixty-eight million Americans. Joseph

Kennedy may have wanted his sons to be Presidents or senators. But the American voter elected them, not their father.

It was said by some, "We're fed up hearing about the Kennedys." True, the family did not avoid the spotlight and may at times have focused it on themselves. But no one was forced to look.

They had a quality inbred from the very fact of their family life. They were large in number, and such families develop a group cohesion and purpose just from their own size. In a neighborhood, it is the family with the flock of children that draws the other youngsters. Add money. Add a father who felt that this money would free his children to do the worthwhile, a father who for all his ability to elbow his way to the pot of gold as well as any American who has tried, did so no more roughly than some and a good deal less so than others. Stipulate that politics was in his inheritance, both as a son and as an Irish son. Stipulate that he was not a man so greedy for riches that he did not give concern for his nation. Equate this in some form of balance sheet. Was it surprising, then, that his sons became what they became? (Was it any less surprising that another great family of wealth, the Rockefellers, gave their name to the governors of two states?)

Stipulate that Joseph P. Kennedy, in wanting what he wanted and in his sons wanting what he wanted, saw them move into prominence that drew the fire, the actual fire, of another side of America.

Stipulate all that. Then, had not this nation witnessed true tragedy, classic tragedy, tragedy in which it was not only audience?

Perhaps the aged patriarch, looking out over the dunes to Nantucket Sound, might have agreed, might have uttered the word that remained to him. The repeated "no no no no," the word that meant yes.

# Index

# Bibliography

The Associated Press, *The Torch Is Passed*, New York: 1963.

The Associated Press, *The World in 1964*, New York: 1965.

Burns, James MacGregor, *John Kennedy: A Political Profile*, New York: Harcourt, Brace and World, Inc., 1959.

Cutler, John Henry, *Honey Fitz: Three Steps to the White House*, New York: Bobbs-Merrill Co., Inc., 1962.

Dinneeh, Joseph F., *Joseph P. Kennedy Family*, Boston: Little, Brown and Co., 1960.

Donovan, Robert J., *PT 109*, New York: McGraw-Hill Co., Inc., 1961.

Duncliffe, William J., *The Life and Times of Joseph P. Kennedy*, New York: Macfadden-Bartell, 1965.

Friedman, Stanley P., *The Magnificent Kennedy Women*, Derby, Conn.: Monarch Books, Inc., 1964.

Gardner, Gerald, ed., *The Quotable Mr. Kennedy*, New York: (Abelard-Schuman Ltd.) Popular Library, 1962.

Johnson, Haynes and M. Artime, José Peréz San Román, E. Oliva, E. Ruiz-Williams, *The Bay of Pigs*, New York: Norton and Co., 1964.

Kennedy, John F., ed., *As We Remember Joe*, Cambridge, Mass.: The University Press, 1945.

Kimball, Penn, *Bobby Kennedy and the New Politics*, Englewood Cliffs, N. J.: Prentice-Hall, Inc., 1968.

Laing, Margaret, *The Next Kennedy*, New York: Coward-McCann, Inc., 1968.

Lieberson, Goddard and J. Meyers, eds., *John Fitzgerald Kennedy: As We Remember Him*, New York: Atheneum, 1965.

McCarthy, Joe, *The Remarkable Kennedys*, New York: The Dial Press, 1960.

Manchester, William, *The Death of a President*, New York: Harper and Row, 1967.

Opotowsky, Stan, *The Kennedy Government*, New York: (E. P. Dutton and Co., Inc.) Popular Library, 1961.

Quirk, Lawrence J., *Robert Francis Kennedy: The Man and the Politician*, Los Angeles, Calif.: Holloway House Publishing Co., 1968

*Report of the President's Commission on the Assassination of President Kennedy*, Washington, D.C.: United States Government Printing Office, 1964.

Rovere, Richard H., *Senator Joe McCarthy*, New York: Harcourt, Brace and World, Inc., 1959.

Salinger, Pierre, *With Kennedy*, New York: Doubleday, 1966.

Salinger, Pierre and S. Vanocur, eds., *A Tribute to John F. Kennedy*, Chicago: (Encyclopedia Britannica) Atheneum, 1964.

Schaap, Dick, *R.F.K.*, New York: New American Library, 1968.

Schlesinger, Arthur M., Jr., *A Thousand Days: John F. Kennedy in the White House*, Boston: Houghton Mifflin Co., 1965.

Sobel, Robert, *The Big Board*, New York: (Free Press) Macmillan, 1965.

Sorensen, Theodore C., *Kennedy*, New York: Harper and Row, 1965.

Tregaskis, Richard, *John Kennedy: War Hero*, New York: Dell Publishing Co., Inc., 1962.

Whalen, Richard J., *The Founding Father*, New York: New American Library, 1966.

White, Theodore, H., *The Making of the President 1960*, New York: Atheneum, 1961.

Wittke, Carl, *The Irish in America*, Baton Rouge, La.: Louisiana State University Press, 1956.

Woodham-Smith, Cecil, *The Great Hunger*, New York: Harper and Row, 1962.